RAO'S
CLASSICS

ALSO FROM RAO'S RESTAURANTS

RAO'S CLASSICS

More than 140 Italian Favorites from
the Legendary New York Restaurant

FRANK PELLEGRINO
SENIOR and **JUNIOR**

with **JOSEPH RICCOBENE**

ST. MARTIN'S PRESS
NEW YORK

www.stmartins.com

The Library of Congress Cataloging-in-Publication Data is available upon request.

ISBN 978-1-250-00628-8 (hardcover)
ISBN 978-1-250-03824-1 (e-book)

Book design by Susan Walsh

Our books may be purchased in bulk for promotional, educational, or business use. Please contact your local bookseller or the Macmillan Corporate and Premium Sales Department at 1-800-221-7945, extension 5442, or by e-mail at MacmillanSpecialMarkets@macmillan.com.

First Edition: November 2016

10 9 8 7 6 5 4 3 2 1

*This book is for Josephine Pellegrino,
wife and mother extraordinaire*

One evening as I was about to leave my apartment and go to the restaurant I called out to my wife and said, "Josephine, I'm going to work and I will see you later." Josephine came out of the kitchen and, with a bemused expression on her face, said, "You call that work?" To which I replied, with a quizzical expression on my face, "Of course I do." To which she replied, "You mean singing and dancing with all the pretty women? Hugging all of your customers and friends? Telling jokes? Swapping funny stories? Having a scotch or two? And then sitting with some friends and customers to enjoy a late supper? Work?" We both started laughing and I realized Josephine's description of what I did at the restaurant would be hard to call work. None the less it is work. Making people happy, providing them with an experience, helping them to forget their troubles for a few hours, transporting them to another time and place just through their senses, that's the real work I do. It's what all the people in the restaurant and hospitality business do. It's a great business filled with great people. So I will continue to tell Josephine I'm going to work and she will laugh and be waiting for me when I get home.

Frank Sr.
Southhampton New York
August 21, 2016

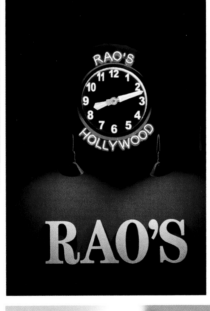

CONTENTS

ACKNOWLEDGMENTS

My culinary and management teams were critical to the preparation of this book and deserve special thanks. Their contributions to our restaurants and to this book are examples of the philosophy that has underpinned our family's hard work over the last century. Both teams consist of ambassadors of hospitality who work hard. They serve as our inspiration as we move toward the future and evolve and improve our business.

As Senior always points out, a restaurant is only as good as the people who support it. We express our appreciation and gratitude to our guests, all of whom have made Rao's what it is today. The majority of our guests, in their own way, have championed our evolution.

Regardless of geography, our visits to New York City, Las Vegas, and Hollywood are filled with anticipation, knowing that when we hit the ground in any of these cities, we have a home and family waiting there. We salute our culinary and management teams in NYC, Las Vegas, and Hollywood: Executive Chefs Dino Gatto, Fatimah Madyun, James Palermo, Laura Augsberger, and Michael Lanza are all priceless. Special homage to our sous chefs, Lydia Vicens, Paulie, Dominick and Rosie, and their teams. Based in New York, Tommy Mara, Nicky "the Vest" Zaloumis, Joe Ciccone, Dee Mendoza, and Jessica Danowsky, and the indispensable Susan Paolercio have been superlative for decades. Special shout-outs to Hilton Pacheco, Marc Melvin, and Big Mike, all also up in Harlem. To our Las Vegas team go big kudos: Marie Joe Tabet, Andrea Cisneros, and our front-of-house servers, bartenders, busboys, and runners. And a special thanks to the executive team at Caesars Palace, who provide a peerless setting and unbeatable ambiance. A special hosanna goes up for our hostess and part-time house photographer, the irrepressible Marisa Posner. Big ups go out as well to the Hollywood team: Patrick Hickey, Big Lou, Johnny Roast Beef, Adrian, Kevin, Jason, Mark T, Lena, and Magic Marc C. And to all the waiters and bartenders out there in Movieland at the former Hollywood Canteen, with its unique karma.

Special thanks to our dear friend and house scribe, Joseph Riccobene, whose writing in this book captures the history and character that makes Rao's magic. Thanks also to our literary agent and dear friend, Eddie Breslin, who has helped forge and guide each of our four books. A hearty thumbs-up also to recipe organizers Gracie and Raine Boscos, and to recipe editor Chris Peterson. To our dear friend and world-renowned photographer, Timothy White, we extend gratitude for capturing the very special photograph of a father and son that graces the back jacket of this book.

We can't possibly overpraise the team at St. Martin's Press, who were marvelous: Publisher Sally Richardson, Executive Editor Elizabeth Beier, Editorial Assistant Nicole Williams, and Managing Editor Amelie Littel. Their direction, support, and dedication were unrelenting. We salute them for the opportunity they extended to us to further articulate the Rao's story.

Rao's is a celebration of people and the special moments of joyful simplicity total team efforts produce. Serving outstanding food enriches some of the most important elements in life: love, friendship, conviviality, and pleasure.

Like charity, love and support begin at home. That's why we tip the brim of our caps to Josephine, Senior's wife and Junior's mother; Angela, Senior's daughter and Junior's sister; and Caroline, Junior's wife. All three of these graces are steadier and more stable than Rocks of Gibraltar, and our enduring and ever-growing love for them is so great it defies description.

Thanks, everyone,
The Franks, Senior and Junior

NOTE FROM THE AUTHOR

Rao's Classics is a nostalgic, generational recipe book with a story to tell. Steeped in Italian culture dating back to the turn of the century, Rao's on 114th Street and Pleasant Avenue in East Harlem is the focal point, setting, and backdrop of the narrative.

One of my earliest memories dates back to 1976, on a late autumn Sunday afternoon. I was seven years old and visiting my great-aunt and uncle, Annie and Vincent, for Sunday dinner with my parents. Their brownstone, and the birthplace of my great-uncle Vincent in 1903, was just fifty feet away from the ruby red doors of where Rao's still stands today.

This book is a journey through eras of tranquility and turbulence, and of times of celebration followed by sudden downturns. In a city forever in flux, Rao's is as close to constant as it gets.

The universality of this culinary experience spans the considerable chasms between the greatest generation, baby boomers, Generation X, and millennials. When we break bread at the restaurant the distinctions blur, these generations merge, and my father, Frank Pellegrino, Sr., and I stand together instead of years apart. Intergenerational appreciation has shaped our present-day hospitality, food culture, and social interaction at Rao's New York, Rao's Las Vegas, and Rao's Hollywood.

Stories peopled by a vibrant cast of notable Rao's characters—from the postman to personalities of stage, screen, literature, sports, and music—are as much the heart of this book as our popular meatballs or lemon chicken.

Society bombards us with endless information, distracting technological gizmos, and tight and frantic schedules that never relent. The superfast pace of our lives diverts us from breaking bread with our family and friends. I want to inspire you to put aside your gadgets and create your own precious moments and memories while preparing meals together with family and friends at home. It is my hope that these stories and recipes will provide a greater understanding of the roots of our family, and possibly remind you of your own. Into this mix I will drizzle my thoughts and insights on Italian culture, from the tenement to the table. The ethos of this book and of Rao's stands in stark contrast to our impersonal culture of fast food/slow death and the tragedy of eating in isolation.

Together we can rekindle the family fire and with the press of a button turn off the social media. I will show you how to create delicious meals that inspire precious moments and generate memories that will last a lifetime.

Enjoy!

—*Frank J. Pellegrino, Jr.*

Introduction

It all started after school on a warm and sunny June afternoon in 1982. I was in the sixth grade at Boardman Junior High School, on the South Shore of Long Island, New York.

Looking forward to the end of another school year and planning for a carefree summer, I was a happy camper. I anticipated upcoming summer days spent boogie boarding at the beach, lounging poolside with friends, or out cycling on my BMX bike. These summer plans abruptly changed when, my father, Frank, Sr., summoned me to his office . . . my grandmother's kitchen table.

What did I do now? I paused to wonder; did one of my teachers call from school to report that I wasn't going to pass the sixth grade? *Did so-and-so rat me out for some shenanigans my crew of friends and I perpetrated?* To my surprise, it wasn't any of that. Dad greeted me with a big smile and asked me to take a seat. Nervously I sat down at the opposite end of the table, just out of his physical reach, in fear of a surprise attack.

"François!" my father called. My name in French lingered briefly in the air, delivered only as a singer could. Then he said, "Guess what, my boy! You've got a job this summer!" My silent response was, *Ah, what? But . . . But . . . My summer plans . . .*

It was the beginning of the rest of my life.

As I reminisce about my beginnings at Rao's, I am excited to share with you some personal stories and recipes that have touched my heart and were my introduction and inspiration for a life spent providing hospitality.

I think of my Aunt Anna and Uncle Vincent at their home for Sunday dinner. Upon entering the house, the aroma of Sunday Gravy permeated the brownstone. The familiar scent made me feel right at home, just the way I felt at my grandmother's. My Aunt Anna, impeccably dressed as always, in cashmere and silk, was tending to the stove braising the meats for the gravy, pensively looking for the short ribs.

I marveled at my uncle Vincent, as he unlocked the roll-down gate of what appeared to this seven-year-old to be an ironclad fortress. Uncle Vincent, sporting his trademark Stetson, was huge to me, straight out of a John Ford film. He had a six-foot frame that towered over me, and hands so big they could have served as baseball mitts. His chiseled features were accentuated by a pair of robust lightly tinted brown spectacles with Coke bottle lenses. As the steel gate rose with a clatter, the red facade of Rao's was made plain. I recall old glass doors, held together by unique double-steel door-handle strips; a long, high-pitched creak followed the swing of the opening doors. As I entered, I was startled by a deep groan, something like a grizzly bear. In a deep voice, my uncle said, "Don't worry, it's only Jocko." Jocko was a beautiful black Labrador, who, in tandem with an ornery German shepherd named Rip, kept guard over the restaurant when it was closed. As we stepped into the dimly lit kitchen, the smell of gas from the pilot lights on the well-used Garland stove, reminiscent of an old steam locomotive, permeated the air. After turning on the kitchen lights, Uncle Vincent walked toward the back of the tiny kitchen to a massive four-door white refrigerator and freezer unit right out of the early sixties. This refrigerator/freezer spanned the entire back wall of the kitchen. It looked just like the freezer doors on the old-school white Good Humor ice-cream trucks that parked on the block when we ran out in summer. To my surprise, it wasn't an ice cream cone Uncle Vincent reached for when he opened the heavy-duty latch on the refrigerator door, but a rack of beef short ribs. I watched my uncle handle the rack with ease as he placed it atop the band saw he had just turned on. Wow! Like a warm knife slicing through butter, Uncle Vincent broke down those ribs with the whining band saw and quickly wrapped them in some butcher paper. With a smile, he said, "One day I'll show you how to use the saw . . . so long as you do not tell your aunt." I was over the moon with excitement; this place was so cool!

MOST IMPORTANT INGREDIENTS

I am forever being asked three questions by friends, guests, and journalists. One: "What are your go-to ingredients?" Two: "How do you make a good cooking experience at home?" Three: "Cooking is so much work, don't you tire of it?"

The answers to these three questions are far more difficult than one would think. Each represents a facet of a tapestry that one weaves when one creatively expresses oneself in their kitchen. Think of yourself as an artist before a blank canvas. The canvas is your foundation, the ingredients are the colors that sit upon your palette. You can go big, robust, and colorful like Monet, or you may venture off into the esoteric, you know, Picasso. Or, it may be more practical to subscribe to a more fundamental approach, like Bob Ross.

Answering the above questions for yourself, while factoring in the numerous challenges of daily life, will determine what style of cuisine best suits your needs, making for the most enjoyable cooking experience possible. That being said, here are my answers to the three questions.

In my pantry, I keep dried goods with long shelf lives. Grains, such as white and whole grain rice, Arborio rice, cornmeal/polenta, couscous, lentils, cannellini/Roman beans in dried and canned versions, all-purpose flour, dried yeast, bread crumbs, Wondra. As for pasta, usually four cuts of dried pasta: a long pasta such as linguine, great for light and quickly prepared sauces such as clam sauce or *aglio e olio*; rigatoni, ideal for hardier sauces like Filetto di Pomodoro con Pancetta as a quick marinara; short fusilli, for its ability to hold up to a more robust sauce such as pasta with broccoli or a primavera; farfalle, which means "butterfly" in Italian, and is sometimes referred to as bow tie pasta, is terrific for soups. With a wink, I always have on hand a box of gluten-free pasta, for some of my more health-conscious guests. After all, no dietary concern should get in the way of a great dish of pasta. Additionally, I keep an inventory of bulk ingredients, including: kosher salt, black pepper, crushed red pepper flakes, corn oil, vegetable oil, pure olive oil, extra-virgin olive oil, red wine, balsamic and white vinegars, and cheeses such as fresh mozzarella, shredded mozzarella, Parmigiano Reggiano and Pecorino Romano. There are a few specialty items here as well, for those rare impromptu, in a pinch, chichi moments: truffle essence/ oil can change a midnight snack into an unforgettable indulgence.

SOME BASIC TIPS AND PROCEDURES

Before starting to cook the recipes in this book, review some of the basic and simple recipes we use at home and in the restaurant. You will find them helpful in achieving the best results not only for our dishes, but for any genre of cuisine you cook at home.

Flavored Olive Oil
Makes 1 cup

1 cup fine quality olive oil
4 garlic cloves, peeled and smashed

In a large sauté pan, over a medium-low heat, add the olive oil and garlic. Sauté the garlic until it begins to shimmy in the oil and takes on a deep golden hue. Remove the garlic and discard. Pour the garlic oil into a sealable glass or plastic container and reserve at room temperature.
The oil is ideal for frying and sautéing vegetables, meats, and fish and is a terrific accoutrement for bread, salads, and charcuterie plates.

Preparing Garlic

Every day in our restaurants we use hundreds of cloves of garlic. After separating them, we soak them in a bowl of warm hot water for 15 minutes, to make them easier to peel, before easing off their paper-thin skins. We leave some cloves whole and run others through a garlic press, for soups and sautés.

Keep in mind; seasoning is akin to temperature (medium-rare, medium, and well-done) for meats and fish. Less is more: it is very difficult to reverse the seasoning or temperature of a dish. However, you can always add more heat or seasoning without having to start the preparation all over again.

Vinegared Hot and Sweet Cherry Peppers or Sweet Bell Peppers

A must-have that lends a zesty flavor to many dishes! From frittatas to fried cutlets and pasta, these babies will lend an additional flavor dimension, particularly if you are fond of spicy foods.

Bread Crumbs

In the restaurants, we make our bread crumbs from our leftover Italian bread. The process is a bit time-consuming and arduous to do without an industrial grater/grinder.

Our primary reason for preparing our own is greater control over the flavor of our seasoned bread crumbs, which we use for everything from Mozzarella en Carrozza to Veal Milanese.

Buy unseasoned bread crumbs and season them to your taste. Add, salt, pepper, parsley, freshly minced garlic, grated cheese, or any other seasoning that tickles your fancy. Your additions will add a personal flavor touch to your dishes, and separate yours from dishes made in anybody else's kitchen.

WINE PAIRINGS

It's Italian cuisine—never have food without wine or wine without food.

Italian food has such intense flavors, wine can rinse and reset your taste buds so each bite can taste like the first. In a Japanese restaurant you eat ginger between bites of sushi—wine is Italian ginger!

When pairing food and wine, remember it's an adventure. There's always a reason to try a new wine or new combination. And always remember, in the end, what you like trumps all (except never drink a tannic full-bodied wine like cabernet with cherry peppers: it will taste like you bit into bitter steel!).

Make sure you have enough wine for the meal, and that means enough to drink while cooking *and* eating. Whenever I prepare a meal for myself or others the feast begins over the stove. I like to enjoy wine with all the individual ingredients while cooking as I test for "quality control" while preparing the meal. This can, of course, lead to a shortage of these ingredients when it's completed! The solution to this was—like many things in my life—inspired by football. When you go to tackle someone, you never run to where they are, you run toward where they're going to be. With that in mind I always put a little extra of everything in any dish. Anticipating the tendency to graze, and knowing how much has to be there when it's done; that's the way my quantities never fall short and never miss the target.

In the list that follows, I've paired the dishes with reasonable vintages off of our list in Hollywood, You can almost never go wrong with Sangiovese, a varietal whose most famous types are Chianti, Brunello, and Vino Nobile.

1. Marinara Sauce: Chianti Colli Senesi from Sienna or a heavier Montepulciano d'Abruzzo, from Amorino
2. Fusilli with Cabbage and Sausage: this one screams for di Lenardo Sauvignon Blanc from Friuli
3. Linguine and Clams: Verdicchio dei Castelli di Jesi, "Bucci" or just a simple Pinot Grigio, Borgo Conventi from the Collio region
4. Spaghetti Aglio Olio: Borgo Conventi Pinot Grigio or for red, a light Valpolicella like Zenato Ripassa
5. Spaghetti with Zucchini and Yellow Squash: Venica Sauvignon Blanc, Venica or Pio Cesare "Dolcetto d'Alba"
6. 30-Minute Tomato and Basil: Vino Nobile di Montepulciano, "La Braccesca," Antinori
7. Pasta and Broccoli: for red, "Nero d'Avola," Morgante, and for white, Sauvignon Blanc, Venica
8. Sunday Gravy: go big with a "Brunello Di Montalcino," Castiglion Del Bosco
9. Ravioli Purses with Dried Cranberries, Sage, and Bread Crumbs: Pinot Nero (Italian Pinot Noir) "Stiftskellerei Neustift," Abbazia di Novacella
10. Lasagna: take your pick from the classics such as, Chianti Classico, "Brunello di Montalcino," Castiglion del Bosco if you are on budget, Valdicava if you want the best

11. Giampotta: Di Lenardo Sauvignon Blanc or "Serra" Paitin Barbaresco
12. Spaghetti Carbonara: LA Scolca, "Black Label," Gavi di Gavi, or for red, Aglianico, Feudi San Gregorio, "Rubrato"
13. Fresh Pasta with Peas and Ham: Chardonnay "Bramito," Castello della Sala, or a nice Pinot Noir
14. Orecchiette with Rabe and Sausage: "Serra" Barbaresco Paitin or Chianti Classico Riserva
15. Filetto di Pomodoro: Barbera d'Alba "Campolive," Paitin, or for more body, Amarone della Valpolicella Classico, "Costa Sera," Masi
16. Manicotti: "Rosso di Montalcinoc Casanova di Neri Sant'Antimo Rosso"
17. Southern Pesto: Sauvignon Blanc, Gavi or Barbera
18. Eggplant Parmigiana: Amarone, Chianti, Chardonnay
19. Lobster Fra Diavolo: Berlucchi, "Cuvée 61," Ros è Franciacorta or Robert Eymael "Monchof," Riesling
20. Shells with Ricotta: Barbaresco, "Serra," Paitin or Chardonnay
21. Asparagus Risotto: Sauvignon Blanc or Bramito Chardonnay
22. Risotto Milanese: Greco di Tufo, Feudi di San Gregorio or Chardonnay
23. Risotto Frutte di Mare: Verdicchio dei Castelli di JesiBucci or a White Burgundy
24. Polenta with Sausage and Mushrooms: Barbaresco, Brunello, Pinot Noir

Not everyone can have a Sassicaia with every meal. Sommeliers and restaurateurs sometimes take for granted the fact that we work with the best wines in the world every day and forget that most people drink simple regional table wine with dinner. You don't have to break the bank to find a wine you can enjoy. I love finding gems for under ten or fifteen dollars that drink like a million bucks, they're out there.

Some of my favorite wines on a budget are:

- Villa Antinori, Chianti Classico
- Cecchi, Chianti Classico
- Borgo Conventi, Pinot Grigio
- Principessa Gavia, Gavi
- 14 Hands, Cabernet Sauvignon
- 14 Hands, Merlot
- Casillero Del Diablo, Cabernet Sauvignon
- Estancia, Pinot Noir
- Petite Petit, Petite Syrah

—*Big Lou, Sommelier at Rao's Hollywoo*d

TEN TABLES AT A TIME
Recipes And Other Secrets

EATING & EXPERIENCE

Aristotle taught us that there's nothing in the intellect that wasn't first in the senses. From birth we are sensual beings, exploring and evaluating our environment, encountering stimuli, embracing, confronting, engaging, and ingesting as we make our way through. We all understand that a picture's worth a thousand words, Thomas Mann has suggested that music is a "foretaste of Heaven," commercials extol the "touch" and "feel" of cotton, olfaction brings both flowers and fetor to vivid life, and, of course, there's no accounting for taste. Yet all of our senses conspire when we enter the alimentary arena. Marcel Proust provides the classic example of gastronomical sense memory in his novel *In Search of Lost Time*. Volume One of his works includes the episode of the madeleine, where the author reflects upon a languid winter of ennui in Combray, a commune in his native France. One afternoon his mother prepares, as an elixir of sorts, a cup of tea, accompanied by "plump little cakes known as '*petites madeleines,*' which look as though they had been molded in the fluted scallop of a pilgrim's shell." The taste and texture of the pastries, comingled with the tea, serve as a catalyst for a torrent of meaningful memories.

Food has transportive power. Its cultivation, preparation, and enjoyment is central to every aspect of our existence, from sustenance, to courting, to religious celebrations, rites of passage, and holidays. From the staff of life to the king of condiments, from the Frigidaire to the county fair, be it ten-pound roast or holy host, foodie fashions or plain K rations, foodstuffs are both essential and evocative. What does your Proustian memory consist of? Mine goes like this:

I do recall a space confined,
And cruets filled with blood-red wine,
White boxes bound with baker's twine.
The nuts and berries cheese and bread,
Fresh pasta strewn across a bed,
Santino raging, full of lead.
A dish that teemed with nonpareils,
Intoxicating sights and smells,
The time and care that love compels.
As mother cooked with fretful pace,
The smelts were gone without a trace,
But she fried extra, just in case.
The hats and gloves, the suits and ties,
The dipping cookies, cakes and pies,
And lessons learned from men most wise.
Chocolate turtles, panna cotta,
ungulates fresh from the slaughter,
No one heard of bottled water.

The baked stuffed shrimp, fillet of sole,
And white beans swathed in escarole,
The dulcet tones of Nat King Cole.
Pizzelles stacked like poker chips,
The rich black steaming coffee drips,
While anise essence coats the lips.
The sun descends behind the trees,
On ancient homelands, overseas,
As we go forth with memories.

MEATBALL DIPLOMACY

The meatball, or *polpette,* is a mainstay of the Italian kitchen. Its rich density and protein provided the nutritional ballast for a community of aspiring immigrants. Unlike pizza that has been endlessly bastardized and experimented with (cheese-filled crust, pineapple toppings, and dipping sauces among other travesties), the meatball has remained relatively untainted by marketing or media makeover.

We must acknowledge that the name "meatball" is unflattering, connoting rotund Italian guys, distressed and distended, like the afflicted fella in Alka Seltzer's '70s "Agita" campaign, who sat at the edge of his bed, plaintively repeating, "I can't believe I ate the whole thing." Furthermore, the meatball is often relegated to the confines of a hero or insinuated into a side order of soft and stringy spaghetti, resting atop a paper placemat bearing the Italian boot, a gondola, the Leaning Tower of Pisa, and the obligatory wicker (*fiasco*) bottle of Chianti. Also, there's

only so much one can do with a meatball. From time immemorial, a meatball consists of a mixture of ground beef, pork, and veal, bound by egg and bread, and seasoned with parsley, garlic, grated cheese, salt, and pepper. Once formed, it is fried—or baked, if you want to significantly cut down on cleanup time or you are paying lip service to health concerns. Sure, some Sicilians have introduced raisins or mint, pine nuts and ricotta (regional wrinkles, really) into the mix; but at the end of the day, a meatball is still a meatball.

How does Rao's elevate the meatball from sub-shop staple to the toast of the table?

Size Matters: I am loath to be considered puerile or prurient, but Rao's has big balls. How big? Calibrating by eye, I'd say by a factor of about three to one, that is three traditional Nana meatballs to one of Rao's awesome orbs. But this is not size for size's sake; the greater girth allows the meatball to be cooked in degrees, growing gradually pink toward the center, a moist, tender core protected by a crusty outer shell, served plain or bathed in vibrant marinara sauce.

The Scene: Wednesday may be Prince Spaghetti day in Boston's North End, but at Rao's, Wednesday is meatball night. Once a week, the kitchen cranks out platters of steaming meatballs, making the midweek seating an experience not to be missed. At Rao's, on any given night, you could indulge yourself with Chicken Scarpariello, Steak

Pizzaiola, Seafood Salad, and Lobster fra Diavolo, but meatballs are reserved exclusively for Wednesday night. Wednesday means meatballs, and for Rao's habitués the terms are practically interchangeable. The association was almost Pavlovian, and gradually a scene grew out of it. Could it possibly get any *more* difficult to get into Rao's? Meatballs were gaining ground.

No one is suggesting that we invented meatballs, but I think it's fair to say that we were complicit in their resurgence. I remember my father preparing them on *Late Night* with Conan O'Brien, the gangly redhead and the meticulously attired man about town, Irish and Italian, Harvard and Hun-Fourteenth. Many a deal's been brokered over these dollops of gustatory goodness. They are homespun and wholesome; they

provide an authentic experience for the many restaurant visitors who did not grow up in an Italian milieu. Today, they are served as a stand-alone item, no longer the sidekick or sandwich stuffer. Today they are made with great care and choice ingredients, deep-fried to perfection. Sure, they made their name in East Harlem, but have since been rolled out in Las Vegas, and now the belle of the ball in Los Angeles O.A.R.—only at Rao's.

Foodball

From late summer to the dead of winter, Sunday sits at the splendid intersection of food and football. The two are a potent double helix that has stratospherically increased bottom lines for the NFL and food purveyors. Since 1970 we've had *Monday*

Night Football, the NFL Network premiered in 2003, and three years on we saw the advent of *Thursday Night Football*. During roughly the same period, food-related programming has gone from homey PBS programs like *The Romagnolis' Table* and *The Galloping Gourmet* to 24/7 cable networks featuring celebrity chefs and competitive cooking. How powerful and mutually influential is this relationship? Consider the fact that tailgating has evolved into an absolute art form. Gone are the days of burgers and hot dogs, while Iron Chefs (Flay, Batali, Morimoto) face off at Kitchen Stadium in uncompromising opposition.

Labor Day cookouts double as delirious celebrations for the kickoff of a new NFL season. After a long summer of boring box scores from a fading former pastime, the return of football is indeed cause for unfettered celebration. As autumn temperatures plummet, pumpkin ales and the low glow of the parking lot grill keep grease-painted, shirtless fans warm. Then comes Thanksgiving: the pigskin is as essential to this national holiday as the turkey. We give thanks, we eat to excess, fortifying ourselves in anticipation of another uncompromising winter, and then we watch the games, the Cowboys and Lions part of the bill of fare. The Italian Thanksgiving is less Norman Rockwell and more a Vespers Liturgy, as the bird debuts well after nightfall, around the third quarter of the second game, due to the fact that it is preceded by antipasto, arancini, artichokes, stuffed peppers, meat sauce, braciole, and mostaccioli. Then, after the

winter solstice, as the days grow imperceptibly longer and the polar vortices descend, teams vie for wildcard berths, division titles, and the all-important home field advantage. Libations flow more liberally in the NFL's classic cold-weather cities, and regional dishes reflect the time of year. There's hearty "chowduh" with crunchy Oysterettes up and down the New England states, hot coals char the steaks in the Steel City when memories of six Lombardi Trophies don't suffice, the Bears have their beers and their brats, there's Frozen Tundra Chili in Green Bay, Dungeness Crab soup works like a charm for Ravens fans, Philly has its cheesesteaks (Pat's or Geno's?), Spicy Buffalo Wings always fit the bill for the brave souls in frigid Orchard Park, and those who bolster the Broncos will eat pretty much anything since Colorado's legalization of recreational marijuana.

Giants fans, however, have the annual Dino Gatto tailgate extravaganza, where the Rao's executive chef brings the heat all the way from East Harlem; we're talking meatballs for three hundred, pig on a spit, bottle service, and dignitaries aplenty, 2015's soiree was attended by NFL Commissioner Roger Goodell, who actually pitched in at a carving station. O.A.R.

With the New Year, chili and stew come just in time for the Wildcard Weekend and the Divisional Round. The penultimate, Championship Weekend (preferable to Super Bowl Sunday for many football purists) is an all-day affair, and here we see the culinary influence from South of the Border, the salsa, guacamole, nachos with refried beans and jalapeños, bolstered by Jamaican jerk wings or oxtail with butter beans, before we return stateside for Texas-size portions of pulled pork, brisket, and ribs.

By the time the "big game" finally rolls around, after a two-week interregnum of relentless hype and prognostication, most of our teams are, sadly, out of the running, and all that's left of our once-promising football season are Super Bowl commercials and the promise of another halftime performance by a pop prince or princess.

But once again, the calendar harmonizes perfectly with the NFL schedule, as Lent follows on the heels of Super Bowl Sunday, and fasting is certainly in order.

ETRUSCAN PLACES

Who are the Italians? We have to go all the way back to a people known as the Etruscans for this one. Flourishing on the banks of the Tyrrhenian sea circa 700 BC, these Italian ancestors established language, literacy, and governance while producing art, mythology, jewels, earthenware, sculptures, cave murals, and sarcophagi that would resonate to the time of the Renaissance. This ancient culture and many of its customs formed the basis of an inchoate commonwealth that was eventually absorbed and co-opted by the bands of opportunistic forces that would ultimately constitute the Roman Republic. Much of the heraldry associated with glorious

Rome is attributable to the inhabitants of Etruria. For instance, the emblematic Roman fasces, depicted as a bundle of bound birch rods, is an icon of strength through unity that was adopted from the Etruscans; today, these symbols pop up in depictions of American authority. Gilt fasces featuring protruding axe blades are featured prominently in the well of the House Chamber, on collectible relief coins, flanking the seat of the Lincoln Memorial, and they can even be found, on a grand scale, running several stories into the desert sky at Caesars Palace in Las Vegas. The Etruscan diet, as gleaned from funerary art and oblations, featured fish, game, spelt bread, pulses, olives, cheeses, and other foodstuffs associated with the bounty of the Mediterranean. Though the Etruscans were known to cook with garlic and onions, pasta (made with durum flour) would not arrive until after Marco Polo's thirteenth-century expedition to the East, and the tomato would not debut in Italy till after the Colombian exchange, when the indispensable golden balls finally made their way via sea voyage from Peru. Giuseppi Sassatelli's chapter on Etruscan gastronomy, in Jean-Louis Flandrin's *Food: A Culinary History* says, "The Tyrrhenians prepare sumptuous repasts twice a day on carpets of many colors and with silver goblets of all kinds, and a crowd of beautiful slaves, dressed in precious garments."

Sassatelli proceeds to paint a portrait of astute farmers cultivating fertile land, and of proficient hunters wielding hand-crafted weapons to kill what they could not breed, protracted feasts, precision utensils, boar on a spit, amphorae brimming with wine, and some festive fellow gaily plucking the lyre by the fire. Funiculì Funiculà?

So who, in today's context, is Italian? The fifteen million or so Americans who claim Italian heritage? Or should the designation be exclusive to those born on that storied peninsula bathed by the Adriatic and Mediterranean? What about the remote islanders on Corsica and Sicily, with their multitude of foreign influences, Norman, Spanish, North African, and Greek among them, are they Italian? Is your father Italian, or your mother? Have you no Italian ancestors, but have travelled extensively from the Hellenic ruins of Agrigento to the Eternal City to the Lakes and the Alps and the watery home of the Doges, mastering the many tongues and regional tastes along the way? Italians everywhere display a variety of physical types, some quite paradoxically, like the redheaded Sicilians in the Straits of Messina or the brown-eyed brunettes from Bergamo, in the northern reaches of Italy's Butter Belt. Millennia of marauders have encoded the Italian people with a kaleidoscopic genetic palette. Perhaps this was the cost of Italia's "fatal gift of beauty," as Lord Byron remarked.

Dialects further divide the cosmopolitan Italian north from the *Mezzogiorno* (Rome and all territories south), perhaps more decisively than actual international borders with, say, France and Switzerland. While the mother tongue (Tuscan Italian) flows beautifully with a fine bottle of Montepulciano and a bowl of ribollita, conversely, a Sicilian compatriot living in what was once known as Magna Graecia (Greater Greece) prefers to braise his rabbit with a measure of Marsala wine, i.e., *Mars al Allah,* from Arabic (the Port of God).

Whether they hail from Trieste, New Orleans, Buenos Aires, Victoria, or Toronto, Italians share common values, customs, and idiosyncrasies. The great Yale University president and former Major League Baseball Commissioner A. Bartlett Giamatti referred to this shared sensibility as *filial piety,* that is, "The fierce delight in being descended from a culture that created or transmitted many of the core values, secular and religious, of western civilization." (*The Italian Americans*, Allon Schoener, 1987)

Despite their pronounced differences in complexion, dialect, disposition, socio-economic station, and geographical location, the sacred, single unifying factor of all Italians is the family, be they Remus and Romulus desperately seeking sustenance, huddled 'neath the teat of a succoring she-wolf, Michelangelo's heartwarming "Holy Family," Da Vinci's fraternal "Last Supper," or Tony Soprano dispensing dour advice to his disillusioned son, telling him that "in the end your friends will always let you down. Family, they're the ones you can depend on."

If family is the quintessence of Italian culture, then the kitchen is the epicenter of the Italian family and the dinner table is where traditions are upheld, where memories are forged, where we give thanks, where young and old see eye to eye, where disputes end, where we take our time, where we join hands, where we gather in sorrow and celebration, where the family unit bonds, as symbolized long ago by those bound birch rods of ancient Etruria.

GOODFELLAS

It was 1989, and for ninety-three years some of New York's most colorful characters had come and gone at Rao's. They were known by their sobriquets, by their cars, gaits, fashions, habits, and, of course, by their appetites. Some were master craftsmen; some took a shot in the arts or gravitated to law enforcement, while others elected to take the perceived path of least resistance and enlist in a certain nefarious Sicilian co-operative that flourished in the shadows of American industry. Inevitably, Hollywood came calling: Warner Brothers was backing a film adaptation of Nick Pileggi's mob biography *Wiseguy: Life in a Mafia Family*. The studio settled on a more succinct title, *Goodfellas*, and, in the name of authenticity, began informal casting at Rao's. The joint, as it's known, is situated on an urban cul-de-sac, buffered by the FDR Drive and Jefferson Park; partially obscured by the imposing Manhattan Center for Science and Mathematics, Rao's literally stands alone, its vermillion façade conspicuous against the tenements and jalopies that dominate this historic hardscrabble neighborhood. The place teems with history and "well respected

men," many of whom frequented this place without pretense in the days of Prohibition and beyond; this singular site, eternally trimmed in garland and boxwood roping, all that felicity compressed beneath a nine foot, tin-stamped ceiling; the joint jumps like no other and serves as the epicenter of a vibrant, at times fraught, scene that has captivated visitors for decades.

Did "Dutch" Schultz conceive of the City's first lottery at table "O"? Maybe so, maybe not. Did John Gotti dine at Rao's? Once. But before you label the place a "mob joint," please consider the fact that Elie Wiesel had also broken bread there.

East Harlem was the crucible of Italian assimilation and activity, a bustling base of operations to the aforementioned tradesmen, seamstresses, stevedores, laborers, clergy, cobblers, anarchists, and cooks, as well as a stomping ground for the underhanded and opportunistic. One such man was Giovanni Ignazio Dioguardi; born in 1914, on New York's Lower East Side, he is reported to have been an associate of the Lucchese crime family, where he was simply known as "Johnny Dio."

In an inspired move, Rao's owner, my father, a seasoned performer in his own right, was cast by Martin Scorsese to play the role of Johnny Dio in *Goodfellas*. He appears in several scenes, but most memorably, and appropriately, in a cooking sequence. The story goes like this, during downtime, between camera setups, Frank was overheard reminiscing passionately about the days of

old New York with Charles Scorsese, Martin Scorsese's father. When it came time to shoot, the director approached Frank and asked him to recollect old New York again, and a classic scene was born.

With Bobby Darin's "Beyond the Sea" playing in the background, we see a group of incarcerated Mafiosi, Frank Pellegrino, Paul Sorvino, Ray Liotta, and Charles Scorsese, happily preparing an epic feast, momentarily oblivious to their Spartan accommodations. I remember the now-famous banter as Frank pan-fried steaks; he was dressed in a scarlet bathrobe, brandishing a two-pronged fork like a conductor's baton, stogie protruding from his profile, at once mild and menacing, "Vinnie, how do you like yours?" "Rare, medium rare." "Medium rare," he retorted, "Mmm, an aristocrat." And then, brilliantly

interspersed with the Henry Hill voiceover, Frank Pellegrino began to wax nostalgic and extempore about those idyllic days long past, "everyone in the neighborhood had respect, you loved one another, you left your doors open," he elaborated, while a large cauldron bubbled in front of him: tomatoes, veal, beef, and pork; "Ya gotta have the pork;" Sunday Gravy.

SUNDAYS

Sundays aren't quite the same anymore. Attendance at church is down; family togetherness is eroding under the weight of technology, and schedules and corporations have encroached on our domestic bill of fare. It wasn't long ago that Dominos was a game played in Spanish Harlem, the Subway was an urban transportation service, and Papa John was the Bishop of Rome. Today, these purveyors of pasta and pizza offer promises like "better ingredients" and assure us that their food will arrive at the door in fifteen minutes or less. What a departure from yesteryear, when fast food was a frittata (peppers and eggs), served with a loaf of bread, raised in an inferno by a local merchant called Joe the Baker.

From this tradition sprang *fare la spesa*, shopping, not at a supermarket, with gleaming aisles and conveniently demarcated sections, but in different, often far-flung locations, because Dominick the butcher had the most tender veal, "Artichoke" Mo had the freshest produce, the best confectioner could be all the way downtown (anywhere below Ninetieth Street to residents of East Harlem), fishmonger, vintner, a dizzying interborough gauntlet. While the route was often fractured, the foods were whole indeed.

THE HEATED TERM

"If you can't stand the heat, get out of the kitchen." This line is particularly relevant to the birth of Rao's. It was August 1896, and New York City was in the grip of a devastating heat wave. Sustained temperatures in the nineties coupled with relentless humidity made life in Manhattan's tenements unbearable. The city's police commissioner, a young patrician firebrand named Theodore

Roosevelt, referred to this urban calamity (that claimed an estimated 1,300 lives) as "The Heated Term." Conditions were less than ideal for inaugurating a restaurant. But forged in the fire as the curtain came down on the nineteenth century, Rao's has lasted through economic hardship, two World Wars, race riots, low hems, miniskirts, many mayoralties, Y2K, 9/11, Sandy, and beyond.

THE ROOM

On any given night at Rao's you will hear Frank Pellegrino say, "I just have no place to put you." He may be resigned when he delivers the news, or disappointed, sometimes frustrated, and at other times relieved, but always frank. The joint is big-time, but the square footage is small, the sunken entrance offers diners incredible street-level sight lines of shiny black stretch Maybachs or a convertible Carrera; young lovers, hand in hand, emerging from Jefferson Park; white-haired men conferring just beyond the intrusive glow of the lamppost; the necklace of coruscating lights on the Triborough Bridge; Dave Collins, Nick Rondi, and Frank Trepeddi

eating Patsy's Pizza, al fresco, behind the cement and wrought iron parapets that mark the narrow entrance where 114th Street and Pleasant Avenue converge to form a vertex that vaguely resembles the prow of a rollicking pirate ship. Inside, past the bar where Bobby V and Charlie DeMonte reminisce over drinks, is the stockroom that doubles as an informal green room, a raw space populated by lawyers, agents, politicians, and tradesmen making deals and exchanging pleasantries over the drone of the walk-in freezer, next to palettes of canned tomatoes, gallons of Filippo Berio, and cases of pasta. It is the proverbial "smoke-filled room." The office, adjacent to the stockroom, is the smallest space on the premises. Reminiscent of Fibber McGee and

Molly's closet, it is overflowing with bric-a-brac, test products, souvenirs, and mementos. There is a wall-mounted coatrack, a safe, Joe Ciccone tapping away on an adding machine, and more recently, cable television. There is always a game on TV in the office, and you never know who will stick their head in the door to check a score. One night, I retreated, as I often do, to the office, where I stood, taking in a game—Rangers, Mets, Knicks, I can't be certain—until I detected someone in the periphery. I did not turn my head until he asked, "What's the score?" It was none other than Paul Anka; O.A.R.

Rao's is a microcosm of Gotham itself; space is scarce and highly coveted, every square inch is spoken for, and the rents are exorbitant. Rent may not be the most suitable term, but certain tables at Rao's are allotted to regular patrons, and those tables are occasionally auctioned off, with the proceeds (tens of thousands for a single table) benefitting the renter's favorite charities. Space is finite, but human ingenuity is unfathomable: Rao's regulars can be resourceful when it comes to carving out a pied-à-terre in this hottest of urban markets. Former New York City detective, Fox News Channel analyst, *Goodfellas* alum ("bye-bye dickhead"), and East Harlem original Bo Dietl, raised the bar where maximizing precious space is concerned. Bo has a table every Thursday night, and has since 1977. It is a traditional six-top occupying a significant swath of space before a large picture window looking out onto Pleasant Avenue. It is favorably situated

at the south end of Nicky "Vest's" bustling bar, and occasionally subject to strange, Tornado Alley–like weather patterns as it lies at the midpoint of the heat emanating from the kitchen and the draft infiltrating from the front door, as smokers and cell phone enthusiasts come and go, almost incessantly. Bo traditionally holds court from a seat that faces the picture window as well as assorted framed photos of himself dining with Anna and Vincent Rao or his *Wolf of Wall Street* scene partner, Leonardo DiCaprio (their scene was shot at Rao's). There is also a picture of a young, strapping Bo, svelte with dark hair, circa 1990, receiving a citation from George Herbert Walker Bush, aka Bush 41, or, as Frank Pellegrino might say, "the good Bush." From this vantage, Bo is the de facto greeter, the jovial familiar face, the bon vivant, looking nowhere while seeing everything, his white beard finely trimmed, ruddy cheeks, sidearm protruding from the vent of a hand-tailored suit. Bo knows the pols, Bo knows the stars, Bo knows the jocks, the real estate magnates, and the hedge fund fat cats. You know what else Bo knows? He knows eight is greater than six. And so it was that during a late afternoon "family meal," Bo arrived at Rao's, rolling what could only be described as a large, circular, laminated wooden disk into the restaurant. "What the hell is that?" asked Mo, a neighborhood fixture, his trusty beige pit bull, Cinnamon, at his side. Bo said nothing, carefully navigating the entrance, moving eagerly into the unoccupied dining room.

Since Bo's table, located by the front door,

was occupied by staff as they dined on pasta broccoli and lemon chicken, he rolled his disk past the bar to the second of the three six-tops, provoking strange looks as he leveraged it atop the unset table, immediately increasing the table-top circumference and therefore the potential seating capacity by a count of two. Voila! Bo had successfully engineered an eight-top, effectively shoehorning more diners into a joint already bursting at the seams, particularly in those unbridled days prior to Mayor Bloomberg's smoking ban, when drinks flowed and smoke billowed overhead well into the predawn hours. Back then, in the mid-to-late '90s, Frankie Junior (simply known as Junior) was still a fixture at the Joint; these were the days prior to his western migration (today he presides over Rao's Vegas and Rao's L.A.). Junior would pull up a seat, essentially becoming another diner, establishing eye contact, before carefully tailoring a meal to the appetites of his guests. He'd start with a few questions: "Any vegetarians in your party?" (There are no menus.) "Everybody eat fish?" he'd continue. "How 'bout some baked clams and seafood salad?" The diners might nod cautiously, if they are first-timers. "No worries folks, anything you don't like . . ." Junior effortlessly tilts his head toward Frank Senior, "is on him."

Standing next to Frank is a tall, silver-haired, handsome blue-eyed man, Ron Straci. A lawyer by trade, he is Frank's cousin, and partner in sublime. So while Frank is the undeniable master of ceremonies, capable of whipping the room into a frenzy with an impromptu sing-along, "Ronnie" is the perfect foil, embedded at the bar or by the jukebox, gently laying a hand on your shoulder, asking after your family, happy to expound on the issues of the day and offer you a drink while rhapsodizing about the Golden Age of Hollywood: "*The Four Feathers* was on Turner last night, ever seen it?" Invariably a gravelly voice from the gallery would chime in, "*Four Feathers*, 1939, John Clements and Ralph Richardson," and just like that, we're off and running.

Some nights the gods and goddesses of American cinema were the topic of nostalgic conversation, other times it was something altogether different, like the evening Sophia Loren walked through the door, or did she simply materialize? The Room has been the setting for countless magic moments over the decades, like a standing ovation (the first of its kind at Rao's) for legendary Yankee closer Mariano Rivera, in the waning days of his final season. Even dyed-in-the wool Met fans (this means you, Tommy), joined the applause for the humble Hall of Famer in waiting. Jay-Z shot his "Death of Auto-Tune" video during off hours at the Joint, The New York Giants celebrated their stunning Super Bowl XLII victory on 114th Street, Nobel Peace Prize–winner Elie Wiesel graced Rao's with a visit, as did "Hammerin'" Hank Aaron, Neil Young, Madonna. One night Celine Dion, Gloria Estefan, Danny DeVito, and Jim Carrey sat at the same table. You want more? Jimmy Fallon, Shaquille O'Neal, Hillary Clinton, Whoopi Goldberg, Francis Ford Coppola, Billy Joel,

Muhammad Ali, Denzel Washington, Joe Montana, Cardinal Dolan. Consider the "Hopperesque" tableau of Frank Pellegrino, Keith Richards, and Rod Stewart seated at the bar, coddling single tumblers of malt whiskey, riffing on their shared appreciation of American roots music, from the Delta blues to the legends of Chess Records. By this point in the evening the kitchen has long been closed, Jessica is folding linen napkins for tomorrow night's service, Tommy Mara, the Joint's jester/ waiter/concierge (you name it), just wishes everyone would go home. Then, we hear the six ascending bass notes of the Temptations' 1964 standard "My Girl" from the jukebox and the three men spontaneously break into song, vocalizing as if before a packed house. There were probably more witnesses when Moses got his marching orders from the burning bush, but it happened at Rao's, up the avenue, on the block, in The Room.

For Frank Pellegrino, music is always part of the calculus, from the crooners, jazz singers, and pop recording artists of his formative years, to the layered a cappella harmonies known as "doo-wop" pioneered in the '50s by African Americans (The Harptones, the Penguins, the Chords, the Cadillacs). Italians eventually came to prominence on the doo-wop scene. There was Johnny Maestro (Johnny Mastrangelo) of the Crests, Larry Chance (Larry Figueiredo) of the Earls, Danny Terranova of Danny and the Juniors; while subgenres of this nascent rock and roll movement produced Dion DiMucci, Bobby Darin, and Frankie Valli. Pellegrino, like many

of his generation, came under the spell of this melody and idyllic notion of a "Sunday Kind of Love," the adolescent quandaries of a "Teenager in Love," the breathless longing in a number "Dedicated to the One I Love." It would be summarily swept away by a cultural tsunami known as the Summer of Love, but not before Pellegrino fronted a '60s vocal group of his own called The Holidaes. A badly damaged vocal cord, the demands of family, and the sea-change that touched off when the Beatles touched down at Kennedy Airport caused Pellegrino to consider a course correction. He continued to perform on cruise ships, at nightclubs, and at festivals, but he deftly adapted his repertoire, selecting dramatic, lyrically complex compositions that relied less on his vocals, and more on his presence, timing, and distinct phrasing. Favorites were compositions like Charles Aznavour's self referential "Le Cabotin" (The Ham), or a stirring arrangement (performed as a duet) that seamlessly fused the verses of Rodgers and Hart's whimsical "My Funny Valentine" with those of Leon Russell's heart-rending "A Song for You;" the result of this inspired musical fusion, combined with Pellegrino's poignant reading, was a powerful meditation on the eternal themes of love and loss. Seismic cultural changes were not limited to popular culture as the tumultuous '60s bled into the chaotic '70s. Crime, persistent unemployment, and the scourge of the drug trade had transformed not just the old neighborhood, but all of New York City. East Harlem's own Salvatore "Sonny"

Grosso, along with his partner Eddie Egan, had infiltrated the notorious Marseilles heroin cartel, coordinating a sensational undercover sting that resulted in the seizure of 112 pounds of processed poppy with an estimated street value of 32 million dollars. Their exploits were immortalized in William Friedkin's Academy Award–winning film *The French Connection*. Sonny, a Monday night mainstay at Rao's, lost his father at a young age, and vividly recalls an episode from that difficult time. He speaks of an elegantly attired man with a topcoat draped over his shoulders, flanked by two "tree trunks," making an entrance at Farenga's Funeral Home, where he offered his condolences and reassurances to the bereft Grosso family. Then this charismatic "man

of respect" faintly gestured to his underlings, who, on command, knelt before the open casket on his behalf. This demonstration of absolute authority left quite an impression on young Sonny, who by his own admission was no angel, but ultimately joined the force in 1954 and rose to prominence, adroitly navigating the precarious gray area between the black hats and the guys in blue. New York City was in transition and the insular enclave on and around 114th Street was not spared: second and third generation Italian made their way, en masse, for the serenity and security of the suburbs, while Hispanics were fast filling an old neighborhood that was once exclusively populated by immigrants from Naples, Calabria, and Sicily. The

Organized Crime Control Act of 1970 sounded the death knell for the unassuming men who maintained order and pacified their respective precincts while discreetly plying their trade. Mass incarceration, internecine fighting, and widespread informing ensued, leaving a vacuum to be filled by opportunistic miscreants and street gangs. It seemed all that remained of old East Harlem was Our Lady of Mount Carmel Church . . . and Rao's.

These were the given circumstances when Frank Pellegrino stepped to the fore, to work alongside his uncle, Vincent Rao and his aunt, the inimitable Anna Pellegrino Rao, the doyenne of the dining room, who served as the inspiration for Mia Farrow's character, Tina Vitale, in Woody Allen's comedy *Broadway Danny Rose*. As for Frank Pellegrino, what was true then is true today: there is no task too small and there is no stage too big. Armed with this credo and an indefatigable work ethic, he set about the task of taking Rao's into the future. With an understanding ingrained from having worked on the floor, in the kitchen, and behind the "stick," he emphasized the fundamentals, training his attention on the details. Never intending to do things "big," he insisted on doing things *well*. He cultivated chefs who would remain meticulously faithful to the Joint's red sauce roots, while allowing space to innovate, experiment, and expand the spectrum of dishes: lamb shank with polenta, soft-shell crab, pesto risotto with spinach. On St. Paddy's Day of 2005, he even offered patrons corned beef and cabbage. O.A.R.

Though Frank Pellegrino is an authority on Italian food and culture, he is known, at times, to go off script. I have seen him dispatch staff to White Castle for late-night burgers; one afternoon at Rao's in Las Vegas he ordered a Reuben and a side of fries from the Forum Food Court; he has a genuine passion for hot dogs, and between you and me, he is experimenting with Pat LaFrieda on a customized wiener: *Frank's Franks,* anyone? But the story that takes the cake is the time he hosted executives from Lou Carvell's advertising agency at Rao's. It was an afternoon meeting, and Dino had a vat of sauce on the fire, peppers were roasting in the oven, clams were being scrubbed, the scent of sautéed garlic and fresh-cut *prezzemolo* perfumed the air. Eddie was prepping Mozzarella en Carozza, the scorched and seeded loaves had just arrived from Sullivan Street; everyone was primed for the feast as Frank finally summoned us to the table. "You're gonna love this," Frank said as he gently placed a napkin in his lap. And then, "as I do live by food," Tommy abruptly entered the restaurant with chicken pot pies from KFC.

Frank Pellegrino wants you have a good time, and toward that end, the food is alpha and omega. Accolades and acclaim are great, but what really matters is the respect of one's peers. And Frank's got that: the top tier of the culinary world has beaten a path to his red door, *sui generis* talents like Jean-Georges Vongerichten, Masayoshi Takayama, Giuseppe Cipriani, Bobby Flay, Mario Batali, Martha,

Ina, Emeril, and Guy. One evening I wandered into the stockroom, where I happened upon Master Pastry Chef Jaques Torres, spreading chocolate frosting on a massive, layered sheet cake that he had prepared at his kitchen in Red Hook and transported to East Harlem. Diners were delighted as they indulged in this lighter-than-air confection. Fast forward to the following afternoon: a man whizzes down 114th Street on something resembling an Italian Vespa, not the typical mode of transportation in East Harlem. The man dismounts and removes his bulbous black helmet to reveal that he's Jacques Torres. Frank thanks him for his gesture the evening before. Then Torres asks if it would be okay if he returned that night—just for drinks, he's quick to qualify—with his legendary countryman, Jacques Pépin. "No one debones a chicken like that man," Frank said. "Such incredible knife skills," he continued.

No one could have envisioned classical French chefs coming to the place back in 1896 when bedraggled immigrants, subsisting on little more than hope, lined up with buckets outside Joe and Charlie Rao's saloon for beer from Ehert's brewery.

It is often difficult for staff to convey steaming platters from the kitchen to the tables, their tortuous routes punctuated with a flurry of "scuse me, scuse me, watch your back, comin' through," and if "D" is carrying stacked sixteen-compartment glass racks, he will necessarily take the shortcut through the stockroom to the bar. It is the Joint's version of the Khyber Pass. The music—everything from Hank Williams to Daft Punk on the new touch screen digital juke box—and robust conversation (Rao's can get quite loud) only add to the challenge. If Frank Pellegrino gets up and sings, then all bets are off, people abandon their stations and, depending on the hour, they may stand on tables and chairs, sing out with abandon, fueled by carbs and cocktails, to send the room spinning off its axis. What is it about this place that loosens inhibitions and lends itself to such gaiety? The late great Robert Goulet once played the room, as did Grammy Award–winner Steve Tyrell, but everyone loves an underdog, especially Frank Pellegrino, and therefore no one will ever forget the Monday night when Sonny Grosso showed up for dinner with a greenhorn named Michael Amante.

Over the years, many enterprises have been initiated at Rao's. It has long been the place to take special clients when it's time to close the deal. It is well documented that John F. Kennedy, Jr., and American Media honcho David Pecker, came up with *George* magazine in a booth at Rao's, and more than a few show business careers have been launched from the East Harlem eatery. There's no telling what can happen when you take your chances in the room, it is the unpredictable nature of working live. Sometimes a single performance, in the right venue, can lead to acclaim and other times, unqualified disaster. Michael Amante arrived at Rao's as a protégé of Sonny Grosso, who asked his old friend Frank if the young man with the matinee idol looks could sing for the overflow crowd.

Frank immediately acquiesced; standing before his patrons, he stayed the jukebox with a wave of his hand and introduced Amante, who received polite applause. The young man hastily set up small, portable speakers and after a bracing breath, cued an instrumental backing track. It was an oldie but goodie, with a high degree of difficulty, "Nessun Dorma," from Giacomo Puccini's unfinished opera, *Turandot*. From the moment Amante opened his mouth, the room was spellbound. By the time he finished, with stentorian force, powerfully exclaiming, *Vincero . . . Vincero . . . Vincero!*, it was apparent that his was the voice of a bona fide tenor with a four octave range. In short order, Amante was headlining a sold-out performance at New York's National Historic Landmark theater, Town Hall; stadium engagements and a performance for Pope John Paul II would follow.

There's a code of behavior so powerful that it has been attributed to Lao-Tzu and spoken by Ossie Davis as "Da Mayor" in Spike Lee's *Do the Right Thing*. It goes like this: "Those who know, don't tell, and those who tell, don't know."

With this idea informing all that follows (as well as everything that preceded), here's an incident that all involved would prefer to forget. So why discuss it at all? To set the record straight? To offer some lurid details concerning the feral nature of man? I suppose the answer would be because it happened in The Room.

A young woman appearing in the role of Cosette in the Broadway production of *Les Miserables* was singing "Don't Rain on My Parade," at Rao's and the diners were receptive and respectful, except for a man at the bar who is alleged to have uttered unkind words. An older man (known by the street sobriquet "Lump Lump"), with roots in the more nefarious aspects of the neighborhood, admonished the heckler, words were exchanged, threats issued, the older man drew a gun, and fired. All hell broke loose. The media had a field day with this act of violence, *New York* magazine ran a sensational cover, "Murder at Rao's," *Law and Order* rushed one of their patented "ripped from the headlines" episodes into production with the not so subtle title "Everybody Loves Raimondo's," and in the name of verisimilitude—adding insult to injury—the producers cast Bo Dietl in the role of the shooter.

Rao's emerged unscathed by the ugly incident. It never missed a beat. One thinks of how Umberto's Clam House and Sparks Steakhouse thrived in the wake of gangland violence, such is our morbid fascination, but Rao's was already, far and away, the toughest ticket in town, and Frank Pellegrino consistently went out of his way to deflect attention and tamp down the wild speculation concerning the restaurant's supposed mob ties (lest we forget he played an FBI agent on *The Sopranos*). He needed this calamity and the ensuing media crush like he needed another reservation request. In the months and years ahead the wild vicissitudes came fast and furious, Rao's had gone from a name to a brand. Their sauce, and growing line of food products, was gaining a foothold not only with boutique purveyors, but with major supermarket chains as well. There were cookbooks, CDs (remember CDs?), and talk of expansion: Las Vegas was on the tip of everyone's tongue. But there were dark days as well, times when it appeared the end was near, not for Rao's, but for Frank Pellegrino himself.

Following routine surgery, Frank was prescribed the anticoagulant heparin. As days passed, rather than improving he grew gradually weaker. It was determined that he was bleeding internally, and in dire condition. Emergency measures were required to stanch the bleeding: he was subsequently intubated and placed in a medically induced coma where he hovered near death for several days as family and friends kept vigil. With Pellegrino's privacy in mind, his prolonged absence from the restaurant was explained through various deflections, excuses, and flat-out lies. Explanations as to Frank's whereabouts, at times absurdly contradictory, became an inside routine that provided some cathartic lightheartedness during this otherwise agonizing ordeal.

Against long odds, Frank's condition began to improve; upon regaining consciousness, he requested a cup of coffee. I recall Frank lying in bed, still very weak and understandably disoriented, watching Ronald Reagan's funeral on TV, quietly taking in the tens of thousands that reverentially filed past the catafalque as Reagan's body lay in state in the Capitol rotunda. At one point, Frank, a staunch and uncompromising Democrat,

slowly turned to his visitors and deadpanned, "Was I wrong?" He was back.

Frank loves people but identifies with turtles. The turtle, with its impregnable exterior, methodical and plodding style, resilience, and pluck (be careful when he snaps), is his avatar. His astrologically assigned beast is the bull, and there are similarities that can be drawn, but turtles can be found everywhere in Frank's world, encrusted in his cuff links where they peer out cautiously from the sleeves of his suits, embroidered in his dress shirts, or seamlessly blending in among the many tchotchkes in the windows at Rao's. So it makes perfect sense that his return to The Room was neither trumpeted nor triumphant, as he eased back into his role, tortoiselike, without fuss or fanfare. There were Frank sightings in the afternoons, when he would visit the restaurant, comforted, no doubt, by the familiar sight of Lydia Vicens and Paulie Sanchez prepping the kitchen, as they've done for so many years. After coffee he would pore over a logjam of mail, assisted by his gatekeeper, right arm, and aide-de-camp, Cousin Susan Pallercio, while receiving a steady stream of visitors and well-wishers. Of course, he also began to feed people; hearty chicken soup from a massive steaming stockpot with shredded tender white meat, carrots, celery, and tubettini to the tooth; braised short ribs; stuffed mushrooms; stuffed artichokes; frittata, minestra; arugula with tomatoes and ricotta salata; sausage and broccoli rabe; hard-boiled eggs with

 orange segments, drizzled extra-virgin olive

oil, and wizened black olives; filetto di pomodoro; pasta e Lenticchie, or Cecci, or Fagioli; or Carbonara, or all' Amatriciana. The revitalizing herbs and nightshades, the lubricating oils and gelatinous fats, the rugged roots and fortifying stalks, the succulent marrow—all the healing power of hospitality.

Rested and fully restored, Frank Pellegrino was no worse for wear, and after years of speculation, and courting by the sultans of The Strip, he made it official, at long last, the eastside Italian eatery was heading to Vegas. But would the experience translate? Was Rao's a Moveable Feast? This was a no-brainer; Rao's stormed Caesars Palace, occupying a space that reimagined the original joint on a monumental scale. The result was something almost spiritual, particularly the poolside portico, where Pellegrino can often be found with coffee and cigarettes, girded by Corinthian columns. Rao's and Vegas proved to be perfectly and potently attuned. But could they do it in L.A.?

Rao's at Caesars Palace is, if you will, a big-budget film, outfitted with expensive props, A-list stars and CGI. What Frank Pellegrino Junior envisioned as he drove west through the monotony of the Mojave Desert was more of an independent film, a hand-crafted noir, set on a darkened corridor. Junior, acting in concert with location scouts, settled on the old Hollywood Canteen, a genuine relic of the studio system, whose parking lot houses a film storage depository. The original was located about 6 miles away on Cahuenga Boulevard, and catered to U.S. servicemen from 1942 until the end of the Second World War in 1945. The Seward Street incarnation operated in the heart of what Charles Perry of the *Los Angeles Times* called "Real Hollywood . . . not Hollywood Boulevard with its strange nocturnal life forms," but rather a place that "radiates backstage film-biz nostalgia," adding "Seward Street is a street you'd probably never have any reason to drive down unless you were getting some film reels developed." A painstaking renovation produced a faithful facsimile, similar in square footage and style to the East Harlem original, but now that set design was achieved, could they recreate the food? The answer was . . . not exactly. Not that the kitchen wasn't capable of turning out tried-and-true Rao's dishes, but what Frankie Junior soon discovered was that Angelinos were a breed apart from the patrons and palates he'd catered to for the vast majority of his life. Veal was verboten in the elevated consciousness of the western. Steak Pizzaiola and Pork Chops with Cherry Peppers were staples back home, but in L.A., fish was a favorite. So they threw out the script and improvised relentlessly in the kitchen, placing greater emphasis on an array of vibrant *contorni*: grilled cucuzza (from the gourd family), beet salad with pistachio-crusted goat cheese, pasta aglio e olio (gluten free?), and cioppino (a savory fish stew with San Francisco roots). To his credit, Frankie Junior was quick to deduce that the only meat his Hollywood patrons appreciated was the gregarious Goodfella Johnny "Roast Beef," so he hired him on as maître d'hotel. It's certainly not a chain, and don't call it a franchise: each restaurant expresses itself uniquely, as the Rao's experience continues to evolve. Legendary concert promoter Bill Graham once said of the Grateful Dead: "They're not the best at what they do, they're the only ones that do what they do." From the dying embers of the nineteenth century to the present day, in New York and Las Vegas and Los Angeles, Rao's remains a singular experience. When you go out to dinner you eat till you're content, but when you go to Rao's you're part of the event. From the moment you cross the threshold, it's your night, the Christmas lights twinkle atop the awning at the bar, "Build Me Up Buttercup" has you moving in your seat as the Caprese Salad with Burrata Cheese arrives, just ahead of the Fritto Misto (with its side of velvety Remoulade), the bartender, wearing a sequined vest worthy of Bob Mackie, approaches with a bottle of wine. There is an unusual air of occasion. 10:30 already?

The laws that govern time seem not to apply at Rao's L.A.: an older man leaves with a doggie bag, a young woman enters with a Birkin bag, Frank Pellegrino approaches, places a hand on your shoulder, asks a question: "Are you having a good time?"

THE FEAST AMONG US

March 17 comes conspicuously each year with a "sea of green" and the rousing call of bagpipes, as Hibernians raucously celebrate Saint Patrick, who, according to legend, drove the snakes from the Emerald Isle. This Irish feast day features parades, the dyeing of the Chicago River, step dancing and, of course, copious amounts of beer. Then, two days later, on the nineteenth, the Italians modestly celebrate the Feast of Saint Joseph. March 19 is so sacred a date that it doubles as Father's Day in Italy, and elsewhere in Catholic Europe.

On this occasion, we acknowledge the man whose name anchors all three branches of desert monotheism—Joseph, Yosef, and Yusef—a man of unfathomable faith who freely accepted that his wife, Mary, was with child by means of a virgin birth; saintly indeed. If you are of Italian heritage and your name is Joseph, St. Joseph's is akin to a birthday: You will receive cards, calls, and a pastry known as Zeppole San Giuseppi, a deep-fried golden fritter, distinguished by spiraling ridges formed from the stainless-steel star-tip of a pastry bag, that encloses silky yellow custard dusted with confectioners' sugar and is topped with a maroon Amarena cherry (not the more juvenile and decidedly less dramatic Maraschino variety).

Food and faith have always had a symbiotic relationship: the Israelites were miraculously sustained by manna from heaven during their exodus from Egypt; Jesus is said to have multiplied loaves and fishes, thereby feeding four thousand of the faithful at Tabgha; Islamic writings likewise tell of fabulous tales of increase, and if your religion is rock and roll, you'll remember that Wavy Gravy provided "breakfast in bed for four hundred thousand" on Max Yasgur's farm. This food/faith dynamic applies to adherents across a multitude of traditions, even including agnostics, for as the English poet Edward Young once remarked, "Some wish they did, but no man disbelieves."

Consider Januarius, the fourth-century Bishop of Benevento, who was seized and spirited to a sulphuric crater by Roman centurions, where he was beheaded on the orders of the Emperor Diocletian. Miracles, specifically the miracle of liquefaction, were attributed to the martyred cleric, whose desiccated blood was enshrined in a silver reliquary at the Cathedral of Naples. He is better known to New Yorkers as San Gennaro, a venerated figure whose persecution and dedication to Christ is commemorated with an annual late-summer street festival featuring doodads and dunk tanks, circus barkers and calzones.

We all know the scene well, the green, white, and red heraldry arching across Mulberry Street, creating an atmospheric Italo-tunnel running north from the Church of the Most Precious Blood past Spring Street, the coils of searing sausage and the aroma of caramelized onions, dollops of fried dough buoyantly bobbing in a drum of molten oil, fresh shucked littlenecks served with fragrant lemon wedges and a dab of Tabasco sauce, airy wisps of whirling pink and blue cotton candy, nuts and chocolate by the pound, the Tilt-A-Whirl spinning round, hand-rolled cigars, vintage cars, tropical spirits, novelties, demitasse, confetti, graffiti, Azzurri, spaghetti,

Italian culture world renowned, but looking more like Chinatown.

There's a saint to be celebrated on virtually every day of the liturgical calendar. Saint Anthony of Padua, with his bread and oil, has a quaint Sullivan Street feast beginning on June 13; October 28 marks the feast of Saint Jude, but coordinating a proper block party for this dauntless apostle seems a hopeless cause; Saint Elzear, September 27, may be long gone but he's not forgotten, as *Sopranos* producers put him, and his feast, at the center of an episode called "The Ride;" Saint Lucy, December 13, patron saint of the blind, has an unsettling face: her ceramic likeness is often depicted holding a tray containing two eyeballs; Santa Lucia's is the festival of winter wheat and a celebration of the *solstizio d' inverno*, but it was Saint Teresa of Avila, feast day October 15 (not to be confused with the more chaste Saint Therese of Lisieux whose feast day is celebrated with her only earthly indulgence, chocolate éclairs); Teresa, the Castilian Carmelite, (1515–1582), really "shook up" the Catholic establishment, as she is best known for a mystical, orgasmic encounter with an impish angel or horny devil, who mercilessly pierced the nun's heart with repeated thrusts from a fire-tipped spear, till writhing pleasure and pain became indistinguishable. As Estelle Reiner famously quipped in *When Harry Met Sally*, "I'll have what she's having." The torrid interlude was the subject of an ethereal marble masterpiece by Gian Lorenzo Bernini, *The Ecstasy of Saint Teresa,* that graces the transept of the Cornaro

Chapel in the Church of Santa Maria della Vittoria in Rome. The seventeenth-century baroque house of worship was established as a Marian shrine, in the name of the Discalced Carmelites. This devotion to Mary, Star of the Sea, was central to Italian Catholics who journeyed in dire privation across the Atlantic until, finally, they arrived at the pedestal of the "American Madonna," gifted by the French but designed by a fellow countryman named Bartholdi, a beatific colossus, "lifting her lamp beside the golden door."

Italians immigrated to the United States by the millions from the late nineteenth to the early twentieth century. Most traced their roots to the economically depressed south, where prospects were nonexistent. After centuries of invasion, corruption, natural disaster, and division in their native Italy, these disenfranchised peasants landed in the United States, where they were immediately confronted by an invidious adversary the likes of which they had never encountered: the Irish.

Ireland had, from about the time of the Flight of the Earls in 1607, fallen under British subjugation. So merciless were British colonists that after arriving at County Clare's Burren, with its lunar landscape, on the rugged west coast, one of Oliver Cromwell's generals infamously offered the following: "Not a tree to hang a man, or enough water to drown him—or dirt to bury him." Having survived religious schism and famine at the hands of British tormentors, the Irish set sail for America, and by 1860, 25 percent of New

York City's population was of Irish descent. But the more things change the more they stay the same, as these newly minted Americans from Counties Wexford, Kerry, Kildare, and Cork once again found themselves under the yolk of Anglican overlords. "Irish need not apply" and "No Irish, no Blacks, no Dogs" were the signs of this troubled time. Wisely, the Irish formed a cohesive voting bloc, sought education, infiltrated civil service, the rackets, the Archdiocese and, ultimately, Tammany Hall. By the time the Italians disembarked at Ellis Island, the Irish had established a hard-fought foothold in Manhattan. To gain some perspective, bear in mind that the Irish (among others) had broken ground on the corner of Mott and Prince Streets in 1809, laying the cornerstone of a Cathedral named for Saint Patrick, their patron saint, and that this construction and consecration occurred forty-seven years after the inaugural Saint Patrick's Day Parade, which took place way back in 1762. By comparison, according to a statement by the Franciscan Friars of the Shrine of Saint Anthony of Padua, "In 1850 there were 4,531 Italians in the United States, with only a handful in New York, one of whom was the great Italian liberator Giuseppe Garibaldi, who ran a candle factory in Staten Island."

Naturally, the Irish would not relinquish their gains and perceived the newly arrived hordes from Italy as a budding threat to their ethnic preeminence; perhaps as a ruthless rite of passage, or some code of migratory hazing honoring a heartless pecking order, they would now mimic the degradation they suffered under the WASPs. The Italians were different in every way from the Irish; a great number of them emanated from arid desert climes rather than lush pastures, most of them had severe obsidian eyes, there were anarchists and mafia among them, they drank wine rather than beer, they preferred turbid black coffee to tea, they ate figs and pungent cheese and reeked of garlic, they were perceived to be secretive, clannish, untrusting, and superstitious. But worst of all, they spoke with a foreign tongue; it seemed the only thing these cultures had in common was faith; but even their methods of practice were foreign to each other.

Where the Irish were perhaps more austere, even discreet, in their personal expressions of piety, the Italians maintained a custom of parading life-size statues of their protectors through the streets, accompanied by boisterous brass bands and deafening fireworks displays. Furthermore, many supplicants likely wore pagan amulets known as *cornicello* and Kabbalistic red ribbons designed to ward off *malocchio*, the dreaded "evil eye." Centuries of misunderstanding and deep-seated enmity would be purged in a confrontation of two great cultures, and this apocalyptic battle, one that would rage from Saint Patrick's Cathedral to the City of Seven Hills, would also play out on the streets of East Harlem.

The players in this drama ran the gamut from the most diffident and vulnerable of penitents to the unerring Bishop of Rome; this conflict, though it concerns two tribes of

European extraction, is inherently American, embodying lessons in tolerance, religious freedom, and the thorny issue of immigration, which remains as caustic and contentious today as it was in the tumultuous era of New York. Of course all of the principals (and bit players for that matter) in this pernicious "turf war" have long passed on, though some records survive to shed light upon the strife engendered by what was then known as the city's growing "Italian problem," an issue involving a paucity of Italian priests and houses of worship to administer to the expanding population of expatriates from the sun-baked Mediterranean peninsula. This resentment attained critical mass with the dedication of Our Lady of Mount Carmel Church on 115th Street in East Harlem in 1884. A subtle observation drives home a vital point: East Harlem fixture Joe "Baccala" Pisacano points out the fact that though Our Lady of Mount Carmel is known as an Italian Church, it bears a Celtic Cross at its summit. Joe went on to offer vivid accounts of how the Italian women, in an act of mortification, would walk barefoot on the searing summer macadam, trailing a procession of saint images, before bathing their burnt feet in the pools of a breached johnny pump, steam rising from their scorched soles.

Professor Paul Moses of Brooklyn College provides invaluable insight into this intra-Catholic imbroglio in his *An Unlikely Union: The Love-Hate Story of New York's Irish and Italians*. A sentence excerpted from Joseph Pulitzer's short-lived *New York World* typifies this volatile situation: "English-speaking and Italian elements are at war in the Catholic Church of our Lady of Mount Carmel." Professor Moses reminds us that this conflict was considered a "race war," as the Italians were so utterly other, so alien, and the term "ethnic" had not yet come to wide use. Religious fervor is one thing, but in order to sow real division, in order to orchestrate naked hatred, to maliciously incite and instill palpable fear and hysteria, well, this requires a politician, and so Paul Moses diligently unearths for us the following testimonial gem from Michigan Congressman Melbourne Ford:

They are of a very low order of intelligence. They do not come here with the intention of becoming citizens. They live in miserable sheds like beasts; the food they eat is so meager, scant, unwholesome, and revolting, that it would nauseate and disgust an American workman, and he would find it difficult to sustain life upon it. Their habits are vicious, their customs are disgusting, and the effect of their presence here upon our social conditions is to be deplored.

By 1884, this powder keg was ready to combust. Stouthearted East Harlem émigré Antonio Petrucci, a man about whom biographical details are scant, would lead the emphatic charge for ministerial equality. Described as a devout Catholic, chieftain, protector, politico, saloon owner, and community leader/activist, Petrucci, like a number of his fellow countrymen, had grown tired of the slights, the insults and the indignity of being consigned to the bowels, or "lower church," of Our Lady of Mount Carmel. Ill will—even fisticuffs with clergy— are reported to have ensued as Petrucci went to extraordinary lengths to provide sanctuary for petitioners, ultimately renting a space on 111th Street, where he housed a statue of the Blessed Mother, patroness of his native Polla, Italy, in the Province of Salerno. Antonio Petrucci and his tattered Italian allies from the fledgling *Congregazione del Monte Carmelo* were up against the magisterial Coadjutor Archbishop Michael Corrigan, His Eminence John Cardinal McCloskey, and the unimpeachable Hibernian-dominated Diocese of New York. But the overmatched immigrants, with help from Reverend Emiliano Kirner and the timely intercession of Father Scipione Tofini, made an eleventh-hour appeal to the only entity in the world that could salvage their desperate cause: Vincenzo Gioacchino Pecci, His Holiness Pope Leo XIII.

The progressive pontiff, who championed the adoration of Immaculate Mary, acted with absolute authority, waiving temporal qualifications that fast-tracked Petrucci's miraculous statue for a rare canonical coronation. Dramatically, Pope Leo XIII died just three days after exercising this rare papal prerogative, leaving the matter to his successor, Pope Pius X, who finalized the elevation of this icon, making the "Madonna of East Harlem" one of only four images in the United States crowned with the benison of the Holy See through the Congregation for Divine

Worship and the Discipline of the Sacraments; Pius X gifted the parish a precious emerald gemstone from the Vatican to be set in the Madonna's crown. The ceremony took place on July 10, 1904.

Gary Potter describes the event in his article "Miracle on 115th Street" published at Catholicism.org: *The coronation itself took place outside in nearby Jefferson Park. The Statue of Our Lady was borne in procession from the church to the park while the choir sang and musicians played. Bringing up the rear of the procession was Archbishop Farley. It was he, as the pope's designated representative, who placed the crowns on the heads of the Madonna del Monte Carmelo and the Christ Child.*

At the time of this celebration, in that more distant summer of '04, Rao's was already in its eighth year, sustaining the outcast immigrants of East Harlem, administering to their spiritual needs with bread and wine of a decidedly more terrestrial variety; but for all the papal pomp and circumstance, for all the authority of the Roman Curia, incredibly, the Madonna, with her elaborately brocaded robe and beautifully bedizened crown, remained relegated to the church basement until 1923.

In 1906, emboldened by their victory, reinforced by their growing numbers, and comforted by the old-world customs that they'd brought with them to this boundless continent of opportunity named for one of their intrepid seafaring ancestors, these Italians stepped boldly out of the shadows once and for all. If the puritans, Teutons, and Celts were dismayed by the devotion of these Italians, they would be sent into states of apoplexy after witnessing the ritualistic Dance of the Giglio. The "Dance" owes its existence to traditions from the faithful Neapolitans of Brusciano and nearby Nola, commemorating the feast days of Saint Anthony of Padua (who was actually of Portugal) and the prolific patriarchal poet Saint Paulinus (who was born in Bordeaux). Saint Anthony, whose image is as common to Italian households as that of Saint Francis of Assisi or Saint Francis Albert of Hoboken, is commemorated on June 13 with an East Harlem block party befitting the legendary tonsured friar, who has been depicted all down the ages, by masters ranging from Raphael to El Greco, coddling the infant Jesus while bearing his trademark lily stalk. It is from the word lily that we get the Italian term *giglio* (jee-lee-oh for our friends unfamiliar with Italian phonology.) The giglio, in the case of the East Harlem feast, is a structure said to weigh between three to four tons. Soaring some eighty feet into the air, it is comprised of sturdy wood scaffolding, which at its base has broad tiers to accommodate dignitaries and a fifteen-piece brass band, gradually tapering to a decorative *papier mâché* covered spire. The unwieldy seven-story, cantilevered *torre* (including the bandstand!) is lifted by its protruding, padded I-beams and paraded through the streets on the shoulders of the devoted, through the throngs that come to pay wistful tribute to a neighborhood long vanished. The feast literally envelops Rao's, and for a few summer nights the unprepossessing restaurant blends in seamlessly with the sausage and seafood vendors, the pizza makers, the pennant hawkers, and the bounce house. On these occasions The Room is well beyond capacity, old friends and neighbors stop in for a drink, the heat is only magnified by the humanity. Tommy wipes his brow and throws his hands up in resignation. He has a notion to step outside for a smoke, but tonight there is no escape, even outside is packed. Folding tables and chairs have been set up on Pleasant Avenue to handle the overflow, but on evenings such as this, it's a merry kind of chaos. Back inside, the air conditioner and Nicky "Vest" are working overtime. Tommy emerges from the kitchen with a platter of prickly stuffed artichokes but is immediately stalled by the crowd before he can reach his destination; he curses, but no one can hear him because the charismatic Jimmy Alleva, his red-capped horn section, and a snare drum have just filed into the overtaxed room.

There's something about saints and celebration, about prayer and satiation. And when belief wanes, we maintain at least a cultural connection to the faith of our forefathers. "Many Italians," the defrocked Dominican Giordano Bruno, once observed, "even those who are not particularly religious, regard Catholicism as an indispensable national asset. The Church, for its part, has absorbed the virtues and vices of the Italians in a process of reciprocal conditioning that has made religion a subcultural characteristic."

Rao's has mastered the synergy of faith and food, of taste and tradition, going the extra mile to provide patrons with a genuine, immersive experience. This means that on Christmas Eve, instead of closing and staying home with his family, Frank Pellegrino spends it with yours; once again, the room is a fire marshal's nightmare, packed like a midnight Mass, it is the Feast of the Seven Fishes, the City of Seven Hills, the seven sacraments, the magnificent seven: lobster, polpo, *baccala* salad, shrimp, scallops, calamari, and clams. It's a service, but it's not solemn. Lower your guard and lift up your hearts, this is the sumptuous sodality, the house of hospitality and home cooking and wine-stained glass, the church of cheer, the bastion of blessings, the gift that keeps on giving, the lively night of the living, what Augustine called "the measure beyond measure"—a national treasure.

CRIME & NOURISHMENT

In his mind-bending biography of Prohibition-era gangster Arnold Rothstein, *King of the Jews,* author Nick Tosches illuminates his subject's flawed aura with an aphorism from Saint Augustine of Hippo: "If you can comprehend it, it is not God." In New York, this logic also applies to parking spaces, as in, "If you think you've found a legal parking space, you definitely haven't," and at Rao's it applies to wise guy sightings. "If you think the guy with the death stare, the clear nail polish and the jewels is a made guy, he almost certainly isn't," or, closer to the original Augustinian paradigm, "If you can comprehend it, it is not Gotti." Sure, a sensational and oft-quoted Zagat review that offers superlative scores for food and ambiance also suggests that *unless you're connected to the governor or the godfather, "fuhgeddabout" getting into this outstanding East Harlem Italian restaurant.* As with many Italian restaurants—from Corona, Queens, to Carroll Gardens, Brooklyn, to Arthur Avenue in the Bronx—this gangster mystique just comes with the territory; but what is it about the Joint? The answer lies somewhere between history and circumstance.

If you're looking for a population with a high concentration of alpine skiers you might go to a village situated in a mountainous region. In that vein, there was a preponderance of young, desperate, and industrious Italian men who emigrated to East Harlem at the turn of the twentieth century. . . and they had to eat somewhere.

From the start, the often grotesque face of this *fabbrica di minaccia* has brought shame and undue scrutiny to decent people of Italian extraction. The violent uprising against Charles of Anjou's occupying forces in 1282, known as the Sicilian Vespers, is widely regarded as the event that made the mob.

It was Easter Monday in Palermo when a French soldier is said to have made unwanted advances on a local girl under the guise of a weapons search, driving bands of enraged villagers to insatiable homicidal rage. As the legend goes, anyone suspected of being of Frankish descent was asked to pronounce the word *ciciri,* "chickpea," the essential Sicilian legume. If a voiced "*g*" sound was produced, then the speaker was determined to be French, and his throat was cut. The slaughter was widespread, abruptly ending French rule and ushering in an era of Spanish domination, where we got the honorific title of *Don.*

It would be almost six hundred years before something called the Mafia reached American shores, via South America. In New York, the extortionate *Mano Nero,* or "Black Hand," preyed ruthlessly on their fellow émigrés, kidnapping children and bombing mom-and-pop establishments, bereft of conscience, ethnic identity, or any sense of community. As the scally cap gave way to the fedora and the English language began to flourish in Italian enclaves, the temperance movement culminated in 1920 with Prohibition, and the American gangster was born. There were Jewish mobsters like "Lepke," Schultz, Lansky, Siegel, and the aforementioned Rothstein, there were remorseless Irish "White Handers" on the Brooklyn waterfront, like "Wild" Bill Lovett and "Peg Leg" Lonergan, but it was the Italians—Capone, Luciano, Masseria, Costello, Marcello, Gambino, and Lucchese— who held the country in dreadful thrall, romanticized by the likes of Arthur Miller and Mario Puzo, brilliantly expounded upon by Gay Talese and Nick Pileggi, and mythologized on celluloid by a studio genre that rivaled the mighty Western. Whether it's referred to as the Mafia (Sicily) or 'Ndrangheta (Calabria) or Camorra (Naples), or as the Syndicate, the Commission, or La Cosa Nostra (*our thing*), Italian organized crime remains an all-encompassing experience, from the cryptic oaths, Roman hierarchy, sartorial trends, idiosyncratic appellations, and gut-busting malapropisms to the distinct nomenclature now ingrained in the American lexicon and, last but not least, the fabled haunts that these lawless legends frequented. Rao's was one such place, situated just two blocks from the Palma Boy's Social Club, where the avuncular, cigar-gnawing Anthony "Fat Tony" Salerno, born 1911 in East Harlem, quietly ruled the roost for the Genovese crime family until his RICO conviction in 1986, part of United States Attorney Rudolph Guiliani's era-defining Mafia Commission Trial, which sounded the death knell for the old guard bosses and any notion of omertà while fueling the future mayor's growing lust to rule.

Imagine the figures that might have passed through the Joint's doors in its history. Many men in "the life" called the old neighborhood home, from the rapacious bandits of the horse-and-buggy era to the well-tailored toughs who trolled the city on broad whitewalls past pushcarts. In wartime, elements of organized crime (Lucky Luciano) are said to have aided the Allied landing in Sicily (familiar terrain where the mob processed heroin destined for American neighborhoods) after Patton defeated the Afrika Korps in a decisive duel in the desert.

Then came the Kefauver hearings that blew the lid off the secret society; during nationally televised proceedings Senator Charles Tobey of New Hampshire confronted East Harlem's own Francesco Castiglia, aka Frank Costello (the Prime Minister of the Underworld), posing the following loaded question: "You must have in your mind, some things you've done that you can speak of to your credit as an American citizen, if so what are they?" Costello paused, and then deadpanned to uproarious laughter, "I pay my tax." In the ensuing generational maelstrom, Camelot came to a screeching halt, the Age of Aquarius brought bigger cars and longer sideburns, Joe Colombo belatedly discovered the virtues of civil rights. By the mid-seventies Sinatra was holding court at the Westchester Premiere Theatre for the likes of Carlo Gambino and Paul Castellano while Bob Dylan, of all people, was singing the praises of "Crazy Joe" Gallo. Indeed, *the times were a changing*, but Rao's stayed true, not only to the guiding principles that had established its good name, but to the denizens of the old neighborhood, some of whom were teachers or judges, and others who elected to pursue less upright callings. Angelo "The Jet" Urgitano, who earned his nickname shuttling back and forth between New York and Las Vegas, was a smoldering hybrid of Dean Martin's devil-may-care swagger and Clint Eastwood's strong, silent steeliness. His hair was white and fluffy, like a coiffed cumulus cloud, an effect enhanced by the haze of cigarette smoke he usually spoke through. Though his voice had been reduced to a rasp by a laryngectomy, his mere glance more than compensated for any vocal limitations. If his weighty mien left anything to doubt, The Jet was often seen at Rao's, eating penne rigate with sausage and Savoy cabbage while seated on a barstool, nestled in a nook, in plain view of a sign that unambiguously read, NO FOOD AT THE BAR. One evening, rather late, The Jet slipped out of the restaurant, cigarette in mouth, topcoat carefully draped over his shoulders, each designer footfall registering on the quiet block as if produced by his own personal Foley artist. He approached a mendicant, a simpleton named Vito, who was slumbering by a dumpster; "The Jet" slapped him gently on the cheek, rousing him to sudden consciousness, and tucked a few greenbacks into Vito's shabby coat before vanishing into the night. Unfortunately, "The Jet" was as unwell as he was debonair, and convergent testimonies affirm that when word of this passing reached Rao's his picture inexplicably fell from the wall. O.A.R.

It is no secret that Chazz Palminteri based the character of "JoJo the Whale" in his film *A Bronx Tale* on the larger-life Louis "Gigi" Inglese. Jerry Capeci, O.C. expert, author and purveyor of *Gangland News*, remembers Inglese as a man of great humor and old-school forbearance who, when confronted with a staggering federal prison sentence from the Honorable Kevin Duffy, replied, "Judge, I can't do fifty-six and a half years," to which Duffy replied, "Do the best you can."

"Gigi," who made his name in the contraband crazy seventies, among the likes of "Mr. Untouchable," Nicky Barnes, paid his debt to society, and was released from federal custody in 1995. After a quarter-century of sequestration and chow-room slop, "Gigi" had his first whiff of freedom and roasted peppers when colleagues and contemporaries feted him with a sumptuous dinner at Rao's. He was dressed in a dark suit that contrasted with his pallid skin that shone from perspiration, he was seated at a large table, where his friends presumably debriefed him as to the goings-on of the last twenty-five years, a period of time in which Carter, Reagan, and Clinton accounted for five presidential campaigns, the World Cup had come to the United States, the Internet was still somewhat foreign to most, hip-hop was in ascendancy, and MetroCards were in, as subway tokens had gone the way of the spittoon. Rao's, however, was just as "Gigi" had left it, immune to time and trends, preserved as if contained by some cultural time capsule. Hushed word cautiously made its way through the room that the hulking figure receiving congratulatory pats on the back had just returned from an extended "vacation." His table became the focal point of the room, sly remarks about "Club Fed" circulated, but respect was implicit, for no matter his offenses, however mortal his transgressions, Gigi had served an interminably long stretch in federal prison rather than electing to join the perfidious legion of cooperative informants living in the monotonous purgatory of the Witness Protection Program. As "Gigi" and his crew reminisced over Riserva Ducale, rib-eye steaks, sautéed spinach, and scampi-sopped bread, a friend nudged me in the side and said, "Listen . . ." Someone had selected Roy Rodgers's "Don't Fence Me In" on the jukebox.

The lionization of such men ("Gigi" and "The Jet") presents one with a dilemma of moral relativism. Thoreau said, "Most men lead lives of quiet desperation," and Henry Hill in *Goodfellas* says, "Suckers waited in line" and subscribed to "good government bullshit." These sentiments are perhaps corollaries to a meditation by the Mafia's spiritual leader, Niccolo Machiavelli, who noted, "The trouble is most men prefer to steer a middle course, which is very harmful; for they know not how to be wholly good or wholly bad." The final thought on moral opacity belongs, of course, to Mario Puzo and Francis Ford Coppola's *The Godfather*. The famous scene takes place as Michael Corleone (Al Pacino), the son of a Mafia Don, is strolling down a suburban street with his Irish American girlfriend Kay Adams (Diane Keaton), on an autumn afternoon.

Michael: *"My father is no different than any other powerful man, any man who's responsible for other people like a senator or a president."*
Kay: *"Do you know how naive you sound, Michael? Senators and presidents don't have men killed."*
Michael: *"Oh. Who's being naive, Kay?"*

We should proceed thoughtfully when evaluating exactly who is who upon entering The Room. For instance, consider the genial man with the finely trimmed goatee, Popeye forearms, and uncanny knife skills, known as Dominick "the Butcher" Loiacono. He's a *butcher*, he expertly prepares the choicest steaks, chops, veal, fowl, and mutton for patrons at Rao's. Johnny "Wheels" Focaro has never driven a getaway car, but is a dealer of luxury vehicles in Manhattan, and Frankie "Nose," rest his soul, had an impressive facial appendage, but no dastardly designs. It's certainly true that mobsters—like movie stars—energize a room, heighten the excitement, and (with respect to the former), add a titillating element of danger. Some Rao's regulars speak of feeling disequilibrium upon entering the restaurant, the fluttering of butterflies, the delirious anticipation, because every night is an improvisation, a vital mix of personalities and potentates. Some nights the crackling chemistry is positively dynamic. I am reminded of one poignant occasion when the forces of the "sinister" and "celebrity" were one, when a famous mob boss came a-callin'. This episode took place entirely behind the scenes, in the quiet daylight hours, with iron-clad discretion. Joe Ciccone's cell phone rang, it was a number he did not recognize, from a foreign area code—designated, he later learned, for Italy. Joe answered the phone; it was a man who identified himself as James Gandolfini, the self-effacing star of *The Sopranos*, who may have employed the more informal "Jimmy" upon introducing himself. He needed to procure a table for his friend and fellow *Sopranos* alum Michael Rispoli. Joe said he'd speak to "Frankie" and see what could be done; Gandolfini expressed his sincere appreciation. After receiving the overseas request from Joe, Frank Pellegrino

set about the arduous task of reaching out to those with reservations, cold-calling, horse-trading, appealing, shuffling dates. Ultimately, Frank was able to accommodate Gandolfini's request. Joe Ciccone, for his part, could not for the life of him figure out how the big-souled actor got his cell number; it was all very "Tony Soprano." Joe phoned Gandolfini, who was vacationing in Rome with his son, and informed him that he had a reservation for Rispoli on the specified date. Ever the gentleman, Gandolfini asked if there was anything he could do to reciprocate; hewing to protocol, Joe respectfully declined. The next afternoon a gentleman showed up at Rao's, and on Gandolfini's behalf, offered Joe a substantial gratuity for his invaluable assistance; again, Joe respectfully declined. Gandolfini's largesse was legendary, and this occasion was no exception. "No worries," Joe Ciccone said to the man, "Frankie was glad to do it." Frank Pellegrino was indeed glad to do it and, in hindsight, he was grateful that things worked out as seamlessly as they did. Gandolfini himself had been to Rao's in the past. He and Frank worked together for several seasons on *The Sopranos*, where Frank played his arch nemesis in law enforcement, FBI Bureau Chief Frank Cubitoso. Frank had great appreciation for James Gandolfini's commitment to craft and his magnanimity. This elaborate, international interlude (all performed through back channels and intermediaries) was a fitting, final correspondence. Gandolfini passed away the following day, taking with him a world

of creative possibilities, as well as one of the most iconic Italian characters ever conjured for the screen, not to mention the answer to the beguiling question, how did he get Joe Ciccone's cell number?

HOW THE WEST WAS WON

L.A.'s palm trees, sunshine, beachfront property, and an easy pace are reminiscent of life in the bay of Naples, but far from the urban corner of 114th Street and Pleasant Avenue. At first blush, the idea of New York's flagship Italian restaurant in SoCal sounds like an exercise in absurdity, so utterly antithetical are the two; Chavez Ravine vs. Yankee Stadium, the Mamas and the Papas vs. the Velvet Underground, the Manson Clan vs. Son of Sam, the freeway vs. the subway, earthquakes vs. hurricanes, droughts vs. blackouts, unbearable traffic jams vs. . . . Okay, so we've stumbled upon a tincture of miserable compatibility.

But before you decide that Rao's has gone all expansion happy, let's consider the glacial pace of rolling out restaurants in Las Vegas and eventually Los Angeles. A hundred years in, and after numerous emphatic solicitations, the powers that be finally acquiesced to a Las Vegas location. As Frankie Junior once jested, "When one considers the founders of the strip, it was a very organic evolution." Some might call it a no-brainer, it was also de rigueur, what with Nobu, the Old Homestead, Mesa Grill, Guy Savoy, and Mr.

Chow all housed at Caesars Palace. Since a soft opening in December of '06, followed by an epic introduction in January, the westward migration has proven a stunning success, as a broad spectrum of tourists, from "the whales" to the "little fish," have turned up for salt-baked branzino in the Emperor's Casino. Still, something was different at this "Rome away from Rome." Though the imposing, cylindrical bar (suspended from the ceiling like a spacecraft bent on doom) occupied as much area as the entirety of the original joint, somehow none of the intimacy was lost. One could fly to the western time zone and enter into the delusion-inducing heat and artificial ambiance of the strip, but once you transited the meridian of this 8,000-square-foot reimagined Rao's, there was co-owner Ron Straci, not a photo on the wall, but the dashing man himself, along with Frankie Junior, who pulled up roots and relocated to Vegas. That's two-thirds of the Rao's triumvirate; and when Frank Senior makes the scene (roughly once a month), the joint reeks of Runyon and Rat Pack reverie. Spontaneity and spirit infuse this spacious venue, so rather than singing along with the jukebox, as Frank does in East Harlem, he may invite his old friend and collaborator, Tony Nicolosi (a nimble, versatile guitarist) and his orchestra, where they perform everything from B.B. King to Santana to bebop jazz and the gems of the great American songbook well into the night, as grappa, disgestivos, tartufo, sfogliatelle, and dollops of gelato decorate tables and banquets.

The nights in Vegas have a tendency to mysteriously deliquesce into day; after performing (intermittently) in three sets at Rao's, the inexhaustible Frank Pellegrino once led an entourage to a most improbable setting, a roadhouse, biker/blues honky-tonk called the Sand Dollar Lounge, off the beaten path from the Vegas Strip. We're talking folks in leather vests bearing heavily tattooed muscular arms, rabbinical beards, wheelbarrow beer bellies, unfiltered cigarettes, billiard tables, and Gulf War vets. The Sand Dollar Lounge? What in God's name were we doing here? Well, Frankie Junior's then girlfriend (now wife) Caroline had brought her dear friend, a dynamic force of nature known as Dee Dee Bridgewater, an artist with three Grammys and a Tony to her credit (she originated the role of Glinda the Good Witch of the South in *The Wiz!*).

Somewhere in the gauzy predawn hours, the incomparable Ms. Bridgewater was invited to take the stage with an initially reluctant Frank Pellegrino in tow, and, backed by the Moanin' Blacksnakes, they proceeded to tear through classics like "Mustang Sally," "C.C. Rider," and other rootsy R&B selections. By the time we wandered back to the hotel an apricot preserve had spread itself across the sky.

Many critical relationships were forged during the establishment of the Las Vegas location. Obviously a small army would be required (waiters, waitresses, kitchen, bar, dishwashers, administrative, etc.) for an operation of its scale. An array of applicants with impressive referrals were considered for employment at this new venture that had garnered unprecedented buzz, even by Vegas standards. Then, an aging and dangerously overweight man with wiry gray hair and New York roots turned up for a job. Though his qualifications were dubious (he had previously worked the door at a topless club called the Crazy Horse Too, a notorious nightspot that had recently been shuttered by the FBI), he possessed undeniable charisma, a kind of gritty Gotham gravitas, and a generous girth that comported with the instant "eat-cred" that Rao's has inhered. The man seeking employment was known in the seamier precincts of Sin City as "Bubbles," and after much handwringing by reluctant hotel brass, he was hired to work as a greeter at Rao's. I'm not sure a lot of people would have taken a chance on the beleaguered "Bubbles," born Robert Ubriaco, but as the old maxim goes, to have a friend you've got to be a friend, and that, at its essence, is the ethos that Frank Pellegrino fosters. The appointment of "Bubbles" proved a masterstroke, as patrons were compelled by his genuine warmth and East Coast authenticity. No one can resist his charms; among his many admirers was director Todd Phillips, who cast "Bubbles" to appear opposite "Mr. Las Vegas" himself, Wayne Newton, in the hilariously irreverent closing credits of his blockbuster film *The Hangover*. "Bubbles" had entrée everywhere, he sipped spirits at Ghostbar, high atop the Palms, and had access to every exclusive event on the strip, circumventing security details

and velvet ropes with A-list ease. In addition to the irrepressible "Bubbles," the decidedly more staid general managers, Patrick Hickey and M.J. Tabet, were enlisted to steward this ambitious new enterprise and fast became indispensable assets. But as they say, the rich get richer, and Rao's Las Vegas scored a major coup with the acquisition of Chef de Cuisine Fatimah Madyun, whose versatility allows her to capture the East Harlem flavor of old-world staples like Pasta e Fagioli, the ethereal texture of homemade ravioli, and the succulence of veal chops with cherry peppers while going off the reservation with specials like "couscous with Spanish olives, heirloom tomato, seared scallops, and a red pepper beurre blanc." Fatimah and M.J. (Marie Joe) are integral parts of sustaining success at Caesars, while Patrick Hickey, aka "Tom Hagen," has since been charged with running the latest iteration of Rao Nation, bringing Lobster Fra Diavolo to the City of Angels.

The road to Los Angeles was, as Robert Hunter once wrote, "no simple highway." Literally, the road (from Las Vegas) is a trek through the barren Martian planes of Interstate 15, Frankie Junior at the wheel, burning through American Spirits, sipping lukewarm black filling-station coffee and satellite surfing while Frank Senior rides shotgun, contemplating the scorched topography out the window. We whiz past Joshua trees and tumbleweeds and then finally, a sign, which prompts Frank Senior to ask, "Who the hell lives in Victorville?" We are lost for a response. Now, in a figurative sense, the "road" to Los Angeles was a good deal more arduous. The idea of L.A. (L.A.o's?) had been bandied about for years, many of the restaurant's New York stalwarts spend a great deal of time there; Nick Pileggi, Rob Reiner, Ron Perelman, Steve Tisch, and Joey Hunter, to name a few. This is not to suggest that a prospective Hollywood location would have a built-in clientele, but this initial "crowdsource" would certainly constitute a promising start. Location would be important, to say the least, but where does one begin? Los Angeles was a long way from home.

After scouting sojourns to Santa Monica, Malibu, and Beverly Hills, Ben Weprin, a real estate developer specializing in luxury hotels, came across a unique property with historical cachet, a location that "spoke" to Frankie Junior, it was an unassuming stucco-surfaced space on Seward Street called the Hollywood Canteen. Rao's stands alone on Seward, its pomodoro red facade and classic Hollywood Canteen clock, painstakingly restored, enliven this otherwise tranquil block, just off of Santa Monica Boulevard. In fact, this "out of the way" seclusion, this destination dining, if you will, is a characteristic of the L.A. restaurant that most closely resembles the original Joint back in East Harlem, which lies well beyond the trendy downtown neighborhoods of Chelsea, SoHo, and the Meatpacking District.

Rao's has always been the place for those who wish NOT to be seen, and the solitude of Seward, with its industrial roots and discreet locale, was fitting for a restaurant that arrived in the land of klieg lights under the cover of darkness, and gradually "rolled out" by word of mouth. Over the years, Rao's has faithfully stuck to tradition, shunning the ephemeral, shaking off fads, trends, and passing fancies. I remember a time when an unruly Canadian pop star with a penchant for racing exotic cars was seeking access to Rao's in New York. This TMZ enfant terrible with a ponderous following on social media (from whence he came), a kid for whom every door was opened, had some serious society types advocating on his behalf. A phone call was made, but Tommy Mara (without consulting superiors) rebuffed the solicitation out of hand, with this blunt rejoinder: "No one gives a fuck about Justin Bieber." Would this lovable truculence translate in L.A.? Though every location has its own identity, there is an undeniable New York flavor at each establishment. In the office of the L.A. Rao's, there hangs a photo of the New York team: Dino, Mike, Marco, Hilton, Dominick, Paulie, and Tommy. All smiling, middle fingers defiantly extended, they are a picture of the loyal opposition. But a vibrant scene has flowered in sunny Southern California: there's "Big" Lou Farber, broad-shouldered, shaved head, backwater beard, he is the gregarious sommelier with a background in molecular biology and a knack for, appropriately enough, bringing the Bacchanalia. As it became clear that the L.A. joint would become a reality, Frankie Junior immediately poached the big guy from Caesars Palace, like an opportunistic GM constituting a roster for an expansion team. Johnny "Roast Beef," also drafted for L.A. after playing back-up behind the stick in East Harlem, is another kind of big.

There's no room that can contain this Gleasonian veteran of such memorable films as *Honeymoon in Vegas*, *State of Grace*, and *Goodfellas*. "Beef" is an apt east-west emissary since, by now, he's likely spent more time in L.A. than in his native New York. He sings, he mugs, he speaks extempore on marriage, Mercury in retrograde, and the over/under. As Frank Pellegrino attests, "he's the only one who knows his way around this town," the rest of us are lost, essentially commuting between the hotel and the restaurant, for fear of taking a wrong turn that might condemn us to the perpetuity of a congested cloverleaf. Charlie and Clarisse Shumaker, the co-councilors, have also brought their energy and expertise to this western expedition. Again, Frankie Junior is credited with finding Charlie, a man of great humor and humanity. California kind with unruly white hair, his counterculture cool and laid back vibe is the perfect antidote for a table of taut New Yorkers.

The Los Angeles kitchen has mastered the traditional Rao's dishes and carved out creative space to improvise with a rich variety of ingredients, both imported and harvested from various local farmers' markets in Hollywood, Santa Monica, and at the sprawling Grove. The formerly trained staff worked stints in East Harlem, where they were not only indoctrinated in the scholastic rigor of the Rao's curriculum, but they were also initiated, which is to say exposed to, the withering ridicule and merciless hazing

of Tommy Mara and sous chef Mike "Salty" Lanza. My apologies, but tired clichés come to mind, like "trial by fire" and "if you can't stand the heat . . ." No one's exempt from the ribbing, and the degree to which it's dished out is often directly proportionate to your credibility in the Joint, because as the young people say, "it's all love."

From approximately 1995 we've watched Tommy transition from a fresh-faced kid to a doting father. As we've seen Dino Gatto, undaunted, take the bit in the teeth and carry the kitchen into this second decade of a new millennium, we marvel as Nicky "The Vest" presides and prevails behind the bar, well into his eighth decade of life, a living legend. There's no Human Resources Department at Rao's. Jobs are filled via referral, openings are infrequent and, like the Supreme Court, these are lifetime appointments, positions filled by people whose qualifications far exceed the breadth and discovery of scientific surveys and padded résumés. Emerson said, "An institution is the lengthened shadow of one man." To that point, longtime patron and corporate impresario Henry Marks asserts that Frank Pellegrino transformed the old "Hole" and has been master of ceremonies since the mid-1970s. This is the longest-running "show" off-Broadway, an interactive feast, transforming the hospitality paradigm ten tables at a time.

At a dinner in Las Vegas on New Year's Eve 2015, an attorney from the Bay Area asked Frank, "Why not open in San Francisco?" The logic is sound, San Fran is a

large metropolitan area with a sizeable Italian population. Frank's response was concise, but by no means impolite. "Because that's not what we do," he replied. Expanding on that point, he explained that he has more offers to open restaurants than he could possibly entertain, that he had no interest in a chain (a term he naturally abhors), and that none of the three Rao's locations operated on autopilot. Frank Pellegrino maintains the standard through late nights and early mornings, through untold in-flight hours restively flipping through channels, devouring books, occasionally nodding off, and bitterly glowering at the NO SMOKING sign until finally touching down in the desert. Upon arrival for

another busman's holiday he's busy putting out fires and picking up tabs. [For this project I've been granted free rein, as large a charter as the wind, to blow on whom I please, but were I to expound on Frank Pellegrino's generosity and the many charties he succors, then the plug would be pulled, posthaste; so suffice it to say the man picks up the tabs (bar, dinner, airface, hotel—you name it) with the unconscious ease that others pick up germs.]

His dedication to quality control is what you might expect. Sometimes his notes and observations are as simple as, "Why is this so salty?" Other times his finely calibrated palate will pick up on issues of texture or consistency. One night while eating white bean and cabbage soup, he summoned the sous chef, stirred his soup, and then asked, "Did you puree a portion of the beans?" A cautious beat. "Yeah, Frank," the young man replied, "one-third of the beans were pureed." Frank returned to stirring his too-thin soup, an unsatisfied look on his face. "Should we puree half the beans?" the young man suggested. "I think so," Frank replied, "either that, or you can get me a straw." Frank practices and preaches pride in preparation, scrutiny on a granular level, and passion for the process as guiding principles for putting forth great food.

But to do it with consistency, cross-continent? That takes true dedication and a team united in purpose. The perfecting of Rao's Famous Lemon Chicken for Los Angeles took repeated executions until Frank Senior was satisfied. This is a pretty straightforward dish: broiled chicken, fresh lemon juice, garlic, oregano, olive oil, red wine vinegar, and salt and pepper to taste; *eccolo qua!* For hours on end, as Frank Senior and the culinary team toiled and tinkered in the kitchen, we ate Lemon Chicken all day. "Are you using the right amount of vinegar?" Frank queried. "Are you tossing each batch in the sauce?" So on. Finally, in the midst of chicken fatigue (we'd sampled four or five servings), the battle was joined, a taste-test challenge was announced. Frank and Jay would each make Lemon Chicken, a neutral party would present their dishes, and we would indicate which we preferred. Everyone took a turn, tasting the tender white meat and the elegantly charred skin bathed in an emulsion of oil and fresh citrus juice, seasoned with aromatic herbs. The point is, Frank was willing to make that dish (and any other that required perfecting) over and over, like a Gold Glove shortstop fielding thousands of ground balls, till the technique was second nature, until it was right and repeatable under the glare of the lights and the pressure of the moment. Rao's is nothing if not fundamentally strong, not just in terms of the food, but the way it's experienced by the lifeblood of any establishment; the patrons. We all know imitation is the sincerest form of flattery, and that there are scores of red sauce joints steeped in Sinatra, plating tagliatelle for tough guys; but Rao's holds an almost universal appeal that transcends milieu and the most stubborn stereotype, finding resonance throughout the industry, sometimes in the unlikeliest of places. Swiss-born chef Daniel Humm and his Cornell-educated business partner William Guidara, of the Made Nice hospitality group, recently stated in an interview with New York Eater that they "will introduce a brand new style of service inspired partially by classic East Harlem Italian restaurant Rao's." Humm and Guidara's Eleven Madison Park is a stately "contemporary American restaurant," one of only six restaurants in New York City awarded three Michelin stars. Flattery indeed. The Rao's brand of service, which might be distilled to "give 'em what they want and get outta the way," has clearly taken hold in Los Angeles. Initially open five nights a week, demand was so high that the full seven were soon required, and an old tradition became a new wrinkle in the Rao's repertoire. Sunday Gravy would roll out in Los Angeles. A 32-quart stainless steel pot of slow-cooked Southern Italian hospitality—a cornucopia consisting of hot and sweet sausage, meatballs, braciole, shoulder pork butt, and eye round browned in olive oil, deglazed with red wine, slathered in paste, flecked with garlic, drowned in hand-crushed tomatoes, and cooked for hours to tender perfection. There was trepidation on that opening Sunday, so much so that when the first customers entered, they were greeted with a standing ovation by the full complement of staff. Sunday gravy has been sold out every week since its introduction, similarly the 40-ounce, corn-fed, porterhouse steak, cooked in a cast-iron skillet, is reserved hours in advance by a growing number of devoted meat eaters that balance out So-Cal's robust kale and quinoa crowd.

These days, Frank Pellegrino, though still every inch the New Yorker, is something of a regular in L.A. where he finds himself more and more at home with successive visits. He's yet to get to the beach, nor has he experienced his first seismic tremor, but he's gravitated to some of the city's older institutions, taking in a show at the Hollywood Bowl and enjoying the Grilled Free-Range Chicken Paillard at the Polo Lounge. But as the saying goes, you can take the man out of New York . . . Anyway, on a recent visit I was walking the palmy corridor of the Beverly Hills Hotel and was struck by the loud music emanating from a room in the vicinity of the Sinatra Suite, where Frank

Pellegrino was lodging. As I entered the room, greeted by Frankie Junior, I saw Frank Senior and Steve Tyrell rehearsing for a show at the Friars Club celebrating the centenary of Ol' Blue Eyes.

There they were, seated around a fruit bowl and a laptop manned by Steve's musical director, joyfully duetting on "I've Got the World on a String." As the two traded verses, with panache and improvisational banter, a breeze from the veranda blew the gossamer curtains to dramatic effect, and the late afternoon sun rallied against the rain clouds, so foreign in this area. Frankie Junior smiled as the jaunty number proceeded to the bridge, and though we were all well familiar with the song, on this occasion one line sustained with the power of epiphany: *Life is a beautiful thing.*

—*Joseph Riccobene*
March 2016

ANTIPASTO

Seafood Salad	49
Baked Clams Oreganate	51
Roasted Peppers	53
Mozzarella en Carrozza	55
Mussels and Fennel in Brodo	57
Octopus Salad	58
Zuppa di Clams	58
Charcuterie di Italia	61
Bruschetta	63

The Beginning of "The Feast"

When first-timers arrive at the New York City Rao's, they can be a bit uneasy. It's obvious when they stare at the ruby red façade on the corner of 114th Street and Pleasant Avenue, then glance back over at the street sign to confirm they're in the right place.

Their focus turns to the group of colorful gentlemen gathering three steps below the restaurant's front door. The men halt their discussions and turn their scrutinizing gazes towards these newcomers. Apprehensively, the visitors inevitably point to the old double doors and ask, "Rao's?"

"Who are you dining with tonight?"

"The Nelsons have given us their table."

The piercing stares of the gang morph into big smiles, as the guests are invited in.

They're directed to the bar, bejeweled with Christmas decorations year-round, and are told that Joe will be right over. As Joe approaches, he asks for confirmation that the table's reservation has been gifted to the right group of people.

"Oh yes, the Nelsons told me you were joining us this evening. When you're ready, take the first booth on the right."

The guests settle into the 100-year-old cherry wood booth, and Nicky "the Vest," or D, delivers drinks from the bar to the table.

"Junior will be right over to take your order," they advise.

Just as Senior taught me, I approach the table with a chair in hand, ready to join the guests and discuss the night's offerings. Perplexed, the new patrons ask me for menus. With a big smile, I say, "You're looking at him."

Once everyone is relaxed, I kick into my spiel: "Basically, what we do is appetizers, pasta, then entrées. Do you like seafood?" I ask, and depending on their tastes, on I go. First I describe one of our most popular starters, the seafood salad, and lead into the other options: roasted red peppers (which we're known for), or other seafood choices, like the fritto misto or baked clams. I can see them perk up when I mention the *Mozzarella en Carozza*.

With their order taken, I head into the kitchen and begin preparing the guests' antipasto, taught to me by my Aunt Anna and my father. Allow me to share their lessons with you.

Seafood Salad

This is, by far, one of the most popular dishes Rao's serves. It's also the first recipe I learned when I was fifteen, practicing under the watchful eye of Aunt Anna and my father. I knew I had mastered it when they granted me permission to prepare this dish for our guests. The secret is freshness. If you're buying a whole squid, look for clear eyes, smooth skin, and a fresh, not fishy, smell. Have your fishmonger clean and cut the squid for you. Many markets sell frozen, precut squid rings and tentacles. Stick to fresh. The same goes for the shrimp and the crabmeat. Always handle your crabmeat carefully, leaving the lumps whole, and check closely for cartilage and shell remnants. You don't want crunch in this dish. Serves 4

1 red bell pepper
1 small celery stalk
6 Gaeta olives
¼ pound cleaned, fresh squid (calamari), cut crosswise into 1-inch rings
4 cups water
1 cup fresh lemon juice
2 tablespoons kosher salt, plus more if needed
4 colossal (U-12) shrimp, deveined, butterflied, and tails removed
1 cup olive oil
1 garlic clove, halved
1 teaspoon finely chopped fresh Italian parsley
Freshly ground black pepper
1 cup jumbo lump crabmeat, picked over for cartilage and shells
½ cup cooked lobster meat
2 lemon wedges

First make a *brunoise*: Cut the top and bottom off the bell pepper, seed, and then cut it in half. Cut the celery stalk in half. Julienne both into ¼-inch strips, then cut the strips into ¼-inch dice.

Place the olives on a kitchen towel. Fold the corner over the top of the olives, and smash them with a meat mallet or a small pan. Squeeze each olive to remove the pit, and then chop the olives into pieces the same size as the bell pepper and celery. Set aside.

Put the squid in a colander and rinse with cold water, until completely clean.

In a medium pot over high heat, combine the 4 cups water and squid, ¼ cup of the lemon juice, and the salt and bring to a boil. Reduce to a gentle boil and cook until the squid is very tender, about 5 minutes.

Drain the squid and rinse in cold water until cooled. Cover with a damp towel and set aside.

Bring a small pot full of water to boil over high heat. Add the shrimp. Remove the pot from the heat, drain, and run cold water over the shrimp to stop the cooking.

When cool, gently pat the shrimp dry with paper towels. Cut each shrimp into 8 pieces, cover with a damp towel, and set aside.

In a medium bowl, whisk together the olive oil, the remaining ¾ cup lemon juice, the garlic, and the parsley. Taste the *citronette* and season with salt and pepper to taste. Add the shrimp and squid and toss until evenly coated. Using a slotted spoon, remove the seafood from the citronette, allowing it to

drain completely. Transfer the seafood to a medium serving plate. Reserve the remaining citronette.

With your hands, or using two spoons, form the crabmeat into a quenelle. Center it atop the squid and shrimp.

Add the lobster to the remaining citronette and toss until evenly coated. Remove with the slotted spoon, let drain, and gently place it on top of the crabmeat.

Drizzle ½ cup of the remaining citronette over the salad. Sprinkle with the parsley, garnish with the lemon wedges, and serve in a small bowl or ramekin, sprinkled with the brunoise.

VARIATION

For a terrific variation of this recipe, prepare a small batch of the pesto sauce on page 137. Add the juice of 1 lemon and toss the cooked squid in the mixture. Plate, and build the rest of the salad according to the recipe above.

Baked Clams Oreganate

I've seen many Rao's guests double and triple order these despite anticipating a hearty meal ahead. I enjoy the dish immensely, especially when I see our guests smiling ear to ear after finishing an order of these lip-smacking breaded clams. If you've never shucked clams before or are apprehensive about tackling what can be a frustrating chore, ask your fishmonger to do it for you. Tell him to leave the clams on the half shell and to keep them on ice while transporting them home. Refrigerate them as soon as you get home and keep them on ice when served. The flavor of the clams works in tandem with the strong oregano presence in the recipe. If you prefer a milder oregano flavor, dial back the amount you use, sample the mixture before breading the clams, and adjust that seasoning to suit your own preference. Serves 4

> 2 cups plain bread crumbs
> ½ tablespoon finely chopped fresh Italian parsley
> ½ teaspoon minced garlic
> ½ teaspoon dried oregano
> Kosher salt and freshly ground black pepper
> ½ cup olive oil
> 1 cup chicken broth
> 2 dozen littleneck or cherrystone clams, cleaned and shucked
> 6 lemon wedges
> 6 sprigs fresh Italian parsley

Adjust the oven rack to its lowest possible position. Preheat the oven to 375°F.

In a medium bowl, combine the bread

crumbs, parsley, minced garlic, and oregano, and season to taste with the salt and pepper. Mix with a fork until completely integrated.

Slowly pour the olive oil over the mixture, mixing with a spoon as you pour. Continue mixing until all the oil has been absorbed and the bread crumbs have darkened. Add the chicken broth, ¼ cup at a time, until the bread crumbs have the consistency of wet sand. If the mixture is too wet, mix in more bread crumbs until you reach the desired texture.

Using a teaspoon, place a mound of the bread crumb mixture on top of each clam. With the flat side of the spoon, spread the mixture evenly around the clam bed. Press down around the edges of each clam to secure and seal them, then use the edge of the spoon to gently create ridges in the breading.

For even more presentation pizzazz, hold the back side of the clam toward your body.

With your other hand, hold the edge of the spoon over the stuffed clam. You will notice the contour of the edge of the spoon matches the shell. Working in ¼-inch increments, gently press the edge of the spoon into the mixture from left to right, forming a shell pattern.

Switch the oven to broil. Arrange the clams on a rimmed, shallow baking sheet large enough to hold all of them. Add about ⅛ inch of water to the baking sheet, being careful not to moisten the breading; this will ensure that the clams remain moist while cooking. Cook for 7 minutes, or until the breading is golden brown and crisp.

Remove the baking sheet from the oven and, using tongs, transfer the clams to a serving plate. Mist with lemon juice, garnish with the parsley sprigs and lemon wedges, and serve.

Roasted Peppers

This recipe is dedicated to Annie Sausto. Until her passing, she was the one and only prep cook at Rao's, and had been for decades. She would prepare this heavenly version of simple roasted red peppers daily, because we were sure to run out by closing. Unlike ordinary roasted peppers, this version includes a more complex mix of flavors and textures, courtesy of rich pine nuts and sweet golden raisins. Serves 4

6 red bell peppers
½ cup olive oil
3 tablespoons golden raisins
2 tablespoons pine nuts
1 teaspoon chopped fresh Italian parsley
½ teaspoon minced garlic (optional)
Kosher salt and freshly ground black pepper

Preheat the oven to 375°F. Grease a baking sheet.

Arrange the bell peppers on the baking sheet, leaving at least ¼ inch between each.

Switch the oven to broil, and put the peppers into the oven. (You can also do this on your stovetop if you have a gas range. Hold each pepper with long tongs over the open flame of a burner until the skins have blistered. It's a faster way and produces very nice results.)

As the peppers begin to char, turn them frequently using a pair of long tongs. When the skins have blackened all the way around, transfer the peppers to a large bowl. Cover the bowl tightly with plastic wrap. Set aside and let the peppers steam in their own heat for 20 minutes, or until cool enough to handle.

Rub off and discard the blackened skin. Remove and discard the stems and seeds. Transfer the cleaned peppers to a cutting board and slice lengthwise into ¼-inch strips.

Transfer the strips to a colander, and let drain for at least 30 minutes, or until all the moisture has drained off.

In a medium bowl, combine the roasted peppers, olive oil, raisins, nuts, parsley, and garlic. Season to taste with salt and black pepper and mix well. Let marinate until ready to serve. Before plating, stir all the components together one last time, sprinkle with the chopped parsley, and serve.

Mozzarella en Carrozza

The Italian grilled cheese! This melted mozzarella extravaganza—blanketed with marinara sauce, fresh basil, and fried Italian bread—will win the hearts of young and old alike. Add an extra dimension of flavor by throwing a couple of tablespoons of pitted Gaeta olives into the pan, and sautéing for a minute or so before adding the marinara sauce. Serves 6

12 slices Italian bread, cut into 1-inch thick slices
6 slices fresh mozzarella cheese, cut ½ inch thick
4 large eggs
¼ cup grated Pecorino Romano cheese
½ tsp finely chopped fresh Italian parsley
Kosher salt and freshly ground black pepper
2 cups all-purpose flour
3 cups plain bread crumbs
3 cups Homemade Marinara Sauce (page 113)
½ cup vegetable oil
4 leaves of fresh basil

Trim the crusts from the bread.

Make 6 sandwiches by layering 1 slice of mozzarella on each slice of bread, and covering it with another slice. Trim the sandwiches into perfect squares or rectangles. Gently press to ensure each sandwich is stuck together.

In a medium bowl, combine the eggs, grated cheese, and parsley, and season with salt and pepper. Whisk until completely mixed. Pour into a shallow baking pan or dish.

Put the flour in a shallow bowl or pie plate. Pour the bread crumbs into a similar container.

Arrange the flour, egg wash, bread crumbs, and a sheet of parchment paper in that order, left to right, to create a breading station.

Gently dredge the sandwiches in the flour, shaking off any excess.

Dredge the sandwiches in the egg wash. As you remove each from the egg wash, allow the excess to drip off. Gently press the sandwiches into the bread crumbs, coating them on all sides. Place the breaded sandwiches on the parchment paper.

In a large saucepan over medium-low heat, bring the marinara to a simmer, stirring occasionally.

Line a large plate with a double layer of paper towels.

Heat the oil in a large sauté pan over medium heat. Carefully add the sandwiches, working in batches as necessary to avoid overcrowding the pan. Fry until the bottoms are golden brown. Flip and repeat. Transfer the sandwiches to the paper towel–lined plate.

Scoop 2 large spoonfuls of marinara onto an individual serving plate. Place 1 of the sandwiches on top of the sauce. Repeat to plate the remaining sandwiches. Top each with a dollop of sauce, sprinkle with basil, and serve.

Mussels and Fennel in Brodo

A few years back, the Rao's team was graciously asked to host and judge an episode of Top Chef *at our New York City restaurant. We set up to accommodate Tom Colicchio, Padma Lakshmi, Lorraine Bracco, and Anthony Bourdain. The contestants' first challenge was to prepare an Italian appetizer for the panel. A lovely up-and-coming chef named Antonia Lofaso presented sautéed mussels with fennel, a dish she learned from her Italian grandfather. When he tasted this beautiful presentation, my father was blown away. So much so, that after the show wrapped up, he instructed Chef Dino to incorporate fennel into our own mussels recipe. To this day, the delicate, licorice-tinged broth and hearty shellfish remains a best seller!*

Serves 4

¼ cup olive oil

6 garlic cloves, smashed

½ fennel bulb, trimmed and cut into ¼-inch-thick slices

1 pound mussels, cleaned (discard any that will not close when tapped)

Kosher salt and freshly ground black pepper

1 cup dry white wine

½ lemon

2 tablespoons salted butter

2 tablespoons chopped fresh Italian parsley

Heat the olive oil in a large sauté pan over medium heat, add the garlic, and cook for 30 seconds. Add the fennel slices and continue to cook until the garlic begins to shimmer.

Add the mussels, season with a dash of salt, and a grind of black pepper, and toss.

Add the white wine and bring to a low boil. Cook until the mussels have opened. Using a sieve or your hand to catch any seeds, squeeze the juice from the lemon into the pan. Transfer the mussels to a serving bowl, discarding any that did not open.

Increase the heat to high, add the butter to the pan, and stir until the butter has completely melted. Toss in a pinch of the parsley and cook for about 1 minute. Pour the sauce over the mussels, sprinkle with the remaining parsley, and serve.

Octopus Salad

Most people are a little squeamish when it comes to octopus. Maybe it's the look? Or the way this sea creature has been portrayed as a movie monster? Whatever the case, I've converted many doubters who come into Rao's by simply getting them to try this delectable salad bursting with simple, fresh flavor. The secret is a long boiling period to tenderize the seafood. The salad nearly melts in your mouth, and could not be easier to make. Try it once and experience the enchanting texture and lemon-bright essence of this salad, and I promise you'll be sold. Serves 4

> One 3- to 5-pound Portuguese octopus
> 3 lemons, halved
> 1 or 2 wine corks (optional)
> 1 cup olive oil
> ½ cup pitted Kalamata olives
> Kosher salt and freshly ground black pepper to taste
> ½ cup chopped fresh Italian parsley

Fill a large stockpot three-quarters full with cold water. Add the octopus and 2 of the lemon halves and bring to a boil over high heat. Add a wine cork or two if you like; an old wives' tale claims that this actually works to keep the octopus tender. Boil the octopus for 3 hours.

When the octopus is tender, fill a large, heatproof bowl with ice and cold water. Remove the octopus with tongs and transfer to the ice bath. Set aside to chill for 30 minutes.

Remove the tentacles from the body with a sharp knife. Discard the head. Cut each tentacle, on the diagonal, into ½-inch slices. Transfer the slices to a large bowl.

Add the olive oil and olives and season to taste with the salt and pepper. Using a sieve or your hand to catch the seeds, squeeze in the juice from the 2 remaining lemons and mix well.

Transfer the salad to a large serving platter, sprinkle with the parsley, and serve.

Zuppa di Clams

Regardless of how cold it might be, this rich dish sparkles with fresh flavors that will transport you and your guests to a warm and sunny day on the coast. At Rao's, we use littleneck clams for our zuppa because, although they're the smallest variety, they are some of the most flavorful clams you can buy. Buy them as fresh as possible, and keep them in your refrigerator, covered with a wet towel. I use them the day I buy them, and I'd suggest you do the same. Discard any that do not open during cooking; they may be "mudders," and no one likes "mudders"! If you want a slightly lighter, summery version of this classic soup, leave out the tomatoes and add an additional half cup of white wine. Serves 6

¼ cup olive oil

3 to 4 garlic cloves, smashed

36 littleneck clams, cleaned

Pinch of salt

1 cup canned San Marzano tomatoes, hand
crushed, with juice

2 cups bottled clam juice

1 cup dry white wine

½ teaspoon chopped fresh oregano

Crushed red pepper flakes (optional)

6 fresh basil leaves

1 tablespoon chopped fresh Italian parsley

Kosher salt and freshly ground black pepper

Heat the olive oil in a large sauté pan over medium heat. Add the garlic and sauté for 1 minute. Add the clams and give them a quick toss, adding a pinch of salt.

Add the tomatoes, clam juice, wine, and oregano, and the red pepper flakes, if using. Increase the heat to high, and bring to a boil. Reduce to low, and simmer for 7 minutes. Cover and cook for 5 minutes more, or until the clams have opened and the sauce has reduced by half. Discard any clams that do not open. Stir in the basil and parsley, and season to taste with salt and black pepper.

Using tongs, transfer the clams to a large serving bowl. Pour the sauce over the clams, and serve hot.

Charcuterie di Italia

I make this wonderfully varied plate whenever I entertain guests at my home. It can be used as a starter, a cocktail party tray, or even as a simple and delicious light meal on a balmy summer night. You'll find most of these meats and cheeses at any well-stocked supermarket, but I implore you to buy quality, which may mean finding a true Italian delicatessen or specialty gourmet shop. The cheeses should be sold wrapped in white butcher paper rather than plastic, and the meats are best sliced fresh, rather than prepackaged. Serves 6 to 8

2 cups arugula, washed and dried
¼ pound thinly sliced prosciutto
    (I recommend prosciutto crudo di Parma)
¼ pound thinly sliced Genoa salami
¼ pound thinly sliced soppressata
¼ pound thinly sliced pepperoni
¼ pound thinly sliced mortadella
1 cup mixed olives
1 ripe melon, thinly sliced, rind removed
    (preferably cantaloupe or honeydew)
½ pound wedge Parmigiano Reggiano cheese
½ pound wedge Pecorino Romano cheese
1 loaf fresh-baked Italian bread
1 bottle high-quality, extra-virgin olive oil

Scatter the arugula around a serving platter. On a large cutting board, lay out all of the meats. Roll them into tubes, or simply arrange them in a pleasing composition on the serving platter. Place the mixed olives in a small bowl on the platter, and arrange the melon slices around the bowl.

Arrange the cheeses on the platter, accompanied by a cheese shaver.

Wrap the bread in aluminum foil and warm in the oven for 10 to 15 minutes. Remove the bread and cut it into thick slices. Transfer the slices to a napkin-lined breadbasket.

Serve the platter with the warm bread and a bottle of high-quality extra-virgin olive oil.

Bruschetta

This is simply toasted Italian bread covered with Mother Nature's delights. Rich plum tomatoes, mozzarella, and fresh basil dressed in a red wine vinaigrette awaken your palate with the flavors of spring. This much-beloved recipe is a snap to prepare. Serves 6

1 pound very ripe plum tomatoes, diced
1 pound fresh mozzarella cheese, cubed
10 fresh basil leaves, chopped
¾ cup olive oil
3 tablespoons Italian-style red wine vinegar
4 garlic cloves, minced
½ teaspoon chopped fresh oregano
Kosher salt and freshly ground black pepper
    to taste
½ loaf seedless Italian bread

In a large bowl, combine the tomatoes, mozzarella, basil, olive oil, vinegar, garlic, and oregano, and season with salt and pepper to taste. Let stand for 30 minutes.

Cut the bread into ½-inch slices and toast lightly.

When ready to serve, toss the bruschetta topping, taste, and add additional salt and pepper if needed.

Arrange the toasted bread slices on a large serving platter. Using a spoon, scoop a healthy portion of the topping onto each slice. Drizzle lightly with a small amount of the liquid from the topping, and serve immediately (or the bread will get soggy).

"He said, 'I'm telling my regulars to take standing reservations. What do you want? Once a week, once a month?' I book every other Thursday. It's not a stretch to say Rao's has changed my life. There have been so many friendships formed and lasting images: watching Frankie's son Frank, Jr., grow up, eventually taking over the floor from his dad and becoming a talented restaurateur in his own right; meeting the Rolling Stones, Ted Turner, Jane Fonda, and Woody Allen. There have been governors and presidents and many more celebrities. But the most special memories are of Frankie and Joey Hunter leading the room in song, customers dancing at the bar and between the tables, and Nicky 'Vest' behind the bar making my wife's favorite drink in the world (his vodka gimlet), relaying the story of the vest he has on that night . . . that's Frankie! His theatrical sense of the moment brings a culture to Rao's like no other place."

—PETER BROCK

INSALATA

Rao's Mixed Green Salad

Combine wildly different lettuces, garden-fresh vegetables, and fresh fennel in a salad and you have something special. Dress the salad with olive oil, a spark of Italian red wine vinegar, and a dash of salt, and you have a special Rao's salad that will leave your guests wanting more. Serves 6

1 medium head iceberg lettuce
1 small head radicchio, cleaned and chopped
1 head Belgian endive
1 medium, very ripe tomato
1 small cucumber, peeled and sliced into ¼-inch rounds
½ cup thinly sliced fresh fennel
¼ cup thinly sliced red onion
¾ cup extra-virgin olive oil
1½ tablespoons Italian-style red wine vinegar
Kosher salt and freshly ground black pepper to taste

Core the iceberg lettuce and rinse well with cold water. Tear the lettuce apart and dry thoroughly with paper towels or in a salad spinner. Transfer the lettuce to a large salad bowl. Add the radicchio.

Trim the endive and pull the leaves apart. Rinse it thoroughly and dry well. Chop the endive and add it to the salad bowl.

Core and quarter the tomato and add to the lettuces. Add the cucumber, fennel, and onion.

Drizzle the olive oil and vinegar over the salad and season with salt and pepper to taste. Toss well until the salad is evenly coated, and serve.

Caprese Salad

This delicious party starter won't bog you down in the kitchen. The firm textures of the onions and tomatoes create a wonderful contrast to the soft richness of the mozzarella. They merge on the palate, creating a symphony of flavors that will have your family and friends humming along. Serves 6

7 ripe tomatoes, cored and cut into wedges
½ large red onion, cut into ¼-inch slices
4 garlic cloves, minced
8 to 10 fresh basil leaves, shredded
½ teaspoon chopped fresh oregano
¾ cup pure olive oil
3 tablespoons Italian-style red wine vinegar
Kosher salt and freshly ground black pepper

Two 8-ounce balls burrata cheese, halved (or substitute fresh mozzarella cut into ¼-inch slices)

In a large mixing bowl, combine the tomatoes, onion, garlic, basil, and oregano. Add the olive oil and vinegar and toss to coat. Season to taste with salt and pepper.

Fan out the halved burrata or sliced mozzarella around the edge of a serving plate. Spoon the tomato mixture over the cheese and serve.

Caesar Salad

A Caesar salad crowned with a mound of grated Parmesan may look impressive, but all that clumpy cheese mutes the flavors in the dressing. That's why I use a vegetable peeler to thinly shave a few sparse ribbons over my Caesar—just enough for some salty bursts. Beyond the cheese, this tried-and-true salad holds a key to unlocking your culinary creativity. Pair it with slices of steak, grilled chicken, shrimp, or any other additions you can dream up. You can even turn this simple salad into a hearty stand-alone meal. Hail Caesar! Serves 6 to 8

FOR THE CROUTONS
3 cups torn country bread (1-inch pieces)
3 tablespoons olive oil
Kosher salt and freshly ground black pepper

FOR THE DRESSING
6 anchovy fillets, packed in oil, drained
1 small garlic clove
Pinch of kosher salt
2 large egg yolks
2 tablespoons fresh lemon juice, plus more if needed
¾ teaspoon Dijon mustard
2 tablespoons olive oil
½ cup vegetable oil
3 tablespoons finely grated Parmigiano Reggiano cheese
Kosher salt and freshly ground black pepper
3 heads romaine lettuce, hearts only, leaves separated
Shaved Parmigiano Reggiano, for garnish

To make the croutons: Preheat the oven to 375°F.

In a large bowl, combine the bread and olive oil and toss until the bread is completely coated. Season lightly with salt and pepper.

Spread out the croutons in an even layer on a rimmed baking sheet. Bake until golden brown, 10 to 15 minutes, tossing once or twice to ensure even baking. Set aside.

To make the dressing: Combine the anchovies, garlic, and a pinch of salt in a pestle (use the face of a knife and a cutting board if you don't have a mortar and pestle). Mash together until the mixture has a paste-like consistency. Transfer to a medium bowl.

Add the egg yolks, lemon juice, and mustard and whisk until thoroughly combined.

Whisk in the olive oil, drop by drop. Add the vegetable oil in the same manner, whisking until the dressing is thick and glossy.

Whisk in the grated Parmigiano Reggiano cheese. Season with salt and pepper, taste, and add more lemon juice if needed.

To assemble the salad: In a large salad bowl, combine the lettuce and croutons. Drizzle with the dressing and, using your hands, gently toss the salad. Top with the Parmigiano Reggiano shavings and serve.

Roasted Beet Salad with Goat Cheese

The unique and robust flavor of this roasted root vegetable—bedazzled with golden raisins, crushed pistachios, goat cheese, and balsamic dressing—will have your taste buds popping.
Serves 4 to 6

2 medium red beets
½ cup balsamic vinegar
1 cup vegetable oil
4 teaspoons honey
2 tablespoons Dijon mustard
Kosher salt and freshly ground black pepper
1 pound arugula, rinsed and dried
1¼ cups salted pistachios, toasted and crushed
½ cup golden raisins, soaked in water for 15 minutes, drained
½ cup crumbled goat cheese

Preheat the oven to 375°F. Chill your serving plates.

Wrap each beet in aluminum foil and place on a baking sheet. Roast for 1½ hours, or until the beets are fork-tender. Transfer the beets to a rack or plate and set aside until they are cool to the touch.

Unwrap the beets. Hold one of the beets in a kitchen towel and rub off the skin. Repeat with the second beet. Cut the beets into medium cubes and set aside, reserving ¼ cup of the beets for garnish.

In a medium mixing bowl, combine the vinegar, vegetable oil, honey, mustard, and a dash of salt and pepper. Vigorously whisk the dressing until completely mixed.

In a large bowl, combine the arugula, the larger amount of beets, the pistachios, and raisins. Add half of the dressing, and toss until the salad is evenly coated.

Wearing latex kitchen gloves, gently transfer the salad, letting excess dressing drip off, to the chilled serving plates.

Sprinkle the goat cheese on top of the greens, divide and scatter the ¼ cup reserved beets among the individual servings, and drizzle with the remaining dressing. Serve chilled.

Rao's Pasta Salad

The key to this preparation is the time allotted for the marinating process—the longer the better. If possible, dress and season the tomatoes, mozzarella, and onions a day ahead of time. Cover with plastic wrap and chill in the refrigerator overnight. Serves 6 to 8

12 ripe plum tomatoes, cored, seeded, and diced
1 pound fresh mozzarella cheese, cut into bite-size cubes
2 tablespoons chopped fresh Italian parsley
10 fresh basil leaves, roughly chopped
1 tablespoon finely chopped fresh oregano
2 tablespoons diced red onion
½ tablespoon minced garlic
Kosher salt and freshly ground black pepper
1 cup extra-virgin olive oil
1 pound farfalle

In a large mixing bowl, combine the tomatoes, mozzarella, parsley, basil, oregano, red onion, and garlic. Season to taste with salt and pepper. Add the olive oil and gently mix together. Cover and let stand for at least 30 minutes, or longer if possible.

Fill a large pot with salted water and bring to a boil. Add the fusilli and cook, subtracting 2 minutes from the cooking time directed on the package. Drain the pasta and rinse under cold water.

Add the cooled pasta to the dressing and mix well until evenly coated.

Using a slotted spoon, transfer the pasta to a serving bowl. Top with the remaining dressing, and chill for 30 minutes, or up to 24 hours.

Toss the salad again just before serving and enjoy!

Summer Tortellini Salad

The collection of vibrant vegetables in this salad just amplifies the incredible flavor of the cheese tortellini. A pretty presentation, this salad will also please the palate and satisfy even hearty appetites. Serves 4 to 6

1 ½ pounds frozen cheese tortellini
2 cups olive oil
1 yellow onion, thinly sliced
1 pint cherry tomatoes, rinsed and quartered
1 medium cucumber, peeled, seeded, and diced
1 red bell pepper, seeded and diced
1 yellow bell pepper, seeded and diced
½ cup apple cider vinegar
Kosher salt and freshly ground black pepper
½ cup chopped fresh Italian parsley

Bring a large pot of heavily salted water to a boil. Add the tortellini and cook according to the package directions. Drain and rinse under cold water. Transfer to a large mixing bowl. Drizzle the tortellini with 2 tablespoons of the olive oil and gently toss to coat. Set aside to let cool.

Heat 2 tablespoons of the olive oil in a large sauté pan over medium heat. Add the onion and cook, stirring frequently, until softened, about 10 minutes.

Remove the pan from the heat and allow the onion to cool in the pan, about 5 minutes. Once cooled, add the onion to the tortellini. Add the tomatoes, cucumber, and bell peppers.

In a medium bowl, combine the vinegar and the remaining olive oil. Season to taste with salt and black pepper. Add the parsley and whisk vigorously until completely blended.

Gradually add the dressing to the pasta in small increments until all the dressing has been used, gently tossing the salad between additions.

Transfer the salad to a large serving bowl and chill for 30 minutes. Gently toss again just before serving.

Chef Fatimah's Creamy Tortellini Salad

The eclectic flavors in this creamy salad will invigorate the imaginations of even discerning guests. The unexpected combination of sour cream, dill, and walnuts will whet the appetite and have everyone at your table asking for seconds. Serves 4 to 6

1 pound frozen cheese tortellini
4 tablespoons extra-virgin olive oil
Kosher salt and freshly ground black pepper
1 medium yellow onion, cut into ¼-inch slices
2 cups sour cream
1 cup walnuts, toasted and coarsely chopped
3 medium cucumbers, peeled, seeded, and
    diced
¼ cup finely chopped fresh dill
Juice of 1 lemon

Bring a large pot of salted water to a boil. Add the tortellini and cook according to the package directions. Drain and run under cold water. Transfer the tortellini to a large mixing bowl. Drizzle with 2 tablespoons of the olive oil. Lightly season with salt and pepper and gently toss to coat. Set aside to let cool.

Heat the remaining 2 tablespoons olive oil in a large sauté pan over medium heat. Add the onion, stirring frequently until softened, about 10 minutes.

Allow the onion to cool in the pan, about 5 minutes. Once cooled, add the onion to the tortellini.

Add the sour cream, walnuts, cucumber, dill, and lemon juice. Gently toss until the dressing is well blended and creamy, and the tortellini are evenly coated with dressing. Season to taste with salt and pepper. Cover the salad with plastic wrap and chill for 1 hour.

Toss the salad once more just before serving. Taste, add additional salt and pepper if needed, and serve.

String Bean and Potato Salad

This salad's vinaigrette is a star, with seasoning that makes all the other ingredients shine. Put your own signature on this one, and turn the volume up a little, with an extra squeeze of lemon, a splash more vinegar, or a more generous dash of seasoning. Serves 4 to 6

3 white potatoes, peeled and diced into
    ½-inch cubes
1 pound haricots verts (petite French green
    beans), trimmed
1 red onion, thinly sliced
¼ cup extra-virgin olive oil
½ tablespoon Italian-style red wine vinegar
Juice of 1 lemon
¼ teaspoon minced garlic
Kosher salt and freshly ground black pepper

In a medium saucepot, cover the potatoes with lightly salted water to 1 inch above the top of the potatoes and bring to a boil over high heat. Lower the heat to medium and simmer for 15 minutes, or until the potatoes are fork-tender. Drain and set aside to cool.

Refill the pot halfway with lightly salted cold water. Add the haricots verts, and bring to a boil over high heat. Lower to medium, and simmer for 15 minutes, or until the beans have softened. Drain and cool.

In large serving bowl, combine the cooled potatoes and beans. Add the red onion, olive oil, vinegar, lemon juice, and garlic. Season lightly with salt and pepper and gently toss until completely mixed. Chill the salad for 30 minutes.

Taste, and add salt and pepper as needed. Mix once more and chill for 30 minutes.

Just prior to serving, taste the salad and add more salt and pepper if needed. Toss and serve immediately.

Macaroni Salad

Serves 4 to 6

  1 pound elbow macaroni
  6 hard-boiled eggs, chopped
  ⅔ cup peeled and diced carrots
  ¼ cup diced celery
  ⅔ cup pitted black olives, drained
  ⅓ cup minced yellow onion
  1 cup real mayonnaise
  Kosher salt and freshly ground black pepper
  2 teaspoons sweet paprika

Bring a medium pot of salted water to a boil over high heat. Add the macaroni and cook according to the package directions. Drain and rinse with cold water.

Transfer the pasta to a large mixing bowl. Add the eggs, carrots, celery, olives, and onion and mix to combine.

Using a rubber spatula, fold in the mayonnaise. Season lightly with salt and pepper.

Spoon the salad onto a large serving plate, cover with plastic wrap, and chill for 30 minutes.

When ready to serve, toss again, and generously dust with the paprika.

Egg Salad

Serves 4 to 6

  8 large eggs
  ⅔ cup finely diced carrots
  ⅔ cup finely diced celery
  ⅓ cup finely diced red onion
  Kosher salt and freshly ground black pepper
  1 cup real mayonnaise

Place the eggs carefully into a pot large enough to hold them in a single layer and cover with cold water. Place over high heat and bring to a boil. Remove from the heat, cover tightly, and let stand for 12 minutes.

Meanwhile, fill a large, heatproof bowl with cold water and ice. Using a slotted spoon, transfer the eggs to the bowl with the iced water. Chill the eggs for at least 15 minutes.

Peel the eggs, chop them coarsely, and transfer to a medium bowl. Add the carrots, celery, and red onion. Season lightly with salt and pepper and mix well. Using a rubber spatula, fold in the mayonnaise and mix until completely combined. Taste and add salt and pepper as needed. Cover the salad with plastic wrap and chill for 30 minutes, or until ready to serve.

Tuna and Cannellini Bean Salad

Serves 4 to 6

Three 6-ounce cans tuna, packed in oil, drained
One 12-ounce can cannellini beans, rinsed and
    drained
¼ cup diced red onion
¼ cup extra-virgin olive oil
6 cherry tomatoes, quartered
1 tablespoon finely chopped fresh sage
¼ teaspoon finely chopped fresh tarragon
1 tablespoon finely chopped fresh basil, plus a
    few leaves for garnish
Kosher salt and freshly ground black pepper
4 lemons, halved

Chill your serving plate.

In a large mixing bowl, flake the tuna with a fork. Add the beans, red onion, olive oil, tomatoes, sage, tarragon, and chopped basil, and season lightly with salt and pepper. Mix until completely combined, and let stand for 30 minutes.

When the salad flavors have married, using a sieve or your hands to catch the seeds, squeeze in the lemon juice from the lemon halves. Mix well, taste, and add salt and pepper to taste. Cover the salad with plastic wrap and chill for 30 minutes, or until ready to serve.

Toss the salad again just before serving and spoon onto a chilled serving plate. Garnish with a few leaves of the fresh basil and serve.

Radicchio and Crabmeat Cocktail

Serves 4

1 cup jumbo lump crabmeat, picked over for
    cartilage and shells
5 teaspoons olive oil
Juice of ½ lemon
2 tablespoons real mayonnaise
2 teaspoons Dijon mustard
2 tablespoons frozen peas, thawed
½ teaspoon finely diced celery
½ teaspoon finely diced pitted black olives
Kosher salt and freshly ground black pepper
4 large radicchio leaves
8 cherry tomatoes, halved
2 tablespoons finely chopped fresh Italian
    parsley

In a large mixing bowl, flake the crabmeat well with a fork. Add 1 teaspoon of the olive oil and the lemon juice and mix well.

Add the mayonnaise, mustard, peas, celery, and olives. Gently mix until all ingredients are well combined. Season to taste with salt and pepper and mix again.

Place a radicchio leaf on each serving plate. Fill each leaf with ½ cup of the crabmeat mixture. Drizzle with the remaining 4 teaspoons olive oil.

Garnish with the tomato halves, sprinkle with the parsley, and serve chilled.

Broccoli Salad

Serves 6

- 2 large heads broccoli, trimmed
    and separated into florets
- 2 teaspoons kosher salt
- 1 teaspoon minced garlic
- ½ cup extra-virgin olive oil
- ⅓ cup fresh lemon juice
- 6 lemon wedges

Fill a large bowl with cold water and ice. Line a baking sheet with layers of paper towels.

In a large pot combine the broccoli florets with enough water to cover. Add the salt and bring to a boil over high heat. Reduce the heat to medium-high and cook for 5 minutes, or until the broccoli is fork-tender.

Drain and transfer the broccoli to the ice bath. When completely cool, transfer the broccoli to the lined baking sheet to dry.

In a medium bowl, combine the garlic, olive oil, and lemon juice. Whisk until completely mixed. Add the broccoli to the dressing and gently toss to coat.

Transfer the broccoli to a serving dish, arranging the florets in an attractive presentation. Whisk the remaining dressing, drizzle over the broccoli, garnish with the lemon wedges, and serve.

"After a cold and difficult day of travel with cancelled flights and lost luggage, Beryl Raff and I were guests of Mr. and Mrs. Matthew Fortgang at Rao's last night. You and yours physically and emotionally warmed us. We dined and danced and drank and sang and came back to life. We cannot thank you enough for making us feel, if even for one night, like a part of your family."

—PAUL RUSSEL

SOUPS

Escarole and Bean Soup

Serves 6 to 8

½ cup olive oil
1 garlic clove, minced
4 cups cooked cannellini beans
1 cup reserved bean cooking broth
1 cup chicken broth
2 large bunches escarole, trimmed and
    blanched
Kosher salt and freshly ground black pepper
¼ cup grated Pecorino Romano cheese

Heat the olive oil in a large pot over medium-low heat. Add the garlic and sauté for 2 minutes, or until the garlic begins to shimmer.

Add the beans, bean broth, chicken broth, and blanched escarole, stir to combine, then stir occasionally as the soup comes to a boil. When the soup reaches a boil, season lightly with salt and pepper. Reduce the heat to low and simmer for 15 minutes. If you prefer a thinner soup, add more chicken broth at this point.

Stir the soup well just before serving. Serve piping hot in individual bowls, generously sprinkled with the grated cheese.

Pasta and Peas

Serves 6 to 8

1 pound tubetti or mini shells
½ cup olive oil
3 garlic cloves, smashed
1½ pounds fresh or frozen peas
⅓ cup diced onion
½ cup diced prosciutto
2 cups chicken broth
¼ cup grated Pecorino Romano cheese

Bring a large pot of heavily salted water to a boil over high heat. Add the tubetti and cook until al dente. Drain the pasta, reserving 1 cup of the cooking water.

Heat the olive oil in a large pot over medium-low heat. Add the garlic and sauté for 2 minutes.

Add the peas, onion, and prosciutto. Cook for 4 minutes, or until the onion becomes translucent.

Add the pasta, reserved pasta water, and chicken broth and bring to a boil. Reduce the heat to low and simmer, stirring occasionally, for 10 to 15 minutes. Serve in individual soup bowls, garnished with a sprinkling of the cheese.

Pasta and Beans

Serves 6 to 8

1 pound tubetti (or substitute small macaroni)
2 cups canned San Marzano tomatoes
½ cup olive oil
3 garlic cloves, smashed
1 cup diced onion
⅓ cup diced prosciutto (or substitute pancetta)
4 cups cooked cannellini beans
1 cup reserved bean cooking broth
4 cups chicken broth
Kosher salt and freshly ground black pepper
¼ cup grated Pecorino Romano cheese

Bring a large pot of heavily salted water to a boil over high heat. Add the tubetti and cook until al dente. Drain the pasta and set aside.

Wash your hands and crush the tomatoes in a medium bowl.

Heat the olive oil in a large saucepan over medium-low heat. Add the garlic and sauté for 1 minute. Be careful not to burn the garlic.

Add the onion and prosciutto and cook for 1 minute.

Add the beans and the bean broth. Increase the heat to medium and add the chicken broth. Season lightly with salt and pepper. Bring to a low boil.

Add the tomatoes and cook, uncovered, for 10 minutes. Add the pasta and cook for 5 minutes more.

Serve in individual warmed soup bowls, garnished with a sprinkling of the cheese.

Pasta and Lentils

Serves 6 to 8

4 quarts cold water
1 pound lentils, rinsed and drained
3 large carrots, peeled and diced
3 celery stalks, diced
1 cup diced onion
6 garlic cloves, smashed
½ cup olive oil
1 ½ tablespoons finely chopped fresh Italian parsley
1 teaspoon dried oregano
Kosher salt and freshly ground black pepper
¾ pound fedelini, broken into 2-inch pieces
¼ cup grated Pecorino Romano cheese

Fill a 6-quart saucepan with at least 4 quarts of cold water.

Add the lentils, carrots, celery, onion, and garlic and stir to combine. Add the olive oil, parsley, and oregano, season lightly with salt and pepper, and bring to a boil over high heat. Reduce the heat to low, and simmer for 30 minutes, or until the lentils are just tender.

Increase the heat to high and stir in the fedelini. Bring the soup back to a boil and cook for 1 minute. Serve in individual soup bowls, sprinkled with the grated cheese.

Minestrone

Serves 6 to 8

½ cup olive oil
1 cup chopped yellow onions
¼ cup chopped fresh Italian parsley
1 teaspoon chopped fresh thyme
2 cups diced russet potatoes
2 cups diced carrots
1 cup diced celery
1 cup diced zucchini
1 cup fresh fava beans
1 cup fresh or frozen peas
2 cups canned San Marzano plum tomatoes
4 cups chicken broth
Kosher salt and freshly ground black pepper
2 cups cannellini or kidney beans, cooked
2 tablespoons chopped fresh basil
¼ cup grated Pecorino Romano cheese

Heat the olive oil in a 4-quart stockpot over medium heat. Add the onions, parsley, and thyme and sauté for 7 minutes, or until the onions start to brown.

Add the potatoes, carrots, celery, zucchini, fava beans, and peas, one at a time, stirring in each before adding the next. Sauté for 6 minutes.

Add the tomatoes and broth and season liberally with salt and pepper. Increase the heat to high and bring to a boil. Reduce the heat to medium-low, and simmer for 1 hour, or until the soup has reached your preferred thickness.

Stir in the cooked beans. As you stir, mash some of the cooked beans with the back of your spoon. Cook for 10 minutes, then remove from the heat.

Stir in the basil and serve the soup in individual warmed soup bowls, sprinkled with the grated cheese.

"I was inspired the night we were with you (and your able crew)—not only by how you approached the 'business of your business' but also how, most importantly, you tirelessly made every person there feel the 'Rao vibe,' an intimate connection—an alchemy of food, music, personality, up-close attention and cool stories about the restaurant's colorful history."
—BOB CHANDLER, RUMSON NJ

EGGS

Potato and Egg Frittata

Some people don't like eggs. Of course, some people don't like the Beatles. There's just no explaining it.

The Pellegrinos like eggs.

As a young boy, I spent a lot of time around my grandparents. They owned a grocery store and deli just a few blocks from their home on the South Shore of Long Island. My grandfather, Frank, was better known as "Yankee" (Bronx Bombers, not Brahmin). He would rise every morning at 4:00 A.M. to open the grocery store and prepare the day's deli menu for his patrons. After working the morning shift, he would come home for lunch. More often than not, eggs were on the menu— specifically, egg sandwiches. Light, fluffy, yet substantial and thoroughly satisfying. It was a sentimental favorite, an Italian classic.

As far as I'm concerned, fresh bakery bread is essential to fully complement a delicacy like potatoes and eggs. Serves 4 to 6

¼ cup olive oil
4 fingerling potatoes, scrubbed and cut into
  ¼-inch slices
1 medium onion, diced
Kosher salt and freshly ground black pepper
8 large eggs
¾ cup grated Pecorino Romano cheese
1 tablespoon chopped fresh Italian parsley

Preheat the oven to 325°F.

Heat the olive oil in a large sauté pan over medium heat for 2 minutes. Add the potatoes and fry until tender and golden brown.

Add the onion and season to taste with salt and pepper. Cook until translucent, 3 to 4 minutes.

In a medium mixing bowl, combine the eggs, cheese, and parsley. Season lightly with salt and pepper and whisk until thoroughly mixed. Add the egg mixture to the potatoes and onion. Cook, shaking the pan from side to side so that the egg mixture covers the bottom of the pan.

Using a rubber spatula, softly turn the eggs, letting the liquid from the top flow to the bottom of the pan. Cook until the bottom is set and beginning to brown, 2 to 3 minutes.

Transfer the pan to the center rack of the oven. Switch the oven to broil, and broil for 3 minutes, or until the top begins to brown.

 Transfer the frittata to a serving platter, cut into wedges, and serve.

Peppers and Eggs

Serves 4 to 6

    ¼ cup olive oil
    4 Italian frying peppers, seeded and cut into
        ¼-inch strips
    1 yellow onion, diced
    Kosher salt and freshly ground black pepper
    8 large eggs

Heat the olive oil in a large sauté pan over medium heat for 2 minutes. Add the frying peppers and onion, season with salt and black pepper, and sauté until the vegetables have softened, 4 to 6 minutes.

In a medium mixing bowl, whisk the eggs. Add to the pan and let the egg set briefly. Using a wooden spoon, turn the eggs until any uncooked liquid begins to set, and the eggs are fully cooked.

Transfer the eggs to a serving platter, or make individual sandwiches with the eggs and slices of toasted Italian bread.

Spaghetti Frittata

Serves 6 to 8

    8 large eggs
    1 cup grated Parmigiano Reggiano cheese
    1 cup grated Pecorino Romano cheese
    1 tablespoon chopped fresh Italian parsley
    Freshly ground black pepper
    ½ pound spaghetti, broken into 2- to 3-inch
        pieces, cooked
    2 tablespoons olive oil

Preheat the oven to 325°F.

In a large mixing bowl, combine the eggs, cheeses, parsley, and black pepper to taste. Whisk until completely blended. Add the cooked spaghetti and stir until the pasta is evenly coated.

Heat the olive oil in a large sauté pan over medium heat for 2 minutes. Add the spaghetti and egg mixture and cook until the edges of the frittata begin to brown.

Transfer the pan to the oven and switch to broil. Broil for 4 to 6 minutes, or until the eggs begin to brown on top.

Transfer the frittata to a serving platter, cut into wedges, and serve.

Eggs in Purgatory

Serves 6

⅓ cup olive oil
½ yellow onion, diced
One 28-ounce can San Marzano tomatoes,
    hand crushed with juice
4 fresh basil leaves, chopped
½ teaspoon kosher salt
½ teaspoon freshly ground black pepper
½ teaspoon chopped fresh oregano
12 large eggs

Heat the olive oil in a large nonstick sauté pan over medium heat for 1 minute. Add the onion and cook until translucent, 3 to 4 minutes.

Add the tomatoes, basil, salt, pepper, and oregano. Reduce the heat to medium-low, and simmer, stirring occasionally, for 12 minutes.

Drop the eggs, one at a time, into the sauce. Cook, sunny-side up, for about 5 minutes, or until the eggs are completely cooked.

Remove the pan from the heat, cover, and let rest for 5 minutes before transferring 1 six-ounce ladle of sauce and 2 poached eggs to a warmed individual soup bowl.

Zucchini with Eggs and Cheese

Serves 4

2 pounds small zucchini, sliced into
    ¼-inch rounds
1 heaping teaspoon coarse salt
½ cup olive oil
3 large eggs, lightly beaten
¾ cup grated Parmigiano Reggiano cheese,
    plus extra for serving
Freshly ground black pepper
2 tablespoons chopped fresh Italian parsley

Add the zucchini to a medium sauté pan and cover with water. Bring to a boil over high heat and add the salt. Cook, partially covered, for 2 minutes, or until the zucchini's skin is bright green.

Drain off two-thirds of the water. Return the pan to the stovetop over medium-low heat and gently stir in the olive oil. Bring to a simmer, and cook for 1 minute more.

Pour in the eggs, stirring gently. Increase the heat to medium and simmer until the eggs cook and stick to the zucchini.

Add the grated cheese and season to taste with the pepper. Remove from the heat and stir gently until the cheese melts and becomes slightly stringy, about 1 minute.

Serve in individual warmed bowls, adding a little cooking liquid to each portion. Sprinkle with the parsley and serve with extra cheese at the table.

PIZZA

Pizza Dough

Who doesn't like pizza? We started serving pizzas at the Caesars Palace Rao's for lunch, and they've been a huge hit. Of course, not everyone has a wood-fired pizza oven in their kitchen. But that's okay. With a good pizza stone, pizza pans, or a pizza peel, and a working oven, your kitchen has everything you need to produce some fantastic pies.

Although this recipe calls for the more widely available all-purpose flour, I like to use Italian "00" flour for pizza dough. It is available at many Italian specialty food stores or online from sources such as Amazon.

Feel free to substitute store-bought dough in any of the pizza recipes that follow; however, your best resource would actually be the local pizza parlor. Makes enough dough for two 12-inch pizzas

1 tablespoon olive oil, plus more for the bowls
4 cups all-purpose flour, plus more if needed
   (or substitute Italian OO flour)
1 teaspoon kosher salt
1½ cups lukewarm (105° to 115°F) water
One ¼-ounce envelope active dry yeast
1 teaspoon sugar

TO MAKE THE DOUGH BY HAND
Grease two large bowls with olive oil. Combine the flour and salt in a separate large bowl and set aside.

Pour the water into a medium bowl and sprinkle with the yeast and sugar. Let stand until the yeast softens and the mixture bubbles, about 5 minutes. Stir to dissolve the yeast.

Gradually add the yeast mixture to the flour mixture, mixing with your hands. Add the olive oil and mix until the dough is soft and sticky. If the dough is dry, add a little more water, or add a little more flour if it is too wet.

Turn the dough out onto a lightly floured surface and knead until smooth and elastic, about 10 minutes, adding more flour as needed.

TO MAKE THE DOUGH (WITH A HEAVY-DUTY STANDING ELECTRIC MIXER)

Combine the flour and salt in a large bowl and set aside.

Add the water to the mixer bowl and sprinkle with the yeast and sugar. Let stand until the yeast softens and the mixture looks active (it may or may not bubble), about 5 minutes. Stir to dissolve the yeast.

Blend on low speed with the dough hook attachment, gradually adding flour to make a rough dough. Mix on medium-low, adding more flour as needed, until the dough is smooth and elastic, about 10 minutes.

Shape the dough into a ball, and cut it in half. Put each half into the prepared bowls and roll the dough around to coat with the oil. Cover the bowls with plastic wrap or a dampened kitchen towel. Let stand in a warm place until almost doubled in volume.

Punch the dough down to remove the air, and reroll each ball. Re-cover the bowls, and set the bowls aside to let the dough rise for at least 1 hour more. (If, when you try to stretch the dough into a pizza, it keeps springing back, let it rest for a while longer and it will loosen up.)

Turn the dough out onto a floured work surface. Cut in half, and shape each half into a ball. You can use the dough right away, or put each ball in a 1-gallon resealable plastic bag, and refrigerate until ready to use, but no more than 24 hours. You can also wrap each ball of dough in plastic wrap, slip into a plastic bag, and freeze for up to 1 month. Thaw overnight in the refrigerator before using. If the dough is chilled, let it stand at room temperature for 30 minutes before shaping into a pizza.

Pizza Sauce

For best results when preparing this sauce, use canned San Marzano tomatoes labeled Pomodoro San Marzano dell'Agro Sarnese-Nocerino, *which ensures they are authentic and the quality you want.* Makes 2 cups sauce; enough for 3 pizzas

2 tablespoons olive oil
1 garlic clove, minced
One 28-ounce can San Marzano tomatoes, hand crushed with juice
1 teaspoon kosher salt
1 teaspoon dried oregano
½ teaspoon freshly ground black pepper
3 or 4 whole fresh basil leaves

Heat the olive oil in a large sauté pan over medium heat. Add the garlic and cook, without browning, until softened, about 1 minute. Add the tomatoes, sprinkle with the salt, and bring to a boil, stirring often. Reduce the heat to medium-low.

Add the oregano, pepper, and basil. Simmer, stirring occasionally, until the sauce is thick, 15 to 20 minutes.

Transfer to a bowl and let cool completely.

VARIATIONS

Use the instructions that follow to create a pizza however you like it. Here are some of the toppings we use at Rao's at Caesars Palace:

Sausage: Precook the sausage, slice, and top the pizza just before it goes into the oven.

Margherita: Tomato sauce, mozzarella, and Parmesan cheese, topped with fresh basil leaves.

Pepperoni: Tomato sauce, shredded mozzarella cheese, and 10 to 12 pepperoni slices.

Four Cheese: A white pizza with a small handful of shredded mozzarella, Gruyère, and Fontina cheeses, topped with crumbles of Gorgonzola and drizzle of truffle oil.

Four Seasons: Tomato sauce, shredded mozzarella cheese, topped with handful of sautéed artichokes, diced Gaeta olives, and mushrooms, finished with sliced prosciutto.

Sausage and Ricotta: No red sauce, just shredded mozzarella cheese, sprinkled with fresh rosemary, and finished with 8 to 10 slices of sausage, and 6 to 7 dollops of ricotta cheese.

Broccoli Rabe: Another white pizza, topped with shredded mozzarella cheese, broccoli rabe sautéed with garlic oil, and 7 to 8 dollops of ricotta.

Calzones

Calzone translates from Italian to "trouser leg," because the folded dough looks like pant cuffs.

Ham Calzone

Makes 1 calzone

1 Pizza Dough (page 97)
1 cup ricotta cheese
½ cup shredded mozzarella
½ cup cubed cooked ham
1 egg, beaten
2 tablespoons unsalted butter
½ to 1 teaspoon chopped garlic
Pizza Sauce (page 99, warmed, optional)

Preheat the oven to 450°F.

Flatten the dough as you would for a pizza, leaving it thicker to avoid making holes in the dough. Spread the cheese on one half of the dough, leaving a ½-inch lip where you'll seal the calzone when you fold it over.

Spread the ham evenly on top of the cheese. Fold the dough over and seal the edges with a fork; if the edges don't stick together, brush with a little water or the egg wash used to coat the calzone.

Brush the dough with the beaten egg; this will make it shiny.

Cut two or three ½-inch slashes in the top to release steam from the inside during baking and prevent the calzone from bursting. Place on a baking sheet.

Bake for 10 minutes. Reduce the heat to 400°F, and bake for 10 minutes more.

While the calzone is cooking, combine the butter and garlic in a small pot over medium heat until the butter melts entirely and begins to froth. (Or use a microwave for this—a simpler and quicker option.)

Remove the calzone from the oven and brush with the garlic butter. Cool for 10 to 15 minutes before cutting and serving. Serve with the pizza sauce for dunking, as desired.

Meatball Calzone

When preparing meatballs for this recipe, use three to four ounces of the meatball mixture per ball. The smaller meatballs make for a more manageable eating experience. Alternatively, if you have any leftover meatballs and sauce from the recipe on page 203, use those for the calzone filling. If you are short on marinara sauce, use a store-bought jar of Rao's sauce. Makes 1 calzone

1 Pizza Dough (page 97)
1 cup shredded mozzarella cheese
1 cooked meatball, halved, warmed
¼ cup Homemade Marinara Sauce (page 113)
2 tablespoons unsalted butter
2 garlic cloves, minced

Preheat the oven to 450°F.

Flatten the dough as you would for a pizza, leaving it thicker to avoid making holes in the dough. Spread the cheese across one half of the dough, leaving a ½-inch lip where you'll seal the calzone when you fold it over.

Center the meatball halves on the cheese. Cover with the marinara sauce. Fold the dough over and seal the edges with a fork; if the edges don't stick together, brush with a little water—or with an egg wash.

Cut two or three ½-inch slashes in the top to release steam from the inside during baking and prevent the calzone from bursting. Place on a baking sheet.

Bake for 10 minutes. Reduce the heat to 400°F, and cook for 10 minutes more.

While the calzone is cooking, combine the butter and garlic in a small pot over medium heat until the butter melts entirely and begins to froth. (Or use a microwave for this—a simpler and quicker option.)

Remove the calzone from the oven and brush with the garlic butter. Cool for 10 to 15 minutes before cutting and serving.

Sausage and Pepper Stromboli

This is one of my favorite calzone variations. Before preparing the sausage and peppers, split the raw sausages in half. This will make assembling the stromboli easier. Makes 1 stromboli

2 tablespoons olive oil
1 bell pepper, seeded and cut into ¼-inch slices
¼ yellow onion, cut into ¼-inch slices
1 Pizza Dough (page 97)
1 cup shredded mozzarella cheese
2 cooked Italian sausages, cut into 8 to 12 pieces
2 tablespoons unsalted butter
2 garlic cloves, minced

Preheat the oven to 450°F.

Heat the olive oil in a large sauté pan over medium-high heat. Add the pepper and onion and sauté until softened, about 7 minutes. Set aside to cool. (Cooled peppers and onions ensure that the dough doesn't become too soft and break.)

Flatten the dough out into a rectangle (you can use a small oiled baking sheet as a mold, although the shape doesn't need to be perfect).

Spread the cheese over the dough, leaving a ½-inch edge on three sides. Top the cheese with the sausage, peppers, and onions. Roll the dough, the long way, into a log. Making sure the seam is on the bottom, place on a greased perforated pan. (The edges do not need to be sealed.)

Bake for 10 minutes, then reduce the heat to 400°F, and bake for 10 minutes more. While the stromboli is cooking, combine the butter and garlic in a small pot over medium heat until the butter melts entirely and begins to froth. (Or use a microwave for this—a simpler and quicker option.)

Remove the stromboli from the oven and brush with the garlic butter. Cool for 10 to 15 minutes before cutting and serving.

Margherita Pizza alla Rao's

Makes two 12-inch pizzas

1 recipe Pizza Dough (page 97)
Cornmeal, for the pans
1⅓ cups Pizza Sauce (page 99)
4 tablespoons freshly grated Parmigiano
    Reggiano cheese
1 pound fresh mozzarella cheese, thinly sliced
10 fresh basil leaves

Preheat the oven to 500°F.

Stretch the dough out into two 12-inch circles on two pizza pans; sprinkle some cornmeal under the pizzas to ensure that they don't stick and the crust is crispy.

Spread the first pizza with half the sauce. Sprinkle with half the Parmigiano Reggiano cheese. Top with half of the mozzarella slices, and space 5 basil leaves evenly around the surface. Repeat to make the second pizza.

Bake for 8 to 12 minutes, or until the cheese is bubbly and the crust is golden brown. Slice and serve.

Sausage Pizza

Makes two 12-inch pizzas

3 sweet or hot Italian sausages (about 9
    ounces), pricked with a fork
1 recipe Pizza Dough (page 97)
Cornmeal, for the pans
1⅓ cups Pizza Sauce (page 99)
4 tablespoons freshly grated Parmigiano
    Reggiano cheese
1 pound shredded mozzarella cheese

Preheat the oven to 350°F.

Put the sausages in a baking pan and bake for 15 minutes, or until firm and cooked through. Transfer to a cutting board and let cool. Cut into ¼-inch slices. Set aside.

Increase the oven temperature to 500°F.

Stretch the dough out into two 12-inch circles and place them on two pizza pans; sprinkle some cornmeal under the pizzas to ensure that they don't stick and the crust is crispy.

Spread the first pizza with half the sauce. Sprinkle with half the Parmigiano Reggiano. Top with half the mozzarella, and half the sausage slices. Repeat to make the second pizza.

Bake for 8 to 12 minutes, or until the cheese is bubbly and the crust is golden brown. Slice and serve.

VARIATION

For a pepperoni pizza, substitute 6 ounces of sliced pepperoni for the sausage.

Four Cheese Pizza

The blend of cheeses, along with a drizzle of truffle oil, lend a touch of sophistication to this pizza bianco. Makes two 12-inch pizzas

1 recipe Pizza Dough (page 97)
Cornmeal, for the pans
8 ounces mozzarella cheese, sliced
¾ cup shredded Fontina cheese
¾ cup shredded Gruyère cheese
½ cup crumbled Gorgonzola cheese
Truffle oil, for drizzling
Freshly ground black pepper

Preheat the oven to 500°F.

Stretch the dough out into two 12-inch circles. Place them on two pizza pans; sprinkle some cornmeal under the pizzas to ensure that they don't stick and the crust is crispy.

Visually separate the first pizza into thirds. Spread half the mozzarella on one-third, half the Fontina on another, and half the Gruyère over the final third. Sprinkle half of the Gorgonzola over the entire pizza. Repeat to make the second pizza.

Bake for 8 to 12 minutes, or until the cheese is bubbly and the crust is golden brown.

Drizzle truffle oil over each pizza, and dust each with black pepper. Slice and serve.

"If you're thinking of putting together a bucket list of ten things you'd like to do before you die, then I strongly suggest you add Rao's to your agenda. . . . What's so magical about Rao's? Well, for thing, every time I venture down, I feel as though it's my first time going. It's the same good feeling every time I walk through that door—like a kid walking through the gate for the first time at Disneyland—and the best part is, it never gets old. . . . All I can say is this, 'if there's no Rao's in heaven, I'm not going,' and neither should you!"

—FRANK TREPPEDI

Four Seasons Pizza

This is an old-country variation of a pizza with everything on it. Take liberties with the toppings, and give the pizza your personal touch. Makes two 12-inch pizzas

2/3 cup thawed and coarsely chopped frozen
    artichoke hearts
1 recipe Pizza Dough (page 97)
Cornmeal, for the pans
1 1/3 cups Pizza Sauce (page 99)
4 tablespoons freshly grated Parmigiano
    Reggiano cheese
8 ounces mozzarella cheese, thinly sliced
2/3 cup pitted and coarsely chopped Gaeta olives
1 cup very thinly sliced white mushrooms
2 ounces prosciutto, sliced paper-thin

Preheat the oven to 500°F. Pat the artichokes dry with paper towels. Stretch the dough out into two 12-inch circles. Place them on two pizza pans; sprinkle some cornmeal under the pizzas to ensure that they don't stick.

Spread the first pizza with 2/3 cup of the pizza sauce. Sprinkle with half of the Parmigiano Reggiano. Top with half of the mozzarella slices. Spread half the artichoke hearts on one third of the pizza, half the olives on the second third, and half the mushrooms on the final third. Repeat with the second pizza.

Bake for 8 to 12 minutes, or until the cheese is bubbly and the crust is golden brown.

Top each pizza with half the prosciutto, draping the slices in pleats across the top of each pizza. Slice and serve.

Sausage and Ricotta Pizza

This pizza is sexy and savvy! Add a touch more character to it by using hot sausage and a sprinkle of crushed red pepper flakes. Makes two 12-inch pizzas

3 sweet or hot Italian sausages, pierced with a
    fork
1 recipe Pizza Dough (page 97)
Cornmeal, for the pans
8 ounces mozzarella cheese, thinly sliced
1 1/3 cups ricotta cheese
4 teaspoons finely chopped fresh rosemary

Preheat the oven to 350°F.

Put the sausages in a baking pan and bake for 15 minutes, or until firm and cooked through. Transfer to a cutting board and let cool. Cut into 1/4-inch slices. Set aside.

Increase the oven temperature to 500°F.

Stretch the dough out into two 12-inch circles. Place them on two pizza pans; sprinkle some cornmeal under the pizzas to ensure that they don't stick and the crust is crispy.

Arrange half of the mozzarella over the first pizza. Spoon 6 dollops (half of the total amount) of ricotta across the pizza. Scatter half of the sausage evenly across the top. Repeat with the second pizza.

Bake for 8 to 12 minutes, or until the cheese is bubbly and the crust is golden brown.

Sprinkle the rosemary over the pizzas, slice, and serve.

Broccoli Rabe White Pizza

This bitter green topping, used in conjunction with the ricotta cheese, creates a balance of flavors on this pie. Try not to overload the pizza with the ricotta; a modest amount will provide plenty of flavor and texture without making the pie soggy. Makes two 12-inch pizzas

1 pound broccoli rabe, trimmed and blanched
2 tablespoons olive oil
3 garlic cloves, thinly sliced
1 recipe Pizza Dough (page 97)
Cornmeal, for the pans
8 ounces mozzarella cheese, thinly sliced
1 2/3 cups ricotta cheese

Preheat the oven to 500°F.

Rinse the broccoli rabe well to remove any grit. Shake off the excess water, but do not dry. Coarsely chop the rabe into bite-size pieces.

Heat the olive oil and garlic in a large sauté pan over medium heat, until the garlic turns golden, about 2 minutes. Add the broccoli rabe and cover the pan. Reduce the heat to medium-low and cook, stirring occasionally, until the broccoli rabe is tender, about 20 minutes. Uncover during the last few minutes to evaporate excess water. Drain in a colander. Let cool.

Stretch the dough out into two 12-inch circles. Place them on two pizza pans; sprinkle some cornmeal under the pizzas to ensure that they don't stick and the crust is crispy.

Arrange half of the mozzarella slices over the first pizza. Scatter half of the broccoli rabe evenly over the pizza. Spoon 6 dollops (half of the total amount) of ricotta across the broccoli rabe. Repeat with the second pizza.

Bake for 8 to 12 minutes, or until the cheese is bubbly and the crust is golden brown.

Slice and serve.

PASTA

The Heart and Soul
of the Italian Kitchen

Just thinking of pasta induces anticipation overload. It's a mouthwatering exercise that starts me pondering, "What am I in the mood for today? Seafood? Vegetables? Beef? Pork? Veal?" As that palate-to-brain connection fires up the imagination, I face more decisions. Red sauce? Oil and garlic? Cream sauce? Decisions, decisions, decisions. I yell over to my friends, "What are you in the mood for tonight? Red? White? Cream?" Then, boom, it hits me like a ton of bricks! "No worries, I got it. We'll do a little bit of each."

Over my thirty-four years spent in the kitchen, I've developed an intimate relationship with the pasta dishes that are so much a part of my personal story. Throughout my culinary apprenticeship, my grandmother, aunts, uncles, father, mother, contemporaries, and guests have all had a tremendous impact on how I make pasta. All that input has left me with strong opinions.

Grated cheese with shellfish? Blasphemous! Overcooked pasta? Neanderthal. Gloppy sauce over poorly drained pasta? Inept. These are crimes against Southern Italian cooking, crimes punishable by banishment from the kitchen and dining room.

The notes with the recipes that follow are my way of sharing the personal lessons I've learned from my family. Whether it's beefy or based on basil, creamy, heavy, or light in consistency, allow me to share with you a few ideas for a beautiful evening's pasta delight. I hope you find these recipes as insightful, entertaining, and fun to make as my culinary team and I do!

Homemade Marinara Sauce

This sauce is the backbone of many of Rao's dishes, and the intensely sweet and flavorful San Marzano plum tomatoes are the backbone of the sauce. In the early days, before canned tomatoes and my father's brilliant idea to package our own, it was common for my relatives to gather as many ripe plum tomatoes as possible during the height of the season (July, August, and September). They would spend weeks preparing the sauce and preserving these skinned fruits (whose name in Italian literally translates to "golden apple"*), in an effort to stock up for the rest of the year. Thankfully, today you can find these special San Marzano tomatoes on the shelves of most every supermarket, to enjoy any time of year.* Serves 4

Two 28-ounce cans San Marzano tomatoes
    with juice
¼ cup olive oil
4 ounces pancetta, cubed (optional)
3 tablespoons minced yellow onion
2 garlic cloves, minced

Kosher salt
6 fresh basil leaves, torn
Pinch of fresh oregano
Freshly ground black pepper

Transfer the tomatoes and their juice to a large bowl. Wash your hands and gently crush the tomatoes into a thick, even consistency. Remove and discard any hard cores or stringy membranes.

Heat the olive oil in a deep saucepan over medium heat. If you are using the pancetta, sauté it for 5 minutes, or until all the fat has been rendered. Remove the pancetta and discard.

Add the minced onions to the rendered fat in the pan and sauté until translucent, about 3 minutes. Add the garlic and stir continuously for 30 seconds.

Add the tomatoes and stir with a wooden spoon. Season with salt to taste and increase the heat to high.

When the sauce reaches a boil, immediately reduce to a simmer. Cook for 1 hour, stirring occasionally, until the sauce has thickened. If you prefer a thicker sauce, simmer for an additional 15 minutes.

Stir in the basil, oregano, and black pepper to taste and cook for 5 minutes more. Remove from the heat and use immediately or store.

"Sometimes you get lucky. Thirty years ago I had such an encounter with luck, and I had my first visit to Rao's. Annie and Vincent were still in the kitchen, Frankie was taking orders, and Anthony was working the tables. Nicky 'Vest' was, of course, running the bar. Back then the Mimi Sheraton review in the *New York Times* had put getting a reservation at Rao's on par with scoring Super Bowl tickets. But, somehow, when my mother-in-law had called to book a table, the phone had been answered and 'Frankie No' had become 'Frankie Yes.' Yes, I got lucky, I eventually became a regular at Rao's, each December getting a simple piece of paper from Joe with my reservation dates for next year. One of the unique and cool things people don't know about Rao's, they tell you what dates you'll be coming for dinner."

—PETE ARDITO

Fusilli with Cabbage and Sausage

When my father introduced this Calabrese dish to the restaurant, it was a tough sell. Truth be told, I was hesitant to offer it to our guests until my Aunt Anna and my dad forced me to try. Even so, most guests were reluctant to try the eclectic mix of ingredients. I pleaded with both bosses to have it removed from our verbal menu. I was exhausted of hearing, "No thank you, I'll stick with the shells or filetto." Undeterred, my dad sent an order to every table, whether the guests ordered it or not. Before long, this dish became a must-have for many of our regulars. When New York media personality and ex-NYPD cop Bo Dietl made it a regular dish at his table every Thursday night, word spread. Since then, this hearty pasta creation has been selling itself. Serves 4

¼ cup olive oil

4 garlic cloves, smashed

½ pound sweet Italian sausage, cooked and cut into bite-size pieces

½ pound hot Italian sausage, cooked and cut into bite-size pieces

(or substitute all hot or all sweet as you prefer)

3 cups Homemade Marinara Sauce (page 113)

½ head Savoy cabbage, cored, blanched, and shredded

Kosher salt and freshly ground black pepper

¾ cup chicken broth

1 pound fusilli pasta

2 tablespoons grated Pecorino Romano cheese

2 tablespoons chopped fresh Italian parsley

Heat the olive oil in a large sauté pan over medium heat and add the garlic.

When the garlic begins to shimmer, add the sausage and cook until browned. Add the marinara and cabbage and stir with a wooden spoon until completely blended together. Season to taste with salt and pepper.

Add the chicken broth and bring to a boil. Reduce to low, and simmer for 10 minutes, or until the sauce has thickened.

When the sauce is almost ready, bring a large pot of heavily salted water to a boil over high heat. Add the fusilli and cook until al dente. Drain the pasta and return it to the pot.

Reduce the heat under the pasta to medium-high, and add 5 large spoonfuls of the sausage-and-cabbage sauce and the grated cheese. Cook, stirring, for 2 minutes.

Transfer the pasta to a large serving bowl. Top with the remaining sauce. Sprinkle with parsley and serve hot.

Linguine and Clams

My grandparents served clam sauce every Friday, for as far back as I can remember. It was a staple at the restaurant, too. I can't tell you what I would have done in my boyhood to never see, smell, or taste another clam. That changed when I started working with my Aunt Anna, "the Mistress of the Mollusks." I would marvel as she warmed up a splash of olive oil with a few smashed garlic cloves. She'd take her eyes off the sauté pan to look me dead in the eye and say, "Once the garlic starts to shimmer, take it out of the pan." Soon, I'd hear the staccato sizzle of littleneck clams hitting the scalding oil. She'd season the juices and white wine and bring them all to a delectable boil. A few moments later, my aunt would invert another sauté pan over the bubbling sauce, saying, "It helps the clams open faster." Within a few minutes, the clams opened up and she would remove the covering pan, flooding the kitchen with the scintillating aroma of the sea. I'd watch, mesmerized, as she plucked the clams one by one from the sauce, and then drained the pasta and introduced it to the sauce, so that it could absorb the flavors and achieve a more tender bite. She would gently slide the pan's contents into a large, white serving bowl. Like an artist finishing a canvas she would arrange the clams on top of the pasta, showering the dish with a final light garnish of freshly chopped parsley. I'd watch hungrily as the still-steaming dish headed off to its table. Serves 4

1 pound linguine
¼ cup olive oil
1 garlic clove, smashed
24 littleneck clams, rinsed and scrubbed
¼ cup dry white wine
One 6.5-ounce can clams, chopped, with their juice
Pinch of chopped fresh oregano
3 tablespoons chopped fresh Italian parsley

Bring a large pot of salted water to a boil over high heat. Add the linguine and cook, until al dente. Drain the pasta.

Heat the olive oil in a large sauté pan over medium heat. Add the garlic and sauté until golden brown. Transfer to a small bowl or ramekin.

Add the fresh clams and white wine. Cover and cook for 10 minutes, or until the clams have opened. Discard any that do not open.

Using tongs, transfer the open clams to a large bowl. Increase the heat to high, and add the canned clams and their juice, the oregano, and chopped parsley leaves. Cook for 1 minute, or until the sauce boils.

Transfer the pasta to the sauce and toss until evenly coated, about 1 minute.

Transfer the pasta and sauce to a large serving bowl. Arrange the open clams on top of the pasta, garnish with a sprinkling of chopped parsley, and serve.

VARIATION

Prefer a pink clam sauce? Open a small can of whole plum tomatoes and add 4 to 5 tomatoes to the sauté pan after adding the clams. For a plain clam broth, you can easily prepare the dish without the pasta and serve it as a soup or dunking sauce.

Linguine Aglio e Olio

Garlic and olive oil are at the heart of Italian cooking. Each is so rich and flavorful they can easily stand alone. But the combination is heavenly, to say the least. Integrating these two sublime ingredients into a silky sauce, with the salty essence of anchovies as an accent, is an example of how Italian cuisine draws complex flavors from a simple mix of ingredients. As basic as this dish may at first appear, it requires finesse to execute properly. The secret is to remove the garlic and add it back in for the final presentation, ensuring it never burns. If it does, the bitter taste is impossible to counteract, and you have to start over again. The olive oil carries the flavor and is the backbone of this dish. Use a high-quality olive oil and you'll have made a tried-and-true crowd-pleaser. Serves 4

1 pound linguine
1½ cups olive oil
3 anchovy fillets
1 teaspoon crushed red pepper flakes (optional)
6 garlic cloves, finely minced
2 tablespoons chopped fresh Italian parsley

Bring a large pot of salted water to a boil. Add the linguine and cook until al dente. Drain, reserving 1 cup of the cooking water.

Heat ½ cup of the olive oil in a large sauté pan over medium heat and add the anchovies. Cook until the anchovies begin to dissolve, 3 to 5 minutes. Add the red pepper flakes if using, and the garlic. Watch the garlic closely as you stir it constantly with a wooden spoon. The moment it begins to shimmer, remove the pan from the heat. Even though the pan has been removed from the flame, the garlic will continue to cook. Just as it starts to brown, pour the pan contents through a medium sieve set over a glass measuring cup.

Set aside the measuring cup and transfer the garlic from the sieve to a small dish lined with paper towels.

Return the sauté pan to the stovetop over medium-low heat. Slowly pour the separated oil back into the pan. Once the olive oil is to temperature, about 1 minute, transfer the cooked linguine to the pan. Using tongs, gently toss the pasta for 2 minutes, evenly coating it with the oil.

Transfer the pasta to a medium serving bowl. Add the reserved pasta water to the bowl. Garnish with the reserved garlic, sprinkle with the parsley, and serve.

30-Minute Tomato and Basil

This recipe is a gift from Mother Earth. Think about it: San Marzano tomatoes, virgin olive oil, fresh-picked basil. These are some of the planet's most precious gifts.

Combining them in this dish is a relatively quick process. It's the type of simple and satisfying meal my dad would turn to on a sunny spring afternoon, with his golf buddies all gathered in our kitchen. As the conversation turned to lunch, my dad would ask his favorite question, "Are you guys hungry?" You could hear them answer, in unison, "Yes!" all the way up in my room.

I would come downstairs to investigate. My dad would say, "I want to show you something. Get a can of tomatoes and open it up." I'd grab a huge can of San Marzano tomatoes from the pantry and place it on the kitchen counter. After I opened the can, Dad would tell me to dump the tomatoes into a big mixing bowl. "Wash your hands, then start crushing those tomatoes." I'd start in, and tomato juice and pulp would begin flying everywhere. "Gently," my dad would shout.

As he managed the ingredients in the saucepan, allowing the flavors to fuse, my dad would start the pasta water boiling. "A few more minutes, Frankie." It was a promise as much as a statement. When he finally filled a large serving bowl with his creation, dressing the pasta with the remaining sauce, he'd say, "Let me tell ya, two pounds of pasta is no match for six hungry men!" Serves 4

½ cup olive oil
3 garlic cloves, smashed
One 36-ounce can San Marzano tomatoes, hand crushed with juice
½ cup fresh basil leaves, torn
Kosher salt and freshly ground white pepper
1 pound rigatoni (or substitute any short pasta)

Heat the olive oil in a large sauté pan over low heat and add the garlic. Add the tomatoes and half of the basil and season to taste with salt and pepper. Increase the heat to high and bring the sauce to a boil. Reduce to medium-low, and simmer for 15 minutes, stirring occasionally with a wooden spoon.

While the sauce is simmering, bring a large pot of salted water to a boil over high heat. Add the rigatoni and cook until al dente.

Drain the pasta, and return it to the pot with 1 cup of the sauce. Using a wooden spoon, mix thoroughly for 1 minute over high heat.

Transfer the pasta to a large serving bowl. Top with the remaining sauce, garnish with the remaining basil, and serve.

VARIATION

Incorporate even more flavor into this simple dish by adding diced onion to the olive oil and garlic as they warm in the sauté pan. Or spice things up a bit by adding a tablespoon of hot crushed red pepper flakes.

Pasta and Broccoli

This is one of my Aunt Anna's favorite recipes. It's a hearty, simple dish, and one that is truly Italian. With its subtle yet bold flavor, the recipe satisfies both vegetarians and carnivores. An overwhelming number of our friends and guests in New York, Los Angeles, and Las Vegas have made this dish a popular "sleeper" staple on the menu. I hope it becomes the same in your kitchen. Serves 4

1 pound broccoli, trimmed and cut into bite-size
    pieces
1 pound fusilli
1 cup olive oil
3 garlic cloves, smashed
½ cup chicken broth or blanching water
    (optional)
Kosher salt and freshly ground black pepper
¼ cup grated Pecorino Romano cheese

Fill a 2-quart pot three-quarters full with lightly salted cold water and bring to a boil over high heat. Add the florets and cook just until fork-tender, 6 to 8 minutes. Drain the florets and reserve ½ cup of the cooking water (unless you're using chicken broth). Set aside.

Bring a large pot of salted water to a boil over high heat. Add the fusilli and cook until al dente.

While the pasta cooks, combine ¼ cup of the olive oil and the garlic in a large sauté pan over medium heat. When the garlic starts to shimmer, add the broccoli and the reserved water or the chicken broth. Season lightly with salt and pepper, bring to a simmer, and cook for about 8 minutes.

Drain the pasta and return it to the pot over high heat and stir in the broccoli mixture. Add the cheese and toss until thoroughly mixed in. Taste and adjust the salt and pepper as needed.

Transfer to a large serving bowl and serve.

Sunday Gravy

I've experienced the Sunday Gravy ritual thousands of times, from the age of three. Growing up, every Sunday at around three o'clock in the afternoon, my Grandma Ida would open the front door, step out on the stoop, and scan up and down the block for me. If she couldn't see me, she'd cup her hands around her mouth and holler my name. No matter what I was doing, I'd race home.

Today I'm the one who announces Sunday Gravy.

Of all Rao's recipes, this is the one most meant for family. It's about relatives and friends gathering around a large table, and the recipe will serve six or more hungry people. The feast begins with a visit to a quality butcher, because the heart and soul of this recipe is the meat that fuses, over hours of cooking, with the sweet essence of tomatoes. Makes 2½ quarts sauce

1 pound lean beef, such as eye round
1 pound pork tenderloin
1 pound hot or sweet Italian sausage
1 pound beef braciole
½ cup olive oil
4 garlic cloves, smashed
1 cup water
3 tablespoons tomato paste
Three 35-ounce cans San Marzano tomatoes, hand crushed with juice
Kosher salt and freshly ground black pepper
14 meatballs (see Frankie's Meatballs page 203)
2 pounds rigatoni (or your favorite pasta)

2 tablespoons chopped fresh Italian parsley
5 to 6 fresh basil leaves, shredded

Pat all the meat dry with paper towels.

Heat the olive oil in a large stockpot over medium heat and add the garlic.

Using tongs, add the meats, one type at a time, to the pot. Sear, turning the meat frequently, until nicely browned on all sides. Remove each batch and set aside before browning the next batch. As the garlic cloves turn golden brown, remove them from the pan and discard.

In a mixing bowl, combine the water with the tomato paste and whisk until thoroughly mixed. Add to the pot, stirring with a wooden spoon for 3 minutes.

Add the tomatoes, increase the heat to high, and bring to a boil. Fill an empty tomato can with water and add to the sauce. Bring the sauce back to a boil.

Return the meat to the pot and season lightly with salt and pepper. Boil for 5 minutes.

Reduce to a simmer, partially cover, and cook for 2 hours, stirring frequently, until the meat is almost fall-apart tender and the sauce has reduced by about a half. (If the sauce becomes too thick, add water to the desired consistency.)

About 30 minutes before the end of the

cooking time, add the meatballs to the sauce. Bring a large pot of salted water to boil over high heat. Add the rigatoni and cook until al dente.

Transfer the meat to a large serving platter. Ladle the sauce over the meat and sprinkle with 1 tablespoon of the parsley and a few basil leaves. Cover lightly with aluminum foil and set aside.

Drain the pasta and return it to the pot over high heat. Add 2 cups of the sauce and stir with a wooden spoon to coat.

Transfer the pasta to a large serving bowl and top with the remaining sauce. Garnish with the basil and remaining 1 tablespoon parsley, and serve the meat and pasta while still hot.

VARIATION

For a little more pizzazz, brown and braise neck bones and short ribs along with the other meats.

Fiocchetti with Dried Cranberries and Sage

The Las Vegas team introduced me to this dish, and it has become one of our most requested pastas at Caesars Palace and in Los Angeles. Although it's a bit time-consuming, the recipe is not unusually difficult, and it's simply perfect for sharing with a close friend or two. Think of the cranberries as ruby red drops of amore. The sage and butter are like a warm and rich embracing blanket, while the bread crumbs provide that little bit of crunch that ties the delightful flavors together. Serves 4 to 6

2 tablespoons bread crumbs
1 pound fiocchetti (or substitute gnocchi or
    cheese ravioli)
4 tablespoons (½ stick) salted butter
1 pear, cored, halved, and thinly sliced
10 fresh sage leaves
¼ cup dried cranberries
Kosher salt and white pepper

Place a 3-quart pot filled nearly to the top with salted water over high heat.

In a medium sauté pan over low heat, toast the bread crumbs for about 3 minutes, or until golden brown. Transfer to a small bowl and set aside. Return the pan to the heat.

Add the fiocchetti to the boiling water in the pot, and cook according to the package directions. Drain the pasta.

Add the butter to the sauté pan. When it

begins to clarify and lightly brown, add the pears and 8 of the sage leaves. When the sage begins to crisp and the butter browns, add the cranberries. Cook over low heat for 4 to 6 minutes.

Add the toasted bread crumbs, reserving 1 teaspoon for garnish. Add the pasta, and the reserved pasta water, and increase the heat to medium-high. Mix thoroughly with a wooden

spoon. Season to taste with salt and pepper.

Transfer to a medium serving bowl. Garnish with the reserved bread crumbs and the remaining 2 sage leaves, and serve immediately.

Lasagna

Like Sunday Gravy, lasagna is a staple of the Italian kitchen and one of the key recipes I grew up with. It's perfect for large gatherings, especially holidays or special family events. Guests find a well-made lasagna irresistible. Making this crowd-pleaser isn't hard, but it is time-consuming. You'll need about four hours from start to finish. Personally, I find it easier to make this recipe over the course of two days: One for preparation and assembly, and the second for baking. Once the components are assembled in the baking dish and covered with aluminum foil, you can store the lasagna in your refrigerator for up to two days. Serves 12

Three 28-ounce cans San Marzano tomatoes
½ cup plus 2 tablespoons olive oil
1 cup chopped yellow onion
1 tablespoon minced garlic
2 pounds lean ground beef
1 pound hot or sweet Italian sausage, casings
    removed, meat crumbled
3 tablespoons tomato paste
½ cup red wine
3 cups of water
Kosher salt and freshly ground black pepper
1 pound lasagna noodles
2 pounds drained ricotta cheese
2 cups grated Pecorino Romano cheese
2 large egg yolks
¼ cup chopped fresh Italian parsley
2 cups shredded mozzarella cheese
1 cup chopped fresh basil
1 pound sliced mozzarella cheese

In a large mixing bowl, crush the tomatoes into a soupy pulp with your hands. Remove any hard stem ends or stringy membranes. Set aside.

Heat ½ cup of the olive oil in a large saucepan over medium-low heat for 1 minute. Add the onions and garlic and sauté for 3 minutes. Stir in the beef and sausage and cook for 5 minutes more. Once the meats are browned, transfer them to a bowl using a slotted spoon.

Increase the heat to medium-high and add the tomato paste to the pan. Vigorously stir with a wooden spoon for 30 seconds. Add the wine and cook for 5 minutes.

Add the tomatoes and water and stir until evenly blended. Season to taste with salt and pepper.

Reduce the sauce to a simmer and cook for 2 hours, stirring occasionally. After 1 hour, check the consistency. If the sauce is too thick, add water. When cooked, remove from the heat and let cool. Reserve 3 cups of the cooled sauce.

Bring a large pot of salted water to a boil over high heat and add the remaining 2 tablespoons olive oil. Add the lasagna noodles and cook until al dente, about 10 minutes.

While the lasagna cooks, line a countertop with dampened dish towels or parchment paper. When the lasagna is cooked, remove the pot from the heat and place next to the towels. Using tongs, pick up the individual lasagna noodles and lay them out on top of the towels. Do not overlap the noodles.

In a large mixing bowl, combine the ricotta, 1¾ cups of the grated cheese, egg yolks, parsley and the tomato sauce. Season lightly with salt and pepper and mix well. Set aside.

Preheat the oven to 350°F.

Lightly coat the bottom of a 14 x 10 x 3-inch baking dish with ½ cup of the reserved sauce. Arrange the lasagna noodles, running across the width of the dish. Dab the noodles with tablespoonfuls of the ricotta sauce, spacing them 2 to 3 inches apart. Smear the sauce evenly across the lasagna noodles.

Spread ½ cup of the shredded mozzarella on top of the ricotta sauce. Sprinkle with ¼ cup of the grated Pecorino Romano and ¼ cup of the chopped fresh basil. Repeat the layers until you've used all the ingredients. For the final layer, spread the ricotta sauce on top of the lasagna noodles, and layer the sliced mozzarella on top.

Cover the finished lasagna with a large sheet of greased (olive oil spray works well) aluminum foil and bake for 1 hour.

After 45 minutes, remove the foil and bake uncovered for the last 15 minutes.

Remove from the oven and let the lasagna stand for 15 minutes. While it sets, heat the reserved sauce in a medium pot.

Using a spatula, cut the lasagna into 4-inch squares. Plate and drizzle each serving with the heated sauce, garnish with shredded basil, and serve.

Giambotta

Giambotta is a vegetable stew, kind of the Italian version of ratatouille. It combines eggplant, zucchini, yellow squash, mushrooms, onions, and garlic in a pleasingly light tomato sauce. The complex flavors seduce the palate. The beauty of this recipe is that you can eliminate or increase the amount of any of the vegetables to suit your own tastes. It's also quick and easy to make.

My first experience with giambotta was as a young boy while watching my father prepare the dish. As he was making it, he told me that around the turn of the nineteenth century, when times were tough, his grandmother would make giambotta often. She turned to the dish because it had "legs," and could be reheated throughout the week, no worse for the wear. Today, its price-to-value ratio remains deliciously strong, especially when paired with pasta. Serves 4 to 6

¼ cup olive oil
3 garlic cloves, lightly smashed
1 eggplant, ends trimmed cubed into ¼ x ¼-inch slices
3 medium zucchini, cut into ¼-inch slices
3 medium yellow squash, cut into ¼-inch slices
¼ pound large white mushrooms, stems removed
1 large white onion, cut into ¼-inch rings
Kosher salt and freshly ground black pepper
½ cup dry white wine
6 cups San Marzano tomatoes, hand crushed with juice

Pinch of fresh oregano leaves
6 fresh basil leaves
1 pound spaghetti (or substitute linguine or your
    favorite pasta)
¼ cup grated Pecorino Romano cheese

Heat the olive oil in a large sauté pan over medium heat. Add the garlic and sauté until golden brown. Remove and discard.

Add the eggplant, zucchini, yellow squash, mushrooms, and onion and season liberally with salt and pepper. Cook for 8 minutes, tossing occasionally.

When the vegetables have softened and started to brown, add the wine and increase the heat to medium-high. When the mixture begins to boil, reduce the heat to medium.

Add the tomatoes, stir to combine, and bring the mixture to a boil. Reduce the heat, season lightly with salt and pepper, and simmer for 15 minutes, stirring occasionally.

Stir in the oregano and basil.

While the sauce simmers, bring a large pot of salted water to a boil over high heat, and add the spaghetti. Cook until al dente, and drain.

Return the pasta to the pot over medium-high heat. Add ½ cup of sauce to the pasta and toss with a wooden spoon until thoroughly mixed.

Transfer to a large serving platter or bowl. Spoon the remaining sauce over the pasta, sprinkle with the grated cheese, and serve.

Spaghetti alla Carbonara

If you love bacon and eggs, you'll love this one-of-a-kind pasta. The dish is filling and flavorful, and really fun to prepare, particularly if you are pressed for time and would like to delight your guests. Although the simple ingredients equate to an easy preparation, the recipe requires close attention for the perfect results.

The preparation should take no more than 35 minutes. Chef Fats and I strongly suggest that you set up all the ingredients beforehand, because timing is key.

Chef Fats especially suggests taking your time during the key step of cooking the bacon (or pancetta): "Rendering the fat from bacon or pancetta is a delicate process and is the soul of the dish. You burn it, you lose it." So take it slow, and think flavor! Serves 4 to 6

    4 large eggs
    ¼ cup heavy cream
    ¼ pound bacon or pancetta, cut into small dice
    ¼ cup diced shallots
    2 tablespoons salted butter
    Freshly ground black pepper
    1 pound spaghetti
    ¼ cup grated Pecorino Romano cheese

Bring a large stockpot of salted water to a boil over high heat.

In a medium mixing bowl, combine the eggs and cream. Whisk until extremely well blended (the more incorporated the ingredients are, the smoother the sauce).

Warm a large sauté pan over a medium-low heat. Spread out the bacon or pancetta evenly across the pan.

Gently turn the bacon with a wooden spoon until the cubes are lightly seared all over and golden around the edges, about 10 minutes. Remove the pan and drain the fat.

Remove ¼ cup of the bacon and reserve for garnish. Note that the pan will remain hot and continue to cook the bacon, rendering a little bit more fat.

Return the pan to the stovetop over low heat. Add the shallots, and sauté for about 3 minutes. Add the butter and black pepper to taste. When the butter begins to froth, turn off the heat.

When the pasta water is boiling, add the spaghetti. Subtract 2 minutes from the cooking time recommended on the box.

Drain the pasta, transfer it to the sauté pan with the butter, and place over medium-low heat.

Using tongs, toss the pasta until completely and evenly coated, about 1 minute. Very quickly pour the egg mixture into the pan. Rapidly turn the pasta with the tongs until the eggs begin to slightly thicken. As the sauce thickens, continue to toss the pasta for 1 minute, or until the sauce firms.

Transfer the pasta and sauce to a large serving bowl. Add the grated cheese and toss. Garnish with the reserved bacon or pancetta, and serve immediately.

Pasta with Peas and Ham in a Cream Sauce

Growing up, red sauce was the routine. So my first encounter with a white cream sauce was an epiphany. The novel flavors were, for me, a radical departure from the tyranny of tomatoes. It was a new spin on pasta. It was so completely alien from my Southern Italian instincts that when presented with this Northern Italian delicacy, I was dubious. In fact, I was convinced it was a clever ploy by my family to ensure that pasta was a seven days-a-week proposition. I didn't protest, though. My elders instilled in me a great appreciation for Italian food and culture, and for that I am eternally grateful. However, I'm even more grateful that Grandma granted clemency to those tomatoes every now and again. Serves 4 to 6

1 quart heavy cream
3 tablespoons salted butter
2 tablespoons diced shallots
1 cup fresh or frozen peas
3¼ cups diced cooked ham (¼-inch cubes)
½ teaspoon ground nutmeg
½ cup grated Pecorino Romano cheese, plus more for sprinkling
1 pound spaghetti (or substitute linguine or your favorite pasta)
Freshly ground black pepper

In a medium saucepan over high heat, bring the cream to a boil. Reduce the heat to medium, and cook until the cream has reduced by half. Set aside.

Meanwhile, bring a large pot of cold water to boil over high heat.

Melt 1 tablespoon of the butter in a large sauté pan over medium-low heat. As it melts, add the shallots, peas, and ham and sauté until the shallots are transparent. Add the cream and bring to a boil.

Add the nutmeg, the remaining 2 tablespoons of butter, and the grated cheese. Stir with a wooden spoon until thoroughly integrated. Reduce the heat to low.

Add the pasta to the boiling water and cook until al dente. Using tongs, transfer the pasta from the pot to the sauce. Increase the heat to high and toss the pasta until evenly coated.

Transfer to a medium-size pasta bowl. Garnish with a sprinkle of the grated cheese and a dusting of freshly ground black pepper, and serve.

Orecchiette with Broccoli Rabe and Sausage

West of the Mississippi this dish doesn't receive its fair due. Like many, it took me some time to warm up to broccoli rabe. As a kid I hated that bitter, leafy green. My taste buds have long since evolved, and I've made my peace with this potent vegetable. As for my guests, it's an absolute must. As you acquire your own appreciation for this unique flavor, your fondness will likely only increase over time, until broccoli rabe becomes as essential as good bread and olive oil. Serves 4 to 6

1 pound broccoli rabe
¼ cup olive oil
4 garlic cloves, smashed
1 pound mixed hot and sweet Italian sausage, cut into bite-size pieces
Kosher salt and freshly ground black pepper
1 pound orecchiette
¼ cup grated Pecorino Romano cheese

Rinse the broccoli rabe. Cut off the stems at the base of the florets, and discard the stems.

Bring a large pot of salted cold water to a boil over high heat. Add the florets and blanch for 3 minutes. Drain, reserving a cup of the cooking water. Immediately rinse the broccoli rabe in cold water to stop the cooking and fix the bright green color.

Heat the olive oil in a large sauté pan over medium-high heat. Add the garlic and sausage and sauté until the meat is cooked through.

Add the blanched broccoli rabe and the reserved cooking water and season to taste with salt and pepper.

Increase the heat to medium-high and bring to a boil. Boil for 3 minutes, then lower to a simmer.

Bring a large pot of salted water to a boil over high heat, and add the pasta. Cook until al dente.

Drain the pasta, and return it to the pot over high heat, along with ¾ cup of the sauce. Using a wooden spoon, mix the pasta for 1 minute.

When the pasta is evenly coated, transfer it to a large serving bowl. Spoon the remaining sauce over the top, sprinkle with the grated cheese, and serve.

Filetto di Pomodoro

This incredibly flavorful sauce is a long-standing pillar of the pasta repertoire served at all Rao's restaurants. I got to really know it at seventeen, when I received my first promotion from busboy to waiter. The truth of the matter is, my busboy responsibilities remained intact—which they do to this day.

I had the intimidating task of following in my father's footsteps. It took all the courage I could muster to pull a chair over to one of Rao's tables and deliver "the spiel."

Unpolished and apprehensive, I'd commence: "Welcome to Rao's, I'm Frankie Junior. Basically, what we do is an appetizer, pasta, and entrée. We do it all family style, which means we share." Typically, before I could deliver my next line, I'd be cut off. "Who are you? Frankie's son?" And even before I could answer: "Were gonna start with the seafood salad, clams, and roasted peppers. Then we're gonna have Rigatoni Filetto di Pomodoro. Then we'll see what's next."

It never failed that as soon I delivered the filetto sauce, the regulars would take their first bite of rigatoni and exclaim, "Smells and tastes just like my mother's. Tell Annie it's perfect!"

Serves 4 to 6

⅓ cup olive oil
¾ cup chopped white onion
4 ounces pancetta or prosciutto, diced into
   ¼-inch cubes
6 cups canned San Marzano tomatoes, hand
   crushed with juice
Kosher salt and freshly ground black pepper
8 fresh basil leaves, shredded
Pinch of fresh oregano
1 pound rigatoni (or substitute your favorite
   pasta)
2 tablespoons chopped fresh Italian parsley

Heat the olive oil in a large sauté pan over medium heat, for 30 seconds.

Add the onion and pancetta and sauté for 5 minutes, or until the onion begins to brown and the pancetta starts to crisp.

Gently add the tomatoes and bring to a boil. Reduce the heat to a simmer and cook for 30 minutes, stirring occasionally. Taste and season with salt and pepper as needed, keeping in mind that the pancetta will naturally impart a good portion of its saltiness to the sauce.

After 25 minutes, add the basil and oregano.

When the sauce is done, bring a large pot of salted water to a boil over high heat. Add the rigatoni and cook until al dente.

Drain the pasta and return it to the pot over high heat and add 1 cup of the sauce. Using a wooden spoon, toss the pasta for 1 minute, or until thoroughly coated.

Transfer the pasta to a large serving or pasta bowl, and spoon the remaining sauce over the pasta. Sprinkle with the parsley and serve hot.

Manicotti

Whenever I say the word "manicotti," inside or outside of the restaurant, I see eyes widen and smiles blossom. Young or old, Italian or not, people absolutely love it. For me, the allure of this lush, cheesy, baked wonder is impossible to resist. Almost as good as eating it is starting by making crêpes. Serves 6 to 8

2 large eggs
2 cups whole milk
1 ½ cups all-purpose flour
2 tablespoons vegetable oil
2 cups ricotta cheese
2 large egg yolks
1 cup diced fresh mozzarella cheese
½ cup grated Pecorino Romano cheese
Kosher salt and freshly ground white pepper
3½ cups Homemade Marinara Sauce
    (page 113)
¼ lb. mozzarella, thinly sliced (optional)
⅓ cup chopped fresh Italian parsley

In a medium mixing bowl, combine the eggs and milk and whisk until completely combined. Add the flour and vigorously whisk until the batter is smooth. Set aside to rest for a minimum of 30 minutes.

Spray or lightly brush a 6- to 8-inch nonstick pan with vegetable oil. Warm the pan over medium-low heat for about 1 minute. Set out a sheet of parchment paper.

Using a 6-ounce (or ¾ cup) ladle, scoop the batter into the pan. Swirl the pan to evenly coat the bottom with the batter. Within 30 to 45 seconds, the crêpe will firm. At this point, carefully loosen the edges of the crêpe with a spatula that's been sprayed with cooking spray, flip it over, and cook for another 15 seconds on the opposite side. Once the crêpe has set, slide it out of the pan onto the sheet of parchment paper. Let it cool. Repeat with the remaining batter until you have at least 12 crêpes. (It's wise to make extra in case of breakage . . . or hunger!)

Preheat the oven to 375°F.

In a medium mixing bowl, combine the ricotta, egg yolks, mozzarella, and Pecorino Romano and season with salt and pepper. Mix until completely blended.

Place the bowl next to the parchment paper with the cooled crêpes. Center a heaping tablespoon of the cheese mixture on top of each crêpe. Using the bottom of the spoon, spread the mixture out evenly, covering the entire crêpe. Fold each crêpe in half, forming a half-circle. Fold the corners into the center, and very gently roll the crêpe into a firm cylinder.

When you've filled and rolled all the crêpes, spread the marinara sauce evenly over the bottom of a 13 x 9 x 2-inch baking pan. Place the manicotti on top of the sauce, so that they aren't touching. For an embellished presentation, add an additional slice of mozzarella on top of each.

Bake the manicotti for 12 to 15 minutes, or until the filling begins to ooze and the mozzarella is golden and blistering.

To serve, place two manicotti on each serving plate and top with a dollop of the sauce from the baking dish. Sprinkle with the parsley and enjoy!

Southern Pesto

The color of pesto competes with its decadent, savory flavor for attention. I imagine that the brilliant green and appealing texture of this Genovese dish must have inspired many a master painter from the fourteenth century on. After my first taste as a young boy, I was moved to finger paint on my grandmother's fine white heirloom tablecloth, a prize from the old country. Thank heaven for the divine universal graces that spared my delicate fingers from the cleaver! Serves 4 to 6

5 garlic cloves, minced
¼ cup pitted Gaeta olives
3 anchovy fillets
1 cup extra-virgin olive oil
2 cups fresh basil leaves
¼ cup pine nuts
1 pound linguine (or substitute your favorite pasta)
¼ cup grated Parmigiano Reggiano cheese

Using a large mortar and pestle, mash 2 tablespoons of the garlic, 1 tablespoon of the olives, and 1 anchovy fillet as you pour in ¼ cup of the olive oil.

Add 1 cup of the fresh basil and ¼ cup of the pine nuts. Continue to mash until the leaves start to separate and are evenly combined with the other ingredients.

Once pulverized, add the rest of the basil, another ¼ cup of the olive oil, 1 teaspoon of the garlic, and 1 tablespoon of the olives.

Repeat until all the garlic, basil, olives, and olive oil are used up, and the mixture is fluid. Set aside.

Bring a large pot of salted water to boil over high heat. Add the linguine and cook until al dente.

Drain and return the pasta to the pot over medium-high heat. Add the pesto and grated cheese. Toss with a wooden spoon until the pasta is evenly coated, about 3 minutes.

Transfer to a large serving bowl and serve hot.

Note: A mortar and pestle is the best way to make pesto. But if you can't lay your hands on a set, you can use a food processor or blender instead.

Eggplant Parmigiana

I tried my first rendition of this dish with the intention of impressing my mother and grandmother. One particular Saturday they were out running errands and visiting our old East Harlem neighbors, who had resettled to the South Shore of Long Island. Despite their warnings to never use the stove without supervision, I decided to risk a severe double-barreled scolding. I was sure that I would be pardoned given my exquisite execution and the delicious results. After all, I had watched them both prepare this dish more times than I could count. I'd even helped them with the preparation of the dish. The recipe was how my grandmother first showed me the proper way to crack eggs into a bowl. For a little kid, cracking eggs was as fun as hurling snowballs. Kids being less than precise, she also had to show me how to scoop out bits of shell, using half the egg shell as a cup. That handy and valuable tip has served me well throughout my kitchen career. Second to cracking eggs, whisking the eggs and seasoning them was as exciting as playing with a chemistry set. So as I made my own version of this dish that Saturday, I transformed those eggs into a frothy whirlpool.

The dish turned out great. But despite my thoroughly professional presentation, boy did I get a scolding! Not to worry—from there on out I was given free rein in the kitchen. Serves 4 to 6

3 medium eggplants
6 large eggs
¾ cup grated Parmigiano Reggiano cheese
3 tablespoons finely chopped fresh Italian parsley
½ teaspoon kosher salt
½ teaspoon freshly ground black pepper
1½ cups all-purpose flour
2 cups plain bread crumbs
½ cup vegetable oil
2 cups Homemade Marinara Sauce (page 113)
¾ pound shredded mozzarella cheese
1 cup fresh basil, shredded

Trim the ends off the eggplants, removing at least 1½ inches from each end to ensure the eggplant rounds are uniform. Cut the eggplant into ¼-inch-thick disks.

In a wide, shallow bowl, combine the eggs, ¼ cup of the grated cheese, 2 tablespoons of the parsley, and the salt and pepper. Whisk until completely blended.

Put the flour in a shallow baking pan or pie dish. Put the bread crumbs in a separate baking pan or pie dish. Set up a breading station with the flour, egg wash, bread crumbs, and a baking sheet in that order. Line a plate with paper towels.

I'd suggest you wear latex disposable kitchen gloves to make the breading process easier and less messy.

Lightly dredge an eggplant disk in the flour. Pat off any excess flour.

Dredge the disk in the egg wash and let any excess drip off.

Press the disk down into the bread crumbs, coating it all over. Set the breaded eggplant on the baking sheet. Repeat with the rest of the eggplant, but don't stack the breaded disks.

Heat the vegetable oil in a large sauté pan over medium heat, for 1 minute. Test the oil by dropping a pinch of bread crumbs into the pan; if the crumbs fry quickly, the oil is ready.

Fry the eggplant in batches, leaving a minimum of ¼ inch between disks in the sauté pan. As the outer edge of the eggplant disks turn light golden brown, use tongs to flip the disks.

When the eggplant is golden brown all over, transfer to the paper towel–lined plate. Repeat until all of the eggplant has been fried.

Preheat the oven to 325°F.

In a deep 11 x 6-inch baking dish, spread 1 cup of the marinara sauce evenly across the bottom.

Arrange a layer of the eggplant in the dish with the disks touching.

Cover the eggplant with a thin layer of sauce, and top with an even layer of ¼ cup of the shredded mozzarella, 2 tablespoons of grated cheese, and a scattering of the basil.

Repeat until the layers are stacked three-quarters of the way up the sides of the baking dish.

Top the final layer with sauce, and spread a generous layer of mozzarella and grated cheese on top. Cover the baking dish with aluminum foil.

Bake the eggplant for 1 hour, then remove the foil and increase the oven temperature to 425°F. Bake for 15 minutes more, or until the mozzarella blisters and begins to brown. Remove the baking dish from the oven, and let stand for 15 minutes.

When ready to serve, cut the eggplant into 4-inch squares with a spatula. Top each individual serving with a drizzle of the sauce, garnish with the remaining basil, and serve.

Lobster Fra Diavolo

This pinnacle dish has dazzled our guests for decades. A holiday standard, particularly for Christmas Eve, it has become one of our most requested pastas from coast to coast—and is now a permanent item on our Hollywood menu. Chef Dino and I love this dish so much that we filmed a video tutorial for our respective culinary teammates to ensure its continuity from restaurant to restaurant.

As it turned out, the video became the rave of the group, evoking lots of laughter and inspiration.

That being said, two variations of this recipe are intertwined in this recipe. One is for the squeamish; the other is for those who have no issue with dismantling live lobsters. The first part of the recipe covers cleaning and butchering two medium lobsters, to create a stock that will be the foundation of the lobster sauce.

If you are going to take the live-lobster approach, you'll need latex kitchen gloves to protect your hands, a sharp chef's knife, and an iron will. Serves 4 to 6

2 medium (1½ to 2 lbs.) live lobsters
1 bunch fresh Italian parsley
1 yellow onion
9 garlic cloves, smashed
½ cup olive oil
¼ cup crushed red pepper flakes, plus more for
    sprinkling
One 28-ounce can San Marzano tomatoes,
    hand crushed with juice
12 tablespoons (1½ sticks) salted butter
½ cup canned lobster or store-bought cooked
    lobster meat
½ cup dry white wine
1 teaspoon chopped fresh oregano
Kosher salt and freshly ground black pepper
1 pound linguine
¼ cup chopped fresh Italian parsley

Roughly chop the bunch of parsley, onion, and
5 cloves of the garlic. Transfer to a bowl and
set aside.

Heat ¼ cup of the olive oil in a large
stockpot over medium heat. Add the parsley,
onion, and garlic and cook, stirring, for about
1 minute. Add the lobster bodies and innards
and continue to stir. Add a dash of the red
pepper flakes, or to taste, and stir for 1 minute
more, or until the ingredients are evenly mixed
together.

Add 1½ cups of the tomatoes and 1 quart
of cold water. Simmer for 30 minutes.

Strain the stock through a large sieve
placed over a smaller stockpot. Heat the
strained stock over medium-low heat. Add the
butter and simmer until the stock has reduced
by half, about 40 minutes. This will amplify
the lobster flavor.

Strain the stock a second time to remove
any remaining hard particles, and set aside.

Heat the remainder of the olive oil in a large sauté pan over medium-low heat for 2 minutes.

Add the split lobster tails and claws, and sauté on each side until the shells turn red.

Add the remaining 4 garlic cloves and the canned lobster meat and sauté for 2 minutes. Add the wine, oregano, and remaining red pepper flakes. Season lightly with salt and black pepper and cook for 2 minutes.

Add the remaining tomatoes and simmer for 3 minutes.

Add 2½ cups of the stock to the sauce, and simmer for 15 minutes, or until the sauce has reduced by half.

While the sauce simmers, bring a large pot of salted water to a boil over high heat. Add the linguine and cook until al dente.

Drain the pasta, and return it to the pot over medium heat. Add 1½ cups of the sauce and mix with a wooden spoon until the pasta is evenly coated. Transfer the pasta to a large serving bowl.

Top with the remaining sauce. Arrange the claws and tails on top of the pasta. Garnish with a sprinkle of crushed red pepper flakes and the chopped parsley. Serve hot.

IF YOU'RE USING LIVE LOBSTERS

Chill the lobsters in the freezer for 30 minutes. The cold temperatures will lull them into submission. After they've fallen "asleep," place them on a large cutting board with the claw rubber bands in place. Quickly drive the tip of your chef's knife into the point where the head meets the tail. Bring the knife down, splitting the head in half. This kills the lobster as quickly and humanely as possible.

Remove each claw where it meets the body. Hold the lobster body in one hand and the tail in the other, and rapidly twist the two in opposite directions. Slide your thumb or index finger underneath the shell of the body, right beneath the back of the main body where the tail was removed. Use a little steady force to remove the innards. Set aside in a separate bowl for the stock. Repeat with the second lobster.

Once the lobsters have been separated, wrap the claws in a dish towel and smack with a meat mallet to crack the shells. Set aside. Set the tails on the same towel and use the chef's knife to split the tails in half lengthwise. Set aside with the claws.

IF YOU'RE BUYING PREPARED LOBSTERS

If you're uncomfortable butchering the lobster, have a local fishmonger do this part. You can also buy the lobster parts frozen, but defrost them in the refrigerator the day before making the recipe. Now you can begin making the stock.

Shells with Ricotta

Many of our regular guests in New York—such as Wendy and Stephen Siegel and Sonny Grasso, among other beloved patrons—have made this an everyday pasta choice in the restaurant.

As Rao's has expanded to the West Coast, the dish had to be reinterpreted for our new clientele. In place of medium shells, we use larger shells or fusilli (much to the consternation of our NYC regulars). I forget about these subtle changes when I'm in Las Vegas or Hollywood, until I'm scolded by

visiting patrons from New York.

The fact is, I love this preparation and am determined to keep it in the pasta lineup from coast to coast.

To my dear extended family in New York, I apologize for the embellishments and ask for forgiveness. I assure you, regardless of the size of the pasta, this recipe will knock your socks off. Serves 4

1 pound medium shells
2 cups ricotta cheese
6 cups Homemade Marinara Sauce (page 113),
    or 2 jars store-bought Rao's sauce
¼ cup grated Parmigiano Reggiano cheese
Kosher salt and freshly ground black pepper
2 tablespoons chopped fresh Italian parsley

Bring a large pot of salted water to a boil over high heat. Add the shells and cook until al dente.

While the pasta cooks, combine the ricotta cheese, 4 cups of the marinara sauce, and the grated cheese in a large saucepan over medium heat. Stir continuously until well mixed and hot. Taste and season with salt and pepper as needed. Cover and remove from the burner.

In a deep pot over low heat, warm the remaining marinara sauce.

Drain the pasta and add it to the warming marinara sauce. Increase the heat to medium-high. Toss the pasta with a wooden spoon for 2 minutes, or until evenly coated.

Remove pasta from the heat and stir in ½ cup of the ricotta sauce. Toss for 1 minute more.

Transfer the pasta to a large serving platter or bowl. Top with the remaining marinara sauce. Garnish with a dollop of ricotta cheese and a sprinkle of parsley, and serve hot.

Polenta with Sausage and Mushrooms

Chef Dino prepares this robust and hardy dish as a special in our New York City joint at least once a month, to rave reviews. The last time I was in the New York restaurant, Senior had a hankering for this. Early in the evening, he mentioned that I needed to put the recipe in this book. I said, "So tell me," but Senior just walked out. A couple of hours later, toward the end of service, Senior pulled me into the kitchen. "Dino! Show Frankie how you prepare the sausage, mushrooms, and polenta."

"Right now?"

"No, next week. Yes, now!" Senior retorted.

Man, oh man, was I in store for a real treat, just as you will be when you prepare this rock star recipe. It will have your taste buds singing, not to mention your friends and family. Serves 6

¼ cup olive oil
2 links hot Italian sausage, casings removed,
    meat crumbled
2 links sweet Italian sausage, casings removed,
    meat crumbled
1 garlic clove, sliced
1 cup sliced white button mushrooms
One 28-ounce can San Marzano tomatoes,
    hand crushed with juice
Kosher salt and freshly ground black pepper
Crushed red pepper flakes (optional)
4 cups whole milk
4 tablespoons (½ stick) salted butter
1 ¾ cups cornmeal

Heat the olive oil in a large sauté pan over medium-high heat. Add the sausage and break it up with a wooden spoon to keep the meat from clumping. Add the garlic and mushrooms and cook until the mushrooms are soft and sausage has browned.

Stir in the tomatoes and mix well with the mushrooms and sausage. Reduce to an active simmer. Taste and season with salt and pepper as needed. Cook for 15 minutes. If you like it spicy, you can add crushed red pepper to taste.

While the sausage mixture reduces, combine the milk, butter, and a dash of salt in a medium saucepan over high heat. Bring to a boil, then reduce the heat to medium. Slowly add the cornmeal while whisking continuously. Continue whisking the polenta until it begins to firm up and forms a velvety rich consistency, about 10 minutes. Remove from the heat.

Using a large serving spoon, scoop the polenta into individual serving bowls. Top with a ladle of the sausage and mushroom sauce, and serve hot.

Risotto

Asparagus Risotto and Risotto Milanese are consistently popular favorites among the guests at all three Rao's restaurants. These simple preparations will expand your Italian cooking repertoire. They also come in handy around midweek, when you're out of ideas and no one wants a Sloppy Joe. These instructions are provided courtesy of Chef Dino from New York City (Asparagus Risotto), and Chef Fats from Las Vegas (Risotto Milanese and Risotto Frutti di Mare).

Asparagus Risotto

Chef Dino stepped into the kitchen of Rao's in New York City more than twenty years ago. Since then, he's not only maintained our cuisine, he has made it better. He became the captain of our culinary team and works closely with both Chef Fatimah in Las Vegas and Chef J in Hollywood. Chef Dino is one of the reasons why the New York restaurant is closed on the weekends. Every Sunday, you can find him on the New York Giants' sideline, lending support to Big Blue regardless of where they're playing. His annual tailgate party is an event, and his friendships range deep and wide. You never know who will be stopping by for a bite.

Serves 4

1 pound asparagus, tough ends removed and discarded
2 tablespoons olive oil
½ cup diced onion
1 ½ cups Arborio rice, rinsed
½ cup dry white wine
5 cups chicken broth, hot
4 tablespoons (½ stick) salted butter
¾ cup grated Parmigiano Reggiano cheese
¼ cup shaved Parmigiano Reggiano cheese
1 ounce truffle oil

Bring a large pot of salted water to a boil over high heat. Add the asparagus and cook for 3 minutes. Drain and rinse with cold water until cool. Cut into ½-inch pieces, reserving the tips, and set aside.

Heat the olive oil in a large sauté pan over medium-low heat. Add the onion and sauté until transparent, 4 to 5 minutes. Add the rice and mix with a wooden spoon until the rice is evenly coated, about 2 minutes.

Add the wine and cook, stirring occasionally, until the rice has absorbed most of the wine and is firm and creamy.

Add the hot chicken broth, 1 cup at a time, stirring constantly. Simmer the risotto, stirring frequently, for 20 minutes.

When the risotto has a velvety, creamy consistency and the rice is still al dente, add the butter and asparagus. As the butter melts, stir in the grated cheese and mix well. Stir in the reserved asparagus tips.

Transfer the risotto to a medium serving bowl. Top with the shaved cheese and a drizzle of the truffle oil, and serve immediately.

Risotto Milanese

This Northern Italian dish is simply exquisite on its own or served as a side dish. Its deep, rich saffron flavor and wavy texture will buckle your knees.

At our Las Vegas outpost, Chef Fatimah serves this alongside our Osso Buco (page 189) to the absolute delight of our guests. Serves 4

5 cups chicken broth
½ teaspoon saffron, plus more for dusting
5 tablespoons (½ stick plus 1 tablespoon) salted butter
1 cup diced shallots
1½ cups Arborio rice, rinsed
½ cup dry white wine
¾ cup grated Parmigiano Reggiano cheese

In a large pot over low heat, warm the chicken broth. Add the saffron, stirring occasionally as the broth heats.

Heat a large sauté pan over low heat. Once the pan has warmed, add 3 tablespoons of the butter. Once the butter has melted, add the shallots and sweat until translucent.

Add the rice and stir constantly (this makes what is known as the *soffritto*). Once the rice is evenly coated (now the *tostatura*), add the wine and increase the heat to medium-low. Cook, stirring continuously, until the rice has absorbed most of the wine and is firm and creamy.

Add the broth, 1 cup at a time, stirring constantly for 20 minutes.

Reduce to a simmer, add the remaining 2 tablespoons butter and the grated cheese. Stir until thoroughly mixed and the risotto has a velvety creamy consistency.

Remove from the heat and transfer individual portions to serving plates. Do not spread the risotto; it will find its resting place. Dust with a pinch of saffron and serve immediately.

Risotto Frutti di Mare

At the age of five, I had dreams of becoming the next Jacques Cousteau. I would spend hours in my grandmother's pool with fins, goggles, and a snorkel, until I was wrinkled as a prune. As I swam, I imagined one of my favorite superheroes, Aquaman, swimming alongside me. I was positive we would discover a wealth of friendly sea creatures—shrimp, clams, lobsters, scallops, and maybe even a visit from Neptune himself.

Unfortunately, my fantasies came to an abrupt end with Steven Spielberg's 1975 blockbuster Jaws. *More than four decades later, I'm still filled with fear at the mere thought of a late-night dip in the ocean. I hung up my fins and snorkel, leaving the deep sea to Cousteau. My dreams were undone by the terrifying tale Peter Benchley invented.*

That didn't change my love of seafood in the kitchen. Just like in the ocean, though, you have to take care with seafood you cook. First, buy the freshest you can find from the most reputable source. Second, carefully and thoroughly clean any seafood in your kitchen. Third, keep your knives sharp and be careful how you use them. Most seafood is slippery. Last, keep in mind that most fishmongers are more than happy to do any cleaning and prep necessary for your recipes. Don't be afraid to ask. Serves 6

3 cups dry white wine
12 littleneck clams, cleaned
8 colossal (U-12) shrimp, shelled, deveined and tails removed
½ pound medium sea scallops
¼ pound squid, cleaned and cut into ¼-inch rings
4 ½ tablespoons (½ stick plus ½ tablespoon) salted butter
2 cups Arborio rice, rinsed
¼ cup diced shallots
3 tablespoons chopped fresh Italian parsley

In a 6-quart saucepan over medium-low heat, combine half the white wine and the clams.

Once the clams begin to open, add the shrimp, scallops, and squid. Simmer for 10 minutes to create the base for the fish stock.

When the clams have all fully opened (discard any that do not), using a spider, remove them and the partially cooked seafood from the pot and set aside. Let the stock continue to simmer.

Once the seafood has cooled, remove 6 of the clams from their shells and reserve.

When the stock has reduced by about half, add 3 cups of hot tap water. Stir the stock occasionally as it cooks. The goal is to blend and warm the stock while you continue preparing the risotto.

Melt 3 tablespoons of the butter in a large sauté pan over medium heat. Add the rice and the shallots and cook for 2 minutes, tossing until the rice is coated.

Once the butter has been absorbed, increase the heat to medium. Add ¾ cup of the stock and cook, stirring continuously with a wooden spoon. As the stock is absorbed, about 3 minutes, continue adding stock, one ladle at a time, and cook, stirring continuously, until the rice is al dente, about 15 minutes.

When the rice has a loose, creamy consistency, add the reserved seafood, except for the clams in the shell, and cook for 5 minutes more, stirring continuously.

If the rice becomes too thick, add a half-ladle of stock and some of the remaining wine and reduce to a simmer.

Add the remaining 1½ tablespoons butter and wine. Vigorously stir until the butter has completely melted, and the rice has a velvety texture.

Transfer individual portions of the risotto to shallow serving bowls or plates. Garnish each serving with a clam, sprinkle with the parsley, and serve.

Risotto Primavera

Serves 4

3 tablespoons unsalted butter
¼ cup olive oil
1 celery stalk, diced
1 carrot, peeled and diced
½ yellow onion, diced
1 zucchini, trimmed and diced
1 cup fresh peas, parboiled (defrosted if frozen)
2 asparagus spears, tough ends removed,
    spears cut into bite-size pieces
1 cup Arborio rice, rinsed
½ cup dry white wine
3½ cups chicken broth, warmed
½ cup grated Parmigiano Reggiano cheese
Kosher salt and freshly ground black pepper

In a large sauté pan over medium heat, combine the butter and olive oil. Add the celery, carrot, onion, zucchini, peas, and asparagus and sauté until the onions are translucent.

Add the rice, and stir gently for 3 minutes, or until the rice is a light golden brown.

Add the wine, and stir with a wooden spoon until the mixture comes to a boil.

Add the chicken broth, one cup at a time, stirring continuously and bringing the mixture back to a boil after each addition. Lower to a simmer and continue to cook, stirring.

Add the grated cheese and stir to incorporate. Cook for 20 minutes, stirring occasionally. Taste and season with salt and pepper as needed.

Stir again just before serving and transfer to individual shallow bowls or plates.

Linguine with Anchovies and Hot Cherry Peppers

If you're not fond of spicy dishes, substitute the hot cherry peppers with sweet cherry peppers. However, if you're a bolder eater and would like to raise the heat to eleven, add a tablespoon or two of crushed red pepper flakes to the oil when sautéing the hot cherry peppers—then have the fire department on speed dial! Serves 4

1 pound linguine
1 cup extra-virgin olive oil
4 to 6 anchovy fillets
4 garlic cloves, thinly sliced
5 jarred hot cherry peppers, halved and seeded
Crushed red pepper flakes (optional)
1 tablespoon chopped fresh Italian parsley

Bring a large pot of salted water to a boil over high heat. Add the linguine and cook, subtracting 2 minutes off the time recommended on the package.

While the pasta cooks, combine the olive oil, anchovies, and garlic in a large sauté pan over medium heat. When the garlic has browned, add the cherry peppers and red pepper flakes, if using, and sauté for 3 minutes. Remove the pan from the heat.

Drain the pasta, reserving ½ cup of the water. Return the sauté pan to high heat, add the pasta, and toss for 2 to 3 minutes, or until evenly coated and cooked al dente.

Transfer the pasta to a large serving bowl. Add the reserved pasta water. This balances the oil and ensures that the pasta will not dry up and clump. Sprinkle with the parsley and serve.

Spaghetti with Zucchini and Yellow Squash

Add another dimension of flavor to this recipe with a dash or two of crushed red pepper flakes, introduced when you sauté the zucchini. Serves 4

1 pound spaghetti
¾ cup extra-virgin olive oil
5 garlic cloves, smashed
1 yellow onion, diced
2 zucchini, cut into ¼-inch slices
2 yellow squash, cut into ¼-inch slices
½ teaspoon crushed red pepper flakes
   (optional)
Kosher salt and freshly ground black pepper
¼ cup grated Parmigiano Reggiano cheese

Bring a large pot of heavily salted water to a boil over high heat. Cook the spaghetti according to package directions.

While the pasta water is heating, combine the olive oil and garlic in a large sauté pan over medium-high heat. When the garlic begins to shimmer, add the onion, zucchini, yellow squash, and red pepper flakes, if using. Season lightly with salt and black pepper. Cook for 8 to 10 minutes, tossing occasionally, until the edges of the zucchini and yellow squash begin to crisp and brown. Remove from the heat.

Drain the pasta, reserving ½ cup of the water.

Transfer the pasta to the sauce. Increase the heat to high, and toss with the sauce until the pasta is thoroughly coated.

Transfer to a large serving bowl. Add the reserved pasta water. Sprinkle with the grated cheese, and a dash of crushed red pepper flakes if you like, and serve.

Christmas Eve
Seafood Pasta

This recipe accommodates substitutions. If you aren't fond of any of the seafood here, substitute shellfish such as clams, lobster, or crabs. If you prefer shell-free, add jumbo lump crab or lobster meat. Serves 8

½ cup extra-virgin olive oil
5 garlic cloves, thinly sliced
1 pound squid (calamari), sliced into rings and soaked in milk for 1 to 4 hours
2 pounds mussels, cleaned
1 pound medium (16-20) shrimp, peeled, deveined, and butterflied
½ cup dry white wine
Two 35-ounce cans San Marzano tomatoes, hand crushed with juice

1 cup clam broth
Kosher salt and freshly ground black pepper
2 pounds spaghetti
½ pound lump crabmeat, patted dry
½ teaspoon chopped fresh oregano
8 fresh basil leaves
1 tablespoon chopped fresh Italian parsley

Heat the olive oil in a large sauté pan over medium-high heat. Add the garlic and cook for 1 minute. Add the squid, mussels, shrimp, and wine and cook until the mussels open (discard any that do not).

Using a slotted spoon, remove the squid, shrimp, and mussels from the pan and transfer to a baking sheet. Cover with a sheet of aluminum foil to keep them warm.

Add the tomatoes and clam broth to the pan and bring to a boil. Reduce to a simmer, taste and season with salt and pepper as needed. Continue to simmer for 30 minutes.

While the sauce cooks, bring a large pot of heavily salted water to a boil. Add the spaghetti and cook until al dente.

Return the seafood to the pan, add the crabmeat, and simmer for 15 minutes. Add the oregano and basil.

Drain the pasta and return it to the pot over medium-high heat. Add about 3 ladles of sauce and toss until the pasta is thoroughly coated, about 1 minute.

Transfer to a large serving bowl. Top with the seafood and the remaining sauce, sprinkle with the parsley, and serve.

Spaghetti with Red Crab Sauce

Cleaning crabs can be a real challenge, particularly when they are alive and snappy. To save time, frustration, and stress, ask your fishmonger to clean them for you. Serves 4

½ cup extra-virgin olive oil
12 blue crabs, cleaned
1 yellow onion, chopped
4 garlic cloves, minced
1 teaspoon kosher salt
½ teaspoon crushed red pepper flakes
2 tablespoons chopped fresh Italian parsley
1 teaspoon chopped fresh oregano
½ cup dry white wine
One 35-ounce can San Marzano tomatoes, hand crushed with their juice
1 cup fish stock
Kosher salt and freshly ground black pepper
1 pound spaghetti

Heat the olive oil in a large stockpot over medium-high heat. Add the crabs, onion, garlic, salt, red pepper flakes, 5 teaspoons of the parsley (reserving a teaspoon for garnish), and the oregano. Sauté for 15 minutes, or until the crabs turn red.

Using tongs, remove the crabs and set aside on a baking sheet. Add the wine to the pan and cook for 2 minutes.

Add the tomatoes and the fish stock and bring to a boil. Reduce to low and let simmer. Taste and season with salt and black pepper as needed.

Return the crabs to the pot and simmer for 20 minutes.

While the sauce is simmering, bring a large pot of heavily salted water to a boil over high heat. Cook the spaghetti until al dente.

While the pasta cooks, transfer the crabs to a serving platter, and set aside.

Drain the pasta, and add it to the sauce. Increase the heat to high, and toss the pasta for 2 minutes, or until completely coated.

Transfer to a large pasta bowl, sprinkle with the parsley, and serve with the crabs.

SEAFOOD

Shellfish

When it comes to seafood, cast your nets widely! From periwinkles and razor clams to monkfish and St. Peter's fish, or Dover Sole, be it lobster or shrimp, a seething stew or raw bar, a veritable ocean of options await. Italians are seafarers by nature so it's only natural they would cook the bounty of the sea. Of course, their Catholic faith prescribes periodic prohibitions on red meat. It was a faith, after all, founded by "fishers of men." Great seafood dishes are part of the religious tradition.

Shrimp Parmigiana

Serves 4

- 6 large eggs
- ¼ cup water
- ½ cup grated Pecorino Romano cheese
- 2 tablespoons plus 2 teaspoons finely chopped fresh Italian parsley
- Kosher salt and freshly ground black pepper
- 1 cup all-purpose flour
- 1 cup plain bread crumbs
- 16 colossal (U-12) shrimp, peeled, deveined, butterflied, tails removed
- 2 cups vegetable oil
- ½ pound mozzarella cheese, thinly sliced
- 2 cups Homemade Marinara Sauce (page 113)

In a medium bowl, combine the eggs, water, ¼ cup of the grated cheese, 2 teaspoons of the parsley, and season with salt and pepper. Whisk until completely mixed. Pour the egg wash into a shallow bowl or baking pan. Put the flour in a shallow bowl or baking pan. Pour the bread crumbs into a separate shallow bowl or baking pan.

Arrange the flour, egg wash, bread crumbs, and a baking sheet lined with parchment paper in that order, left to right, to set up a breading station.

Lightly dredge the shrimp in the flour, patting off any excess. Dip the shrimp into the egg wash, allowing any excess to drip off. Press the shrimp into the bread crumbs, coating both sides. Pat off any excess breading and transfer the shrimp to the lined baking sheet.

Preheat the oven to 375°F. Line a plate with paper towels. Grease a rimmed baking sheet.

Heat the vegetable oil in a large sauté pan over medium-high heat for 2 to 3 minutes.

Test the oil to see if it is at the proper temperature by sprinkling a pinch of the bread crumbs into the oil. If the crumbs instantly sizzle, the oil is at the correct temperature.

Using tongs, carefully place the shrimp into the hot oil, working in batches to avoid overcrowding. Fry for 1 to 2 minutes on each side, or until golden brown and crispy.

Transfer the shrimp to the paper towel–lined plate and gently pat each shrimp dry with more paper towels.

Arrange the shrimp on the greased baking sheet, spacing them about ¼ inch apart.

Sprinkle the shrimp with the remaining ¼ cup grated cheese. Top each with a slice of mozzarella and drizzle each with 2 tablespoons of the marinara sauce. Spread the sauce evenly across the mozzarella.

Switch the oven to broil and place the shrimp on the center rack. Broil for 2 minutes, or until the cheese has melted and begun to blister.

Transfer the shrimp to a serving platter, sprinkle with the remaining 2 tablespoons parsley, and serve.

Shrimp Fra Diavolo

Serves 4

¼ cup olive oil
4 garlic cloves, smashed
16 colossal (U-12) shrimp, peeled, deveined, butterflied and tails removed
¾ cup dry white wine
¼ teaspoon finely chopped fresh oregano
1 teaspoon crushed red pepper flakes
Kosher salt and freshly ground black pepper

3 cups canned San Marzano tomatoes, hand crushed with juice
6 fresh basil leaves, torn

Line a plate with paper towels and set aside.

Heat the olive oil in a large sauté pan over medium-high heat. Add 2 cloves of the garlic and cook until the garlic begins to shimmer in the pan.

Using kitchen tongs, carefully place the shrimp into the pan and sauté for 1 minute on each side, or until the shrimp begin to turn opaque.

Transfer to the paper towel–lined plate. Cover the shrimp with a sheet of aluminum foil to keep them warm.

Pour off the oil and garlic from the pan. Return the pan to the heat and add the remaining 2 garlic cloves, the white wine, oregano, and red pepper flakes. Bring to a boil, and cook for 3 minutes.

Stir in the tomatoes and cook for 15 minutes, or until the sauce has thickened slightly. Season with salt and black pepper to taste.

Add the basil and the cooked shrimp, and cook for 3 minutes. Remove the garlic cloves and discard.

Transfer the shrimp to a serving platter, pour the sauce over the shrimp, and serve.

Shrimp Scampi

Serves 4

1 cup all-purpose flour
16 colossal (U-12) shrimp, peeled, deveined, butterflied, tails removed
Kosher salt and freshly ground black pepper
¼ cup olive oil
1 cup dry white wine
1 tablespoon Worcestershire sauce
2 tablespoons minced garlic
2 tablespoons chopped fresh Italian parsley
4 tablespoons (½ stick) salted butter
Juice of 2 lemons
1 lemon, cut into wedges

Place the flour in a wide shallow bowl or baking pan. Lightly dredge the shrimp in the flour, shaking off any excess. Season lightly with salt and pepper. Transfer to a plate covered with paper towels.

Heat the olive oil in a large sauté pan over medium-high heat. Line a plate with paper towels. When the oil begins to shimmer, using tongs, carefully place the shrimp in the pan, working in batches if necessary to avoid overcrowding. Fry for 1 to 2 minutes, turning often. When the shrimp turn opaque, transfer to the paper towel–lined plate.

Once all the shrimp have been cooked, pour off the oil from the pan and return the pan to the heat. Add the wine, Worcestershire sauce, garlic, and a dash of parsley. Stir

until blended. Add in the butter and lemon juice, mix well, and bring to a boil. Return the shrimp to the pan and cook for about 1 minute. Once the shrimp are evenly coated with the sauce, transfer them to a serving plate.

Boil the sauce for 1 minute more, and pour over the shrimp. Sprinkle with the remaining parsley, garnish with the lemon wedges, and serve.

"My grandfather provided table wine to Rao's during Prohibition. He owned the building at 322 East 119th Street. In the basement, he made various schnapps and wines. The wine he sold to the local church and synagogue as well as to the founder of Rao's. And to many others, as well."
—JAY MICHAELSON,
Pembroke Pines, Florida

Shrimp Francese

Serves 4

4 large eggs
½ cup grated Pecorino Romano cheese
2 tablespoons plus 2 teaspoons finely chopped
    fresh Italian parsley
Kosher salt and freshly ground black pepper
1 cup all-purpose flour
16 colossal (U-12) shrimp, peeled, deveined,
    butterflied, and tails removed
¼ cup olive oil
3 garlic cloves, smashed
1 cup dry white wine
2 tablespoons salted butter
Juice of 1 lemon
2 tablespoons minced garlic
1 lemon, cut into wedges

In a medium bowl, combine the eggs, ¼ cup of the Pecorino Romano cheese, and 2 teaspoons of the parsley, and season with salt and pepper. Whisk until completely blended. Pour the egg wash into a shallow bowl or baking pan.

Put the flour in a shallow bowl or baking pan. Arrange the flour, egg wash, and a baking sheet lined with parchment paper in that order, left to right, to set up a breading station. Line a plate with paper towels.

Lightly dredge the shrimp in the flour, shaking off any excess. Dip the shrimp in the egg wash, allowing any excess to drip off. Transfer to the parchment-lined baking sheet.

Heat the olive oil in a large sauté pan over medium heat, and add the garlic cloves. When the garlic begins to shimmer, remove and discard the cloves.

Using tongs, carefully add the shrimp to the pan, working in batches as necessary to avoid overcrowding the pan. Cook the shrimp for 2 minutes on each side. Transfer to the paper towel–lined plate.

Pour off the oil from the pan and return the pan to the heat. Add the wine, butter, lemon juice, and minced garlic, season with salt and pepper, and stir until evenly blended. Bring the sauce to a boil, then return the shrimp to the pan. Cook the shrimp for about 1 minute.

Once they are evenly coated with the sauce, transfer to a serving plate. Boil the sauce for 1 minute more and pour it over the shrimp. Sprinkle with the remaining 2 tablespoons parsley, garnish with the lemon wedges, and serve.

Shrimp Oreganate

Serves 4

1 cup all-purpose flour
16 colossal (U-12) shrimp, peeled, deveined,
    butterflied and tails removed
¼ cup vegetable oil
1 cup dry white wine
Juice of 1 lemon
2 tablespoons minced garlic
2 teaspoons finely chopped fresh oregano
Kosher salt and freshly ground black pepper
¼ cup grated Pecorino Romano cheese
2 tablespoons salted butter
¾ cup plain bread crumbs
2 tablespoons chopped fresh Italian parsley
1 lemon, cut into wedges

Preheat the oven to 400°F. Line a plate with paper towels. Grease a rimmed baking sheet.

Put the flour in a wide shallow bowl or baking pan. Dredge the shrimp in the flour, and shake off any excess.

Heat the vegetable oil in a large sauté pan over medium-high heat for 1 minute.

Using tongs, carefully place the shrimp into the pan. Cook for 1 minute per side, or until the shrimp turn opaque. Transfer the shrimp to the paper towel–lined plate.

Pour off the oil from the pan and return the pan to the heat. Return the shrimp to the pan. Add the wine, lemon juice, garlic, oregano, and a dash of salt and pepper, bring to a boil, and cook for 1 minute.

Using tongs, transfer the shrimp to the greased baking sheet. Pour the sauce over the shrimp. Sprinkle the shrimp with the grated cheese, and place about ½ teaspoon of butter on each shrimp. Generously coat the top of each shrimp with bread crumbs.

Bake the shrimp for 3 minutes. Switch to broil, and broil for 1 minute more, or until the bread crumbs are toasted.

Divide the shrimp among individual serving plates, sprinkle with the parsley, garnish with the lemon wedges, and serve.

Aunt Anna's and Uncle Johnnie's Fried Shrimp

Serves 4

1 cup all-purpose flour
1 tablespoon salt, plus more to taste
1 tablespoon freshly ground black pepper, plus more to taste
16 colossal (U-12) shrimp, peeled, deveined, and butterflied
½ cup olive oil
2 garlic cloves, smashed
2 tablespoons chopped fresh Italian parsley
1 lemon, cut into wedges

In a medium-size shallow baking pan, combine the flour, salt, and pepper and whisk until well mixed. Line a baking sheet with parchment paper. Line a plate with paper towels.

Dredge the shrimp in the seasoned flour, and lightly shake off any excess. Place on the lined baking sheet.

Heat the olive oil in a large sauté pan over medium-high heat for 2 minutes. Add the garlic cloves. When the garlic begins to shimmer, using tongs, carefully place the shrimp into the pan. Sauté for 3 minutes, or until the shrimp turn opaque, working in batches as necessary to avoid overcrowding the pan. Transfer the shrimp to the paper towel–lined plate. Fold the paper towels over the shrimp, to soak up any excess oil.

Transfer the shrimp to a serving platter and dust with salt and pepper. Sprinkle with the parsley, garnish with the lemon wedges, and serve.

Grilled Stuffed Lobster

Serves 4

2½ cups plain bread crumbs
1 tablespoon chopped fresh oregano
2 tablespoons minced garlic
¼ cup plus 1 tablespoon finely chopped fresh Italian parsley
Kosher salt and freshly ground black pepper
¾ cup olive oil
1 cup dry white wine
Two 1½- to 2-pound live lobsters, halved lengthwise, cleaned, claws cracked
2 lemons, cut into wedges

Preheat the grill to 450°F.

In a medium mixing bowl, combine the bread crumbs, oregano, garlic, and ¼ cup of parsley. Season with the salt and pepper and mix thoroughly. Slowly stir in the olive oil and wine, adding small amounts of each at a time, until the bread crumbs have evenly absorbed the oil and darkened in color. They should have the consistency of wet sand.

Place each lobster half on a sheet of aluminum foil large enough to enclose the entire half. Wearing a pair of latex kitchen gloves, place a generous handful of the breading into the lobster's body cavity and tail. Push the breading into all the crevices, evenly coating the bodies and tails.

Loosely wrap each lobster half in the foil, closing it over the top of the breading. Place the lobsters on the grill, shell side down. Close the lid and grill for 10 minutes.

Open the lid and unwrap the aluminum foil, exposing the breading.

Close the lid and cook for 2 minutes more, or until the breading is crisp and toasted.

Transfer the lobster halves to individual serving plates. Sprinkle with the remaining 1 tablespoon parsley, garnish with the lemon wedges, and serve.

Fish

Grilled Branzino

Serves 4

Four 7- to 8-ounce sea bass fillets
1 lemon, halved, half cut into 8 thin slices
3 sprigs fresh thyme, leaves finely chopped
2 sprigs fresh rosemary, leaves only
2 tablespoons finely chopped fresh tarragon
Kosher salt and freshly ground black pepper to
    taste
4 garlic cloves, minced
4 teaspoons (½ stick) salted butter
4 cups arugula, rinsed and dried
1 tablespoon plus 2 teaspoons olive oil
¼ cup finely chopped fresh Italian parsley
1 lemon, cut into wedges

Grease the grill grates and preheat the grill to 400°F.

Place the fillets, skin side down, onto a sheet of parchment paper or aluminum foil. Season each with a misting of lemon juice from the lemon half, the thyme, rosemary, tarragon, salt, and pepper. Divide the garlic among the fillets, spreading it over each, and dot each fillet with a teaspoon of butter. Place two slices of lemon on top of each of the seasoned fillets.

Place the fillets, skin side down, on the grill. Close the lid and cook for 6 to 8 minutes, or until the meat flakes with a fork.

While the fish is cooking, combine the arugula, 1 tablespoon of the olive oil, and a spritz of lemon juice from the lemon half in a medium mixing bowl. Season lightly with salt and pepper. Gently toss until the arugula is evenly coated.

Transfer the arugula to a large serving plate, creating a bed for the fish. (If you're serving the fish in individual portions, divide the arugula among individual plates.)

Using a spatula, transfer the sea bass to the bed of arugula. Drizzle a teaspoon of olive oil on top of each fillet. Sprinkle with parsley, garnish with the lemon wedges, and serve.

My Grandmother's Stuffed Calamari

Serves 8

8 large squid, tentacles cut from the bodies
1 pound ricotta cheese
1 large egg
¼ cup grated Pecorino Romano cheese
2 tablespoons chopped fresh Italian parsley
1 tablespoon kosher salt, plus more as needed
1 tablespoon pepper, plus more as needed
2 cups all-purpose flour
¾ cup olive oil
½ cup dry white wine
2 cups Homemade Marinara Sauce (page 113)

Preheat the oven to 350°F. Line a large baking sheet with parchment paper. Fill a large, heatproof bowl with water and ice.

Put the tentacles in a large pot and add water to cover. Bring to a boil over high heat and cook until tender, 15 to 20 minutes. Drain and transfer to the ice bath. When completely cooled, finely chop the tentacles.

In a large mixing bowl, combine the ricotta, egg, grated cheese, 1 tablespoon of the parsley, and chopped tentacles. Season to taste with salt and pepper and mix until completely combined.

Place the squid bodies on the lined baking sheet. Stuff each body with the ricotta mixture. Close the openings with toothpicks, or a butcher's needle and twine.

Pour the flour into a large baking pan. Season with 1 tablespoon of salt and 1 tablespoon of pepper and whisk to combine.

Dredge each stuffed squid in the seasoned flour, patting off any excess. Transfer the squid to a large sheet of parchment paper.

Heat the olive oil in a large sauté pan over medium heat for about 2 minutes.

Using tongs, carefully place the squid into the pan, working in batches to avoid overcrowding the pan. Cook until the squid are browned on all sides, about 15 minutes. Using the tongs, transfer the squid to a large roasting pan.

Pour off the oil from the sauté pan, and return the pan to the heat. Add the white wine and cook until reduced by half.

Stir in the marinara sauce and cook for 1 minute more. Pour the sauce over the squid in the roasting pan, cover the pan with aluminum foil, and bake until the squid is fork-tender, about 1 hour.

Transfer the squid to a serving platter. Pour any remaining sauce from the roasting pan over the squid. Sprinkle with the remaining 1 tablespoon parsley, and serve.

Fritto Misto

Serves 4

- ¼ pound squid bodies, cleaned and cut into ¼-inch rings
- 1 small zucchini, julienned (use a mandoline, without shredding the seeded part)
- 4 cups whole milk
- 1 quart corn oil
- ½ cup Wondra flour
- ½ cup all-purpose flour
- 1 tablespoon kosher salt, plus more as needed
- 1 tablespoon freshly ground black pepper, plus more as needed
- 4 colossal (U-12) shrimp, peeled, deveined, and butterflied
- 2 tablespoons chopped fresh Italian parsley
- 1 lemon, cut into wedges
- 1 cup Homemade Marinara Sauce (page 113) or Rao's marinara sauce
- 1 cup tartar sauce

In two separate large bowls, cover the squid and zucchini with milk and refrigerate for at least 1 hour.

Heat the corn oil in a fryer or deep pot over high heat, until the oil is 375°F.

While the oil is heating, combine the flours, salt, and pepper in a large mixing bowl and whisk to thoroughly combine.

Wearing latex kitchen gloves, remove the squid and zucchini from the milk, and shake off any excess. Transfer the squid, shrimp, and zucchini to the seasoned flour and gently toss until evenly coated.

Fry the shrimp in the oil until golden brown. Transfer to a large mixing bowl, season to taste with salt and pepper, and toss. Repeat with the squid and zucchini.

Transfer to a serving platter or large serving bowl. Sprinkle with the parsley and garnish with the lemon wedges. Serve with bowls of the marinara and tartar sauces.

Baked Scrod

Serves 4

- Four 8-ounce scrod fillets
- Juice of 1 lemon
- 3 tablespoons dry white wine
- Kosher salt and freshly ground black pepper
- 4 teaspoons unsalted butter
- Paprika to taste
- 2 tablespoons chopped fresh Italian parsley
- 1 lemon, cut into wedges

Preheat the oven to 400°F. Grease a rimmed baking sheet.

Arrange the fillets on the baking sheet, leaving ½ inch between each fillet.

Drizzle the fish with the lemon juice and wine. Season with salt and pepper. Dot each fillet with 1 teaspoon of butter and sprinkle with paprika.

Loosely cover the baking sheet with aluminum foil. Bake for 10 to 13 minutes, or until the fish flakes easily with a fork.

Transfer the fillets to individual plates, sprinkle with the parsley, garnish with the lemon wedges, and serve.

Broiled Fillet of Sole

Serves 4

3 tablespoons olive oil
3 garlic cloves, smashed
Four 8- to 10-ounce fillets grey or lemon sole
½ cup dry white wine
4 teaspoons salted butter
Kosher salt and freshly ground black pepper
4 tablespoons plain bread crumbs
2 tablespoons chopped fresh Italian parsley
1 lemon, sliced

Preheat the broiler.

In a large shallow baking sheet, combine the olive oil and garlic.

Place the fillets on the baking sheet, spacing them about ½ inch apart. Pour the wine over the fillets and top each with 1 teaspoon butter. Sprinkle each fillet with salt, pepper, and bread crumbs. Loosely cover the baking sheet with aluminum foil, and broil the fillets for 6 minutes.

Remove the foil, and broil the fillets for 1 to 2 minutes more, or until the bread crumbs have toasted.

Using a spatula, transfer the fillets to individual plates. Sprinkle each with the parsley, garnish with a lemon slice, and serve.

Swordfish Livornese

Serves 4

1 cup all-purpose flour
Four 6- to 8-ounce swordfish steaks, each ¾ inch thick
¼ cup olive oil
3 tablespoons unsalted butter
1 teaspoon minced garlic
5 anchovy fillets, packed in oil
1 cup dry white wine
½ cup Castelvetrano olives, pitted and halved
4 teaspoons capers, rinsed
1 cup canned San Marzano tomatoes, hand crushed with juice
3 bay leaves
1 teaspoon finely chopped fresh oregano

Put the flour in a wide, shallow bowl or baking pan. Lightly dredge each swordfish steak on both sides in the flour. Pat off any excess and transfer to a clean plate.

Heat the oil in a large sauté pan over medium-high heat, for 2 minutes. Carefully add the swordfish, butter, and garlic. Fry the fish for 1 minute per side. Transfer to a clean plate.

Return the pan to the heat. Add the anchovies, wine, olives, and capers. Stir in the tomatoes, bay leaves, and oregano. Increase the heat to high, and bring to a boil. Cook for 6 minutes, stirring often.

Return the swordfish to the pan and cook for 3 minutes on each side.

Remove and discard the bay leaves. Transfer the steaks to warmed individual plates. Spoon the sauce over the fish, and serve.

Fried Fillet of Sole

Serves 4

4 large eggs
2 tablespoons water
¼ cup grated Pecorino Romano cheese
2 tablespoons plus 2 teaspoons chopped fresh
    Italian parsley
Kosher salt and freshly ground black pepper
1 cup all-purpose flour
1½ cups plain bread crumbs
Four 8- to 10-ounce fillets grey or lemon sole
1 cup vegetable oil
2 lemons, cut into wedges

In medium mixing bowl, combine the eggs, water, cheese, and 2 teaspoons of the parsley. Season with salt and pepper. Whisk until well blended. Put the flour into a wide, shallow bowl or baking pan. Put the bread crumbs in a similar container. Line a plate with parchment paper. Arrange the flour, egg wash, bread crumbs, and parchment-lined plate from left to right, in that order, to set up a breading station. Line another plate with paper towels and set aside.

Gently dredge the fillets in the flour, patting off any excess. Dip each fillet into the egg wash, allowing any excess to drip off. Press both sides of each fillet into the bread crumbs to coat, shaking off any excess, and transfer to the parchment paper–lined plate.

Heat the vegetable oil in a large sauté pan over medium-high heat for 1 minute.

Carefully place the fillets into the pan and pan-fry for 2 to 3 minutes, or until the bread crumbs are golden brown and crisp and the fish has cooked through.

Transfer the fillets to the paper towel–lined plate. Pat the tops of the fillets with paper towels to remove any excess oil.

Serve the fillets family style on a platter, or on individual plates, as you prefer. Sprinkle with the remaining 2 tablespoons parsley and garnish with lemon wedges just before serving.

Fillet of Sole with Lemon, Wine, and Fennel

Serves 4

1 fennel bulb, trimmed and sliced ⅛ inch thick
1 cup all-purpose flour
Four 8- to 10-ounce fillets grey or lemon sole
¾ cup vegetable oil
4 tablespoons (½ stick) salted butter
¾ cup dry white wine
Juice of 1½ lemons
Kosher salt and freshly ground black pepper
2 tablespoons fresh Italian parsley, chopped

Bring a saucepan half full of water to a boil over high heat. Add the fennel and boil for 3 minutes, or until the fennel is tender but still slightly firm. Drain, and rinse the fennel under cold running water. Pat dry with paper towels and set aside.

Put the flour in a wide, shallow bowl or baking pan. Lightly dredge each fillet on both sides in the flour. Pat off any excess and transfer the fillets to a clean plate.

Heat the vegetable oil in a large sauté pan over medium-high heat for 2 minutes. Carefully add the fillets and fry for 3 minutes on each side, or until golden brown.

Pour off the oil from the pan and return the pan to the heat. Add 2 tablespoons of the butter. When the butter has melted, add the wine, fennel, and lemon juice and bring to a boil. Reduce to a simmer and season to taste with salt and pepper. Simmer for 2 minutes.

Using a spatula, transfer the fillets to a warmed serving platter or warmed individual plates. Loosely cover with aluminum foil to keep warm.

Return the pan to the heat and stir in the remaining 2 tablespoons butter. Increase the heat to high and bring to a boil. Boil for 1 minute, or until the sauce has thickened.

Remove the aluminum foil from the serving platter or plates and spoon the fennel and sauce over the fillets. Sprinkle with the parsley, and serve.

Codfish Puttanesca

Serves 4

1 cup all-purpose flour
Four 6- to 8-ounce cod fillets
½ cup olive oil
3 garlic cloves, smashed
5 anchovy fillets, packed in oil
4 teaspoons capers, rinsed
½ cup Gaeta olives, pitted and halved
½ teaspoon crushed red pepper flakes
1 cup canned San Marzano tomatoes, hand crushed with juice
1 tablespoon chopped fresh Italian parsley

Put the flour in a wide, shallow bowl or baking pan. Lightly dredge each fillet on both sides in the flour. Pat off any excess and transfer to a clean plate.

Heat the olive oil in a large sauté pan over medium-high heat, and add the garlic. When the garlic begins to shimmer, carefully place the cod into the pan. Fry the fish for 1 minute on each side. Transfer to a clean plate.

Return the pan to the heat. Add the anchovy, capers, olives, and red pepper flakes and sauté for 2 minutes. Stir in the tomatoes, bring to a simmer, and cook for 6 minutes.

Return the fish to the pan and cook for 3 minutes on each side.

Transfer the fillets to warmed individual plates. Spoon the sauce over the fillets, sprinkle with the parsley, and serve.

Pan-Seared Salmon with Almonds and Asparagus

Serves 4

Four 8-ounce, skin-on salmon fillets
Kosher salt and freshly ground black pepper
1 bunch asparagus, trimmed
½ cup sliced almonds
¼ cup olive oil
2 garlic cloves, smashed
2 tablespoons salted butter
½ lemon
¼ cup dry white wine

Place the salmon, skin side up, on a sheet of aluminum foil. Season generously with salt and pepper.

Bring a large pot of lightly salted water to a boil. Fill a heatproof bowl with ice and cold water. Cook the asparagus for 3 minutes, or until bright green. Transfer immediately to the ice bath.

In a large sauté pan over medium heat, toast the almonds, tossing until they are crisp and golden brown, and set aside.

Return the pan to the heat, and add the olive oil and garlic. When the garlic begins to shimmer, add the salmon, skin side down. Remove and discard the garlic. Cook the salmon for 3 to 4 minutes, or until the skin is crisp and slightly charred.

Turn the fillets and cook for 2 to 3 minutes more. Transfer the fillets to a clean platter.

Pour off the oil and return the pan to the heat. Add the butter, a squeeze of lemon juice, and the wine. Increase the heat to high and bring to a boil. Return the salmon to the pan, skin side up and cook for 20 seconds on each side. Transfer the salmon to individual plates, skin side up.

Add the asparagus to the pan and sauté for 1 minute, or until the asparagus is heated through.

Divide the asparagus among the serving plates. Garnish the fish with the toasted almonds, and serve.

MEAT AND CHICKEN

Veal

Veal is incredibly delicious and can be amazingly tender, but you have to know how to properly prepare it.

For our scallopini dishes, we use pink veal loin because it's less sinewy and richer in flavor.

Pounding veal medallions is essential. If not pounded correctly with a meat tenderizer (mallet), the medallions will be tough, a real challenge to chew. Tenderizing the meat breaks down the tissue, ensuring tenderness and a good-looking presentation.

Cut and pound veal against the grain, or it will be stringy and inedible no matter how much you hammer it. To tenderize veal, cut the top off a plastic, resealable bag. Cut open the sides and unfold the bag. Center a medallion on one side of the fold, and fold over the other side to cover the meat, so that it's sandwiched in the plastic. Gently pound with the spiked, tenderizing side of the mallet. Strike the veal from its center, working your way out to the edges. When you're done, the medallion should be approximately 4 inches in diameter, and no less than a ¼ inch thick.

Veal Saltimbocca

Serves 6

12 veal medallions (about 2 pounds)
12 fresh sage leaves
12 slices prosciutto
1 cup all-purpose flour
¼ cup vegetable oil
¾ cup Marsala wine
½ cup chicken broth
6 tablespoons unsalted butter
Kosher salt and freshly ground black pepper

Pound the veal medallions to a thickness of ¼ inch, using the method described on this page.

Lift the plastic, and lay 1 sage leaf and 1 piece of prosciutto (cut to the size and shape of the medallion) on top of the veal. Fold the plastic back over the medallion. Use the ridged side of the mallet to pound the meats together. Repeat for each veal medallion.

Put the flour in a wide, shallow bowl. Lightly dredge each medallion in the flour. Shake off any excess, put on a plate, and set aside. Repeat until all the medallions have been floured.

Heat the vegetable oil in a large sauté pan over medium-high heat for 3 minutes.

Place 3 to 4 medallions into the pan, without crowding them. Cook for no more than 1 minute on each side, or until the veal begins to brown.

Transfer the medallions to a plate lined with paper towels. Repeat with the remaining medallions.

Veal Marsala

Serves 6

12 veal medallions (about 2 pounds)
1 cup all-purpose flour
¼ cup vegetable oil
2 cups white mushrooms, trimmed and sliced
¾ cup Marsala wine
3 tablespoons unsalted butter
¼ cup chicken broth
Kosher salt and freshly ground black pepper
¼ cup finely chopped fresh Italian parsley

Pound the veal medallions to a thickness of about ¼ inch, using the method described on the opposite page.

Put the flour in a wide, shallow bowl. Lightly dredge each medallion in the flour. Shake off any excess, put on a plate, and set aside. Repeat until all the medallions have been floured.

Heat the vegetable oil in a large sauté pan over medium-high heat for 3 minutes.

Place 3 to 4 medallions into the pan, without crowding them. Cook for no more than 1 minute on each side, or until the veal begins to brown.

Transfer the medallions to a plate lined with paper towels. Repeat with the remaining medallions.

Add the sliced mushrooms to the pan and sauté for 5 minutes, or until they have released most of their juice.

 Pour off excess oil from the pan and return the pan to the burner over medium-low heat.

When all of the medallions have been browned, pour off the remaining oil from the pan and return the pan to the burner over medium-low heat.

Add the wine and, using a wooden spoon, scrape up any browned bits stuck to the pan. Cook for 1 minute. Add the chicken broth, and cook for a few minutes more. Add the butter, and season lightly with salt (go easy—the prosciutto can be salty) and pepper.

Return the medallions to the sauce and cook for 5 to 10 seconds on each side, until each medallion is coated with a nice glaze.

Transfer the medallions to individual serving plates, top each with a small amount of the sauce, and serve.

Add the wine and, using a wooden spoon, scrape up any browned bits stuck to the pan.

Add the butter. When the butter has melted, add the chicken broth and bring to a boil. Reduce to a simmer, and season lightly with salt and pepper.

Add the medallions and cook for about 10 seconds on each side. Transfer to a warm serving plate.

Using a slotted spoon, remove the mushrooms and scatter on top of the veal. Reduce the sauce for 1 minute more.

Spoon the sauce over the veal. Sprinkle with the parsley, and serve.

Veal Piccata

Serves 6

12 veal medallions (about 2 pounds)
1 cup all-purpose flour
¾ cup vegetable oil
3 tablespoons unsalted butter
¾ cup dry white wine
Juice of 1 lemon
Kosher salt and freshly ground black pepper
¼ cup chopped fresh Italian parsley

Pound the veal medallions to a thickness of about ¼ inch, using the method described on page 180.

Put the flour in a wide, shallow bowl. Lightly dredge each medallion in the flour. Shake off any excess, put on a plate, and set aside. Repeat until all the medallions have been floured.

Heat the vegetable oil in a large sauté pan over medium-high heat for 3 minutes. Place 3 to 4 medallions into the pan, without crowding them. Cook for no more than 1 minute on each side, or until the veal begins to brown. Transfer the medallions to a plate lined with paper towels. Repeat with the remaining medallions.

Pour off the oil from the pan and return the pan to the heat. Add the butter. When the butter has melted, add the white wine and lemon juice. Season with salt and pepper. Increase the heat to high and cook for 3 to 4 minutes, or until the sauce has reduced slightly and started to thicken.

Add the veal medallions to the sauce and cook for 30 seconds on each side.

Transfer the glazed medallions to a warmed serving platter. Top with the remaining sauce. Sprinkle with the parsley and serve hot.

Veal Francese

Serves 6

- 12 veal medallions (about 2 pounds)
- 1 cup all-purpose flour
- 4 large eggs
- ¼ cup grated Pecorino Romano cheese
- ¼ cup plus 2 teaspoons chopped fresh Italian parsley
- Kosher salt and freshly ground black pepper
- 1 cup vegetable oil
- ¾ cup dry white wine
- Juice of 1 lemon
- 4 tablespoons (½ stick) unsalted butter

Pound the veal medallions to a thickness of about ¼ inch, using the method described on page 180.

Put the flour in a wide, shallow bowl. Lightly dredge each medallion in the flour and place on a plate lined with parchment paper.

In medium mixing bowl, combine the eggs, cheese, and 2 teaspoons of the parsley, and season with salt and pepper. Whisk until well blended.

Dip each veal medallion into the egg wash and let any excess drip off. Repeat with the remaining medallions and return them all to the parchment paper–lined plate.

Heat the vegetable oil in a large sauté pan over medium-high heat for 2 minutes.

Place 3 to 4 medallions into the pan, without crowding them. Cook for no more than 1 minute on each side, or until the veal is lightly browned. Transfer the medallions to a warmed serving platter.

Pour off the remaining oil from the pan and return the pan to the heat. Add the wine, lemon juice, and butter and season liberally with salt and pepper. Stir until the sauce is completely blended and has thickened, no more than 1 minute.

Return the veal to the pan and glaze for 30 seconds on each side.

Transfer the veal to a warm serving platter. Pour the remaining sauce over the veal, sprinkle with the parsley, and serve hot.

Veal Parmigiano

For a lighter presentation of this dish, buy the mozzarella from a deli and ask the counter person to slice it paper-thin. Top the veal with a dollop of marinara and then lay a thin slice of mozzarella over the sauce. Pull from the center of the slice upward, forming a loose and airy drape. The pockets of air under the cheese will allow the mozzarella to fully melt and blister, creating a wispier and attractive presentation. A moderate sprinkle of shredded mozzarella works the same way. Serves 6

2 pounds veal cutlets
1 cup all-purpose flour
4 large eggs
¾ cup grated Pecorino Romano cheese
¼ cup plus 2 teaspoons chopped fresh Italian
  parsley
Kosher salt and freshly ground black pepper
2 cups plain bread crumbs
1 cup vegetable oil
4 cups Homemade Marinara Sauce
  (page 113)
1½ pounds fresh mozzarella cheese, cut into
  ⅛-inch slices

Pound the veal cutlets to a thickness of about ¼ inch, using the method described on page 180.

Put the flour in a wide, shallow bowl or shallow baking pan. Lightly dredge each medallion in the flour and place on a plate lined with parchment paper. Line a platter with parchment paper and set aside.

In medium mixing bowl, combine the eggs, ¼ cup of the grated cheese, and 2 teaspoons of the parsley, and season with salt and pepper. Whisk until well blended. Put the bread crumbs in a wide, shallow bowl or baking pan. Set out a sheet of parchment paper.

Dip each cutlet into the egg wash and let any excess drip off. Press the cutlet into the bread crumbs, coating both sides. Lightly shake off any excess bread crumbs. Set aside on the parchment paper, so that none of the cutlets are touching. Repeat until all the cutlets are breaded.

Preheat the oven to 400°F. Line a large, flat plate with two layers of paper towels. Grease a large, rimmed baking sheet.

Heat the vegetable oil in a large sauté pan over medium-high heat for 2 minutes.

Lightly season the cutlets with salt and pepper, then carefully place them into the hot oil, working in batches of 3 to 4. Cook for 4 to 6 minutes per side, or until the cutlets are a light golden brown on each side.

Transfer to the paper towel–lined plate, and repeat the process with the remaining cutlets.

Arrange the cutlets on the greased baking sheet, leaving at least ¼ inch between each cutlet.

Spread a large dollop of marinara sauce on top of each cutlet. Spread a little sauce between the cutlets. Sprinkle each cutlet with the remaining grated cheese, and top with two slices of mozzarella per cutlet. Spread a modest dollop of marinara sauce evenly across the mozzarella. This top layer of sauce should be very thin.

Bake for 5 minutes. Once the cheese begins to melt, switch the oven to broil.

Broil the cutlets until the cheese starts to blister and lightly brown.

Remove the baking sheet from the oven and, using a spatula, transfer the cutlets to a serving platter. Sprinkle with the parsley and serve.

Veal Milanese

When you buy the veal chops for this recipe, do yourself a favor and ask your butcher to trim and pound the veal for you. It will save you a lot of time and effort preparing the dish, and reputable butchers won't charge you any more for the prep. I've included the recipe for the chopped salad we serve with our Veal Milanese. Enjoy! Serves 4 to 8

1 cup all-purpose flour
2 cups plain bread crumbs
4 large eggs
¼ cup grated Pecorino Romano cheese
2 teaspoons chopped fresh Italian parsley
Kosher salt and freshly ground black pepper
Four 14-ounce veal chops, trimmed and
    pounded
1 cup vegetable oil

Put the flour in a wide shallow bowl or baking pan. Put the bread crumbs in a similar container.

In a large mixing bowl, combine the eggs, grated cheese, and parsley, and season with salt and pepper. Whisk until completely combined.

Line up the flour, egg wash, and bread crumbs, in that order. Line a baking sheet with parchment paper and place next to the bread crumbs, to create a breading station. Line a large platter or baking sheet with paper towels.

Hold a chop by the bone and lightly dredge in the flour. Gently shake or pat off the excess.

Dip the chop into the egg wash, coating the chop completely. Let any excess drip off. Press the chop into the bread crumbs, coating it on all sides. Gently shake off any excess bread crumbs. Set the chop on the parchment paper–lined baking sheet and repeat breading the rest of the chops.

Heat the vegetable oil in a large sauté pan over medium-high heat for 2 minutes. Carefully lay a chop in the oil, and cook for 3 to 4 minutes per side, or until golden brown all over. Transfer to the large platter or baking sheet lined with paper towels. Repeat with the remaining chops. Gently press the tops of the chops with more paper towels to remove any excess oil.

Transfer the chops to individual plates, add Rao's Chopped Mixed Green Salad for Milanese, and serve.

Rao's Chopped Mixed Green Salad for Milanese

Serves 8

- 1 medium head iceberg lettuce, cored and chopped
- 1 small head radicchio, cored and chopped
- 1 head endive, trimmed and chopped
- 2 medium very ripe tomatoes, chopped
- 1 small cucumber, peeled and sliced
- ½ cup chopped fennel
- ½ cup chopped red onion
- ¾ cup extra-virgin olive oil
- 1½ tablespoons Italian-style red wine vinegar
- Kosher salt and freshly ground black pepper

Combine all the ingredients in a large salad bowl and toss to combine. Serve with the Veal Milanese.

Bobby Flay's Veal Chop Milanese, with Crispy Prosciutto and Tomato and Calabrian Chile Salad

Bobby introduced me to this dish when I was honored and flattered to be a judge on the Food Network show Beat Bobby Flay. *Bobby was kind enough to invite me onto the show numerous times. Let me tell you, the show is legit. This dish, in particular, knocked my socks off. It was so good, that I asked Bobby if I could use the recipe at the restaurant, as a "Bobby Flay Special." The fried egg sets the dish off, adding a warmth of flavor and unique texture that pulls it all together. Molto grazie, Bobby!*

Serves 4

FOR THE SALAD
- 3 anchovy fillets, chopped
- 2 tablespoons extra-virgin olive oil
- 1 teaspoon Calabrian chile oil (from jar of Calabrian chiles)
- 2 Calabrian chiles, in oil, finely diced
- 2 tablespoons red wine vinegar
- Kosher salt and freshly ground black pepper
- 4 ripe plum tomatoes, diced
- 1 tablespoon capers, drained and chopped
- ½ cup torn fresh basil leaves
- 1 head frisée, torn into pieces

FOR THE FRIED PROSCIUTTO
- 1½ cups canola oil
- 4 paper-thin slices prosciutto

FOR THE FRIED EGGS
- 4 tablespoons (½ stick) unsalted butter
- 4 large eggs
- Kosher salt and freshly ground black pepper

FOR THE FRIED VEAL CHOP

4 bone-in veal chops, 1½ inches thick, pounded to ¼ inch thick
Kosher salt and freshly ground black pepper
2 cups all-purpose flour
4 large eggs
1 cup panko bread crumbs
1 cup plain bread crumbs
Canola oil
Finely grated lemon zest

To make the salad: Mash the anchovy fillets with the olive oil and Calabrian chile oil in a large bowl. Add the chiles and vinegar and season with salt and pepper to taste. Stir to combine.

Stir in the tomatoes, capers, and basil. Let sit at room temperature while you prepare the veal. Add the frisée to the salad when ready to serve.

To cook the prosciutto: Heat the canola oil in a small sauté pan over medium heat until it begins to shimmer. Fry the prosciutto, one slice at a time, until crispy, about 45 seconds. Transfer to a baking sheet lined with paper towels to drain for a few minutes.

To fry the eggs: Heat the butter in a large nonstick pan over medium heat until it begins to shimmer. Crack the eggs into the pan, season the tops with salt and pepper, and cook until the whites set and the yolks begin to firm slightly, about 2 minutes.

To cook the veal chops: Preheat the oven to 250°F.

Season the veal on both sides with salt and pepper. Put the flour in a baking dish and season with salt and pepper. Combine the eggs and 2 tablespoons of water in a baking dish, whisk until smooth, and season with salt and pepper. Put the bread crumbs in a baking dish and season with salt and pepper.

Heat a few inches of canola oil in a large cast-iron skillet (you can use 2 skillets to cook faster) over medium heat until it begins to shimmer (350°F on an instant-read thermometer).

Dredge each veal chop in the flour and pat off any excess. Dip in the egg wash and let any excess drip off. Dredge in the bread crumbs on both sides. Transfer to a cooling rack set over a baking sheet.

Fry the veal chops, one or two at a time, depending on how big your pan is, until golden brown, crispy on both sides, and just cooked through, about 5 minutes per side.

Place a chop on each dinner plate, top with an egg, then top with the some of the tomato salad. Break up the crispy prosciutto and scatter on top, garnish with the finely grated lemon zest, and serve.

Osso Buco

Unless you feel comfortable trimming veal
shank, I'd suggest you have a butcher cut the
shanks about 2 inches thick, trim any excess
fat, and tie with twine (twice around). Any
reputable butcher will do that for no extra
charge.

For a heartier and more robust dinner,
prepare Risotto Milanese (page 148) during the
last 45 minutes of the osso buco's cooking time.
When the risotto is finished cooking, spoon it
onto the serving plate and place the osso buco
on top. Ladle some of the juices over the veal,
sprinkle with chopped parsley, and serve hot!
Serves 6

6 veal shanks, cut 2 inches thick and tied with
    kitchen twine
Kosher salt and freshly ground black pepper
2 cups all-purpose flour
¼ cup vegetable oil
1 tablespoon unsalted butter
1 large onion, finely chopped
¾ cup finely chopped celery
¾ cup finely chopped carrots
2 garlic cloves, minced
1½ cups dry white wine
1½ cups canned San Marzano tomatoes, hand
    crushed with juice
2½ cups chicken broth
2½ cups veal stock (or substitute beef stock)
1 tablespoon finely chopped fresh Italian
    parsley

Season the veal shanks generously with salt and pepper.

Add the flour to a large, shallow baking pan or similar container. Set the veal shank in the flour on its bottom. Roll the shank to its side and pat flour all around the shank. Gently tap off any excess. I suggest wearing latex kitchen gloves for this—they will keep your hands and the kitchen tidier. Repeat to coat the remaining veal shanks.

Heat the vegetable oil in a large, heavy bottomed, oven-safe pot or Dutch oven over medium-high heat for 2 minutes. Place the veal shanks, bottom side down, in the pot, working in batches if necessary to avoid overcrowding. Sear each shank on all sides, until golden brown and a light crust has formed. Set the seared shanks aside on a sheet of parchment paper.

Add butter to the pot and melt, then swirl the pot to coat the bottom evenly. Add the onion, celery, carrots, and garlic and sauté for 3 minutes, or until the onion is translucent. Be careful not to burn the garlic.

Add the wine and stir to deglaze the pot, scraping up any browned bits with a wooden spoon.

Preheat the oven to 350°F.

When the liquid has reduced by half, about 25 minutes, return the veal shanks to the pot, bottom side down.

Add the tomato, chicken broth, and veal stock, cover, and simmer for 30 minutes.

Transfer the pot to the preheated oven, and cook, covered, for 2 hours.

If the shanks are not fork-tender after 2 hours, cook for 30 minutes more.

Transfer the shanks to individual serving plates. Mix the juices remaining in the pot until well blended. Pour ½ cup of the juice over the veal. Sprinkle with the parsley, and serve.

Veal Chops Paillard

Serves 6

Six 16-ounce veal chops
¼ cup extra-virgin olive oil
2 tablespoons chopped fresh rosemary
2 tablespoons capers, drained, rinsed, and
    chopped
1 teaspoon kosher salt
½ teaspoon freshly ground black pepper
6 cups arugula, washed and dried
6 lemon wedges for garnish

Preheat the oven to 375°F. Grease a large baking sheet.

Cut the top off a clean, large (gallon-size or larger) resealable plastic food storage bag. Cut the sides to completely open the bag. Place a veal chop centered on one half and fold the plastic over to enclose the chop. Pound with a mallet until the meat is about ¼ inch thick. Be sure the bag you use is large enough to accommodate the chop as it spreads out.

Repeat to prepare the remaining chops.

In a mixing bowl, combine the olive oil, rosemary, capers, salt, and pepper. Stir to thoroughly combine and pour into a shallow baking pan. Hold one of the chops by the bone and drag it through the mixture, coating both sides. Let any excess drip off. Repeat with the remaining chops.

Arrange the seasoned chops on the prepared baking sheet, leaving at least ¼ inch between each chop.

Set up a serving platter or individual serving dishes, and spread arugula on each.

Bake the chops for 4 minutes on each side. Switch to broil, and broil until the tops of the chops are lightly browned, no longer than 45 seconds.

Transfer the chops to the serving platter or plates. Squeeze a lemon wedge over each chop, and serve.

Pan-Seared Veal Chop

Add a bit of panache to this dish by cooking an egg sunny-side up (one egg per chop), then placing the egg on top of the cooked chop. It's an incredible presentation and an even better flavor combination. Serves 4 to 6

> Four to six 16-ounce veal chops, 1½ inches thick
> Kosher salt and freshly ground black pepper
> ¼ cup olive oil
> 3 garlic cloves, smashed
> ¼ cup chopped fresh Italian parsley
> 4 to 6 lemon wedges

Preheat the oven to 400°F.

Liberally season each chop on both sides with salt and pepper.

Heat the olive oil in a large sauté pan over medium heat, and add the garlic. When the garlic begins to shimmer, remove it with tongs and discard.

Add the chops to the pan and fry in batches of two. Sear on both sides, turning once after 4 minutes, or when the chops are a deep, dark brown.

Using tongs, transfer the cooked chops to a baking sheet. Cover with aluminum foil and bake for 6 minutes for medium rare, 8 minutes for medium, and 10 minutes for well done.

Transfer the cooked chops to individual plates or a serving platter.

Sprinkle with the parsley, garnish with a lemon wedge, and serve.

Note: A pan screen comes in handy when searing anything like the chops in this recipe. It prevents the oil from splattering (no one likes splatter). Use a screen equal or larger in diameter to your sauté pan.

Veal Chop Valdostano

Serves 4

Four 16-ounce veal chops, 1½ inch thick
12 slices prosciutto
4 tablespoons golden raisins
4 thin slices mozzarella cheese
4 large eggs
¼ cup grated Pecorino Romano cheese
3 tablespoons plus 2 teaspoons chopped fresh
    Italian parsley
Kosher salt and freshly ground black pepper
2 cups all-purpose flour
1 cup vegetable oil
3 cups white mushrooms
4 tablespoons (½ stick) unsalted butter
2 cups chicken broth
1 cup Marsala wine

Using a very sharp chef's knife, trim the fat and meat off the handle (bone) of the veal chop. (It's much easier to just ask your butcher to do this.) Butterfly each chop to the bone and flip open.

On one side of the butterflied chop, place a slice of prosciutto, 1 tablespoon of golden raisins, another slice of prosciutto, and a slice of mozzarella. Top the mozzarella with a third slice of prosciutto.

Close the chop, and press hard to firmly seal the meat. Pound the edges together with a meat-tenderizing mallet. (For a sturdier seal, use a butcher's needle threaded with kitchen twine, and sew the edges closed.)

In a large mixing bowl, combine the eggs, grated cheese, and 2 teaspoons of the parsley.

Season liberally with salt and pepper and whisk vigorously until thoroughly combined.

Put the flour in a wide, shallow baking pan or bowl. Dredge each chop in the flour coating it all over. Lightly pat or shake off any excess.

Dredge each chop in the egg wash, generously coating the chop all over. Let any excess drip off. Set aside on a large sheet of parchment paper.

In a large sauté pan over medium heat, heat the vegetable oil for 2 to 3 minutes. Gently place the chops in the pan, cooking them in batches if necessary, to avoid overcrowding. Cook for 5 minutes on each side, or until golden brown. Transfer to a clean sheet of parchment paper.

Add the mushrooms to the pan, and sauté for 3 to 4 minutes, or until golden brown.

Add the butter and return the chops to the pan. Add the chicken broth and wine, cover and reduce the heat to low. Simmer for 6 to 10 minutes, or until the chops are tender, turning the chops once.

When the sauce has reduced by half and the chops are evenly coated, transfer them to a warm serving platter or warmed individual plates. Cover with the sauce and mushrooms. Sprinkle with the remaining parsley, and serve.

Beef

Pan-Seared Steak with Mushrooms and Onions

When you sauté the mushrooms and onions, add a nub of butter to the pan for an extra touch of flavor. As the butter melts, toss the mushrooms and onions until they are evenly coated. This will enhance the consistency and texture of juices left behind, while tying all the flavors together. After plating the mushrooms and onions, pour the remaining sauce over the steak. Serves 2 to 4

Two 16-ounce bone-in or -out rib-eye steaks, 1½
    inches thick (or substitute two 6- to 8-ounce
    filet mignon steaks)
Kosher salt and freshly ground black pepper
¼ cup olive oil
3 garlic cloves, smashed
¼ pound white mushrooms, stems removed
½ white onion, thinly sliced
1 tablespoon salted butter
¼ cup dry white wine
3 tablespoons chopped fresh Italian parsley
1 lemon, cut into wedges

Season both sides of the steaks generously with the salt and pepper, and set aside for 10 to 15 minutes.

Preheat the oven to 375°F. Grease a large baking sheet.

Heat the olive oil in a large sauté pan over medium-high heat and add the garlic. When the garlic starts to shimmer, carefully place the steaks in the pan. Cook them one at a time, if your pan isn't large enough to accommodate both without touching. (A pan screen will help contain splatter when pan-frying steak like this. It's an inexpensive way to avoid a lot of mess.)

Cook the steaks on each side for 7 minutes, or until dark brown on each side.

Transfer to the prepared baking sheet. Turn off the heat under the pan; leave the pan on the burner. Loosely cover the steaks with a sheet of aluminum foil and transfer to the oven. Cook for 7 minutes for medium-rare, 10 minutes for medium, and 12 minutes for well-done. Regardless of the cooking time, remove the foil 2 minutes before the steaks are cooked.

Heat the sauté pan over medium-high heat. Add the mushrooms and sauté for 5 minutes, or until they start to brown. Add the onions and season lightly with salt and pepper. Sauté for 4 minutes more, or until the onions are translucent. Add the butter and toss to evenly coat the mushrooms and onions.

Add the wine, and increase the heat to high. Cook, stirring occasionally, until the sauce has reduced by half, about 6 minutes. Taste and season with additional salt and pepper as needed. Add a dash of the parsley and toss until it is evenly distributed throughout. Lower the heat to medium, stir, and watch carefully to avoid burning the vegetables.

Remove the steaks from the oven, and let rest for about 5 minutes before cutting. Slice on a diagonal if serving family style. Transfer to a warmed serving platter (or warmed plates, if serving individual portions).

Spoon the mushrooms, onions, and sauce over the steaks. Sprinkle with the remaining parsley, garnish with the lemon wedges, and serve.

Steak Pizzaiola

Serves 2 to 4

Two 16-ounce bone-in rib-eye steaks, 1½ inches
    thick (or substitute two 6- to 8-ounce filet
    mignon steaks)
Kosher salt and freshly ground black pepper
¼ cup vegetable oil
½ tablespoon minced garlic
2 large bell peppers, seeded and cut into ¼-
    inch slices
1 large white onion, sliced ¼ inch thick
¼ pound button mushrooms, sliced
¼ cup dry white wine
2 cups canned San Marzano tomatoes, hand
    crushed with juice
1 teaspoon chopped fresh Italian parsley

Season both sides of each steak generously
with the salt and black pepper. Let rest for 10
to 15 minutes.

Heat the vegetable oil in a large sauté pan
over medium-high heat and add the garlic.
When the garlic starts to shimmer, carefully
place the steaks in the pan. Cook the steaks
individually if your pan won't accommodate
both steaks without touching.

Sear the steaks on each side for 7 minutes,
or until the meat is dark brown on each
side. Transfer the steaks to a large sheet of
parchment paper.

Add the bell peppers, onions, and
mushrooms to the pan and sauté for 5
minutes, tossing frequently. When the onions
are translucent and the mushrooms have
browned, add the wine and cook for 2 minutes
more.

Add the tomatoes and bring to a boil.
Reduce the heat to medium, and return the
steaks to the pan. Cook for 2 minutes for
medium-rare, 4 minutes for medium, and 6
minutes for well-done. If the sauce reduces
too much, add ¼ cup more of white wine.

Transfer the steaks to a cutting board and
let rest for 5 minutes.

If serving family style, slice the steaks on
a diagonal and transfer to a warmed serving
platter. If serving individually, place each steak
on a warmed plate. Spoon the sauce over the
steaks, sprinkle with the parsley and serve.

Bacon-Wrapped Filet Mignon

Serves 4

Four 8-ounce filet mignon steaks
2 teaspoons kosher salt
1 teaspoon freshly ground black pepper
1 tablespoon garlic powder
4 strips bacon, at least ⅛ inch thick
¼ cup olive oil
4 garlic cloves, smashed
4 ounces Gorgonzola cheese, crumbled

Generously season each steak on both sides with salt, pepper, and garlic powder and set aside for 10 to 15 minutes.

Wrap a slice of bacon around each filet and secure with butcher's twine.

Preheat the oven to 375°F. Grease a rimmed baking sheet.

TO COOK ON THE STOVETOP:

Heat the olive oil in a large sauté pan over medium-high heat and add the garlic. When the garlic begins to shimmer, carefully place the steaks into the pan, cooking in batches if your pan will not accommodate all the steaks without touching. Sear for 4 minutes on each side.

When the meat is dark brown, transfer the steaks to the prepared baking sheet.

Top each with 1 ounce of the Gorgonzola. Transfer to the oven and bake for 3 to 6 minutes, or until the cheese has melted and is blistering.

Using tongs, transfer the steaks to warmed plates or a warmed serving platter and serve.

TO COOK ON THE GRILL:

If you prefer to grill the steaks, preheat your grill to 400°F. Place the bacon-wrapped filets on the grill and sear for 3 minutes on each side.

Reduce the heat to low, or place the filets on the secondary grill shelf. Sprinkle 1 ounce of the Gorgonzola on top of each filet. Close the grill lid, and allow the cheese to melt, about 2 minutes. Transfer the steaks to plates and serve.

Junior's Grilled Italian Burger

This recipe is based on our meatball recipe, which calls for chopped beef, veal, and pork. Use any variation to create a beef burger, pork burger, or veal burger. You can also substitute American, Gorgonzola, or Gruyère for the provolone. Serves 4

2½ pounds 80-percent lean ground beef
2 cups Roasted Peppers (page 53)

¼ cup chopped fresh Italian parsley
3 cups grated Parmigiano Reggiano cheese
2 cups water
4 teaspoons kosher salt
1 tablespoon freshly ground black pepper
8 slices provolone cheese, ⅛ inch thick
4 hamburger buns
4 large lettuce leaves
1 tomato, sliced ⅛ inch thick
Red Pepper Aioli (optional)

TO COOK ON THE GRILL:

Preheat the grill to 450°F. Line a baking sheet with parchment paper.

While the grill is heating, prepare the burger patties. In a large mixing bowl, combine the beef, roasted peppers, parsley, grated cheese, water, salt, and black pepper. Mix just until all the ingredients are combined.

Scoop a handful of the mixture and form a 1½-inch-thick patty. Transfer to the lined baking sheet. Repeat until all the meat mixture is used.

Grill the burgers for 4 minutes on each side.

When the burgers have turned dark brown and begun to char, top each burger with 2 slices of the provolone cheese. Reduce the heat to low, or place the patties on the secondary grill shelf, and close the lid. Leave the lid closed until the cheese has melted, about 2 minutes.

Place 1 lettuce leaf on the bottom half of each bun. Place the burgers on the lettuce, and top each burger with a tomato slice. Close the burgers and serve.

STOVETOP VARIATION:

Preheat the oven to 375°F. Grease a baking sheet.

Grease a large sauté pan or cast-iron grill pan, and place over medium heat. Sear the burgers for 4 minutes on each side. When the patties are dark brown, transfer to the prepared baking sheet and into the oven and bake for 5 minutes.

Remove the baking sheet from the oven and place 2 slices of provolone cheese on top of each burger. Return to the oven and bake until the cheese has melted.

RED PEPPER AIOLI:

2 egg yolks
1 clove garlic
2 teaspoons fresh lemon juice
¼ teaspoon cayenne pepper
½ teaspoon smoked paprika
½ cup roasted red peppers
¾ cup canola oil
Kosher salt and freshly ground black pepper

Combine the egg yolks, garlic, lemon juice, cayenne pepper, smoked paprika, and peppers in a blender or food processor. Blend on medium-high for 20 seconds. With the blender or processor still running, slowly drizzle in the canola oil until it's completely incorporated. Taste and add salt and pepper as needed. Cover and refrigerate to save for later. Use (within two days) on salads or any type of grilled fish or meat.

Frankie's Meatballs

This is my great-grandmother's meatball recipe, and it has been passed down from generation to generation. First to my Aunt Anna, then to my dad, and then to me.

It's a staple on Rao's menus from coast to coast, and loved by all our guests.

Now, I pass it on to you. Makes 14 meatballs

1 pound lean ground beef
½ pound ground veal
½ pound ground pork
2 large eggs
1 cup grated Pecorino Romano cheese
1½ tablespoons chopped fresh Italian parsley
1 garlic clove, minced
Kosher salt and freshly ground black pepper
2 cups plain bread crumbs
2 cups cold water
1 cup olive oil
1 garlic clove, smashed

In a large mixing bowl, combine the beef, veal, and pork. Wearing latex kitchen gloves, mix the meat with your hands until it is evenly blended.

Add the eggs, cheese, parsley, minced garlic, salt, and pepper. Mix again, until the seasonings are evenly incorporated.

Add the bread crumbs and mix in thoroughly. Slowly add the cold water, ¼ cup at a time, mixing the water in until the mixture is evenly moist throughout. Shape the mixture into 3-inch balls.

Heat the olive oil in a large sauté pan over medium heat and add the smashed garlic.

When the garlic begins to shimmer and turn light brown, remove and discard.

Carefully add the meatballs to the pan, working in batches to avoid overcrowding the pan.

When the bottom of each meatball is browned and slightly crisp, about 5 minutes, turn and cook the other side for 5 minutes more.

Transfer the meatballs to a paper towel–lined plate. Serve hot, or use in your favorite recipe.

Note: If you are making Homemade Marinara Sauce (page 113) or Sunday Gravy (page 123), add the meatballs to the sauce 30 minutes before the sauce has finished cooking.

Beef Spiedini

A dear friend, Vincent Rippa, shared this recipe with us. Vincent's family has a great passion for food. His grandfather was a butcher, and he used to take young Vincent along with him to the slaughterhouse on Saturdays to purchase the meat for his butcher shop. To this day, this dish is a staple in the Rippa home, and I bet it's soon to be one of yours. Serves 6

1½ cups plain bread crumbs
½ cup grated Parmigiano Reggiano cheese
2 tablespoons chopped fresh Italian parsley
¼ cup olive oil
½ pound tri-tip steak, cut into strips 4 to 5
    inches long, pounded ⅛ inch thick
2 tablespoons unsalted butter, melted
Kosher salt and freshly ground black pepper
½ pound prosciutto, thinly sliced
One 16-ounce can San Marzano tomatoes,
    hand crushed with juice

Preheat the oven to 375°F. Grease a rimmed baking sheet well.

In a large mixing bowl, combine the bread crumbs, cheese, parsley, and olive oil. Mix until evenly blended and set aside.

Lay out the meat on a large sheet of parchment paper. Brush the top of each slice with the melted butter. Season each slice with a pinch of salt and pepper. Top with a slice of prosciutto. Sprinkle 1 teaspoon of the bread crumb mixture on top of each slice of prosciutto. Spoon 1 tablespoon of the tomatoes onto the center of each piece of dressed steak. Tightly roll the strips, and secure them with a toothpick or butcher's twine. Arrange the rolls on the prepared baking sheet.

Switch the oven to broil and place the baking sheet on the middle rack of the oven.

Broil the rolls for 3 minutes for medium-rare or 4 minutes for medium, turning the rolls once during the cooking.

Transfer the rolls to a warmed serving platter and serve.

Simple Beef Stew

As a young boy, this was the one hearty dish I would regularly beg my grandmother to make for dinner. Grandma Ida would indulge my requests only during the colder months. Having the recipe in hand, I prepare it for my family year-round. Now I'm the one who is asked to make this stew on a regular basis, regardless of the season. Thank you, Grandma. Serves 6

1 cup all-purpose flour
2 teaspoons kosher salt, plus more as needed
1 teaspoon freshly ground black pepper, plus
    more as needed
2 pounds silver-tip or hanger steak, cut into
    1-inch cubes
¼ cup vegetable oil

1 cup red wine
5 cups beef broth
6 cups canned San Marzano tomatoes, hand crushed with juice
2 white onions, quartered
2 large russet potatoes, peeled and cut into eighths
4 carrots, peeled, and chopped into 1-inch pieces

Put the flour in a wide, shallow bowl or baking pan and season liberally with salt and black pepper. Dredge the meat in the flour, and shake off any excess.

Heat the vegetable oil in a large, heavy-bottomed pot or Dutch oven over medium heat for 3 minutes. Add the beef and brown well on all sides. Using tongs, remove the meat and set aside on a plate.

Add the red wine to the pot and stir to loosen any browned bits stuck to the bottom. Increase the heat to high, and cook until the wine has reduced by half.

Return the beef and any juices to the pot. Add the beef broth and tomatoes and bring to a boil. Season with the salt and pepper and reduce the heat to low. Simmer, partially covered, for 2 hours.

Add the onions, potatoes, and carrots and cook for 45 minutes more.

Taste and season with salt and pepper as needed. Serve in individual bowls. For a heartier presentation, serve the stew over buttered egg noodles.

Beef or Pork Braciole

Makes 10 rolls

1 pound bottom round of beef or lean pork, cut into slices and pounded ¼-inch thick
1 garlic clove, halved
1 cup seasoned bread crumbs
½ cup olive oil, plus more for drizzling
4 cups Homemade Marinara Sauce (page 113)

Rub each slice of meat with a garlic half. (Garlic powder will work, too.)

Sprinkle each slice with the bread crumbs, and drizzle with a small amount of olive oil. Tightly roll each strip, securing it with toothpicks or butcher's twine.

Heat the olive oil in a large sauté pan over high heat. Add the rolls and cook, turning frequently, until the meat is evenly browned, about 6 minutes.

Pour off the excess oil from the pan. Add the marinara sauce and simmer for 1 hour, or until the meat is fork-tender.

If you're preparing Sunday Gravy, place the braciole into the simmering sauce 1 hour before the sauce has finished cooking.

Pork

Pan-Seared Pork Chops

Pressed for time? This dish is a winner; easy to prepare, quick, and delicious. You can substitute veal chops or steak if either of those is more to your taste. If you would like to make this dish a little heartier, serve it with our Roasted Potatoes (page 238), sautéed string beans, or any of Rao's leafy side dishes. Serves 4 to 6

Two to four 16-ounce, double-cut, bone-in pork chops, trimmed
Kosher salt and freshly ground black pepper
½ cup olive oil
2 garlic cloves, smashed
2 tablespoons finely chopped fresh Italian parsley
2 lemons, cut into wedges

Place the pork chops on a sheet of parchment paper and season both sides of the chops generously with salt and pepper. Set aside for 10 to 15 minutes.

Preheat the oven to 375°F. Grease a baking sheet large enough to hold all the chops.

Heat the olive oil in a large sauté pan over medium-high heat and add the garlic.

When the garlic starts to shimmer, carefully place the chops in the pan. Work in batches if your pan isn't large enough to accommodate all the chops without touching.

Sear the chops for 7 minutes on each side, or until each side has a nice crust.

Place the chops on the prepared baking sheet and cover loosely with a large sheet of aluminum foil. Transfer the chops to the oven and bake for 7 minutes for medium-rare, 10 minutes for medium, and 12 minutes for well-done. Regardless of the cooking time, remove the foil 2 minutes before the cooking is complete.

If serving individually, transfer the chops to warmed individual plates. If serving family style, cut the loin of the chops away from the bone and slice them on a diagonal. Transfer the slices to a large, warmed serving platter. Sprinkle with the parsley, garnish with the lemon wedges, and serve.

Pork Chops with Hot and Sweet Cherry Peppers

If you want to make this dish even more special, add eggs to the pan (one for each chop) after you remove the chops. Cook them sunny-side up, and top the chops with the eggs. The creamy yolks will heighten the flavors in the cherry pepper reduction, and will prove irresistible for dipping. Serves 4 to 6

    4 double-cut, bone-in pork chops, trimmed
    Kosher salt and freshly ground black pepper
    ½ cup olive oil
    2 garlic cloves, smashed
    1 cup pickled hot cherry peppers with juice,
        seeded and halved
    1 cup pickled sweet cherry peppers with juice,
        seeded and halved
    1 cup dry white wine
    1 tablespoon unsalted butter
    3 tablespoons finely chopped fresh Italian
        parsley

Place the pork chops on a sheet of parchment paper and generously season both sides of the chops with salt and black pepper. Set aside for 10 to 15 minutes.

Preheat the oven to 375°F. Grease a baking sheet large enough to hold all of the chops.

Heat the olive oil in a large sauté pan over medium-high heat and add the garlic.

When the garlic starts to shimmer, carefully place the chops in the pan. Work in batches if your pan won't accommodate all the chops without touching.

Sear the chops for 7 minutes on each side, or until a nice crust has formed on each side. Place the chops on the prepared baking sheet. Pour off the excess oil from the pan, leaving any browned bits stuck to the bottom. Loosely cover the chops with a large sheet of aluminum foil. Transfer the chops to the oven and bake for 7 minutes for medium-rare, 10 minutes for medium, and 12 minutes for well-done. Regardless of the preferred cooking time, remove the foil 2 minutes before cooking is complete.

Return the sauté pan to the stovetop over medium-high heat. Add the cherry peppers and wine and bring to a boil. Season lightly with salt and black pepper. Continue to cook until the sauce has reduced by half, about 4 minutes. Add the butter and increase the heat to high. Stir until the butter has incorporated into the sauce.

Remove the chops from the oven, and gently return them to the sauce in the pan. Cook for 1 minute on each side to glaze the chops. Reduce the heat to a simmer.

For individual servings, transfer the chops to warmed plates and spoon the sauce and peppers over the chops. Sprinkle with parsley and serve.

If slicing for a family-style presentation, transfer the chops to a cutting board and cover with a sheet of aluminum foil. Let them rest while the sauce continues to reduce. Cut the loin of the chops away from the bone, and slice on the diagonal into ¼-inch slices. Arrange the slices and bones on a large warmed serving platter, and spoon the sauce and peppers over the chops. Sprinkle with parsley and serve hot.

Sausage with Peppers and Onions

Serves 6

½ cup olive oil
3 garlic cloves, smashed
6 sweet Italian sausages
6 hot Italian sausages
3 bell peppers (green, red, and yellow), seeded
　　and cut lengthwise into ¼-inch strips
2 large yellow onions, sliced ¼ inch thick
Kosher salt and freshly ground black pepper

Heat the olive oil in a large sauté pan over medium-high heat and add the garlic. When the garlic begins to shimmer, carefully place the sausages into the pan. Fry the sausages, turning frequently, until they are nicely browned, about 10 minutes. Remove from the pan and set aside.

Add the bell peppers and onions and season with the salt and black pepper. Reduce the heat to medium and cook for 5 minutes more, or until the vegetables are fork-tender.

Return the sausage to the pan and cook for 3 minutes more, turning often.

Using tongs, transfer the sausage to a serving platter.

Toss the peppers and onions one last time, and then spoon on top of the sausages. Serve hot.

"For the past forty-plus years, as an inspired cook and frequent traveler, I can attest to having dined at marvelous restaurants not only in Europe but many across our great country. But dining at Rao's is not just a delicious food experience, it's like going home to family! If you look up the word 'hospitality' in Webster's dictionary, under the definition should be a photo of Rao's on the corner of 114th Street and Pleasant Avenue."

—FRANK SCHIPANI

Braised Short Ribs with String Beans and Tomatoes

Serves 4

¼ cup olive oil
6 garlic cloves, smashed
1½ pounds country-style pork ribs
One 56-ounce can San Marzano tomatoes,
    hand crushed with juice
½ teaspoon dried oregano
Kosher salt and freshly ground black pepper
1 pound string beans, trimmed

Heat the olive oil in a large sauté pan over medium-high heat and add the garlic.

When the garlic begins to shimmer, add the ribs. Brown for 4 minutes on each side.

Add the tomatoes and oregano and season with salt and pepper. Increase the heat to medium-high and bring to a boil. Reduce the heat to low, and simmer, stirring occasionally, until the ribs are fork-tender, about 3 hours.

While the ribs are cooking, bring a large pot of salted water to boil. Add the string beans and cook for about 7 minutes. Drain and rinse under cold water to stop the cooking process and set the color.

When the ribs have about 5 minutes left to cook, add the beans and heat through.

Transfer the beans and ribs to a large warmed serving platter and serve.

Roast Loin of Pork with Potatoes and Onions

Serves 6

One 3- to 4-pound pork loin, trussed
6 sprigs fresh rosemary
3 tablespoons kosher salt
3 tablespoons freshly ground black pepper
3 tablespoons garlic powder
12 fingerling potatoes, scrubbed and quartered
1 onion, cut into ¼-inch slices
1 cup water
¼ cup olive oil
2 tablespoons chopped fresh Italian parsley

Preheat the oven to 350°F.

Place the pork loin on a large sheet of parchment paper. Secure the rosemary sprigs evenly spaced around the loin in the trussing twine. Season the loin with 2 tablespoons of the salt, 2 tablespoons of the pepper, and 2 tablespoons of the garlic powder.

In a large roasting pan, combine the potatoes and onions and season with the remaining 1 tablespoon salt, 1 tablespoon pepper, and 1 tablespoon garlic powder. Add the water and the olive oil to the pan.

Place the loin on a V-shaped roasting rack and set in the roasting pan over the vegetables. Loosely cover with a sheet of aluminum foil, tenting it over the sides, front, and back.

Roast for 45 minutes, or until the internal temperature of the loin registers 135°F (for medium), occasionally turning the potatoes and onions.

After 30 minutes of roasting, remove the foil to allow the meat to brown and crisp.

Remove the loin from the oven, and again loosely cover the roasting pan with foil. Let the meat rest for 15 minutes.

Transfer the loin to a cutting board. Using a sharp carving knife, cut the loin into ¼- to ½-inch slices. Shingle the slices on a warmed serving platter and arrange the potatoes and onions around and on top of the pork. Sprinkle with the parsley and serve.

Lamb

Roast Leg of Lamb

Serves 6

4 garlic cloves, minced
½ cup chopped fresh Italian parsley
½ teaspoon dried rosemary (or substitute 6 sprigs fresh rosemary)
Kosher salt and freshly ground black pepper
½ cup olive oil
One 6-pound leg of lamb, trimmed
3 carrots, peeled and chopped into ¼-inch pieces
3 celery stalks, chopped
1 large onion, cut into ¼-inch slices
6 cups canned San Marzano tomatoes, hand crushed with juice
⅓ cup chicken broth, plus more as needed

Preheat the oven to 325°F.

In a medium mixing bowl, combine the garlic, parsley, rosemary, salt and pepper to taste, and ¼ cup of the olive oil. Whisk until completely blended and the mixture forms a paste.

Generously brush the entire leg of lamb with the garlic-herb mixture.

Coat the bottom of a large roasting pan with the remaining ¼ cup olive oil. Add the carrots, celery, onion, tomatoes, and chicken broth. Set a V-shaped roasting rack in the pan, and place the leg of lamb on the rack. Roast for 1½ hours, basting the lamb every 15 minutes with a basting brush or baster. If the liquid on the bottom of the pan begins to dry up at any point, add ½ cup more of chicken broth to the pan.

Increase the oven temperature to 400°F, and roast the lamb for 30 minutes more, or until a meat thermometer registers 130°F. Remove the lamb from the oven, transfer to a cutting board, and let rest for 15 minutes before carving. As the lamb rests, it will continue to cook to medium.

Carve the meat from the bone and cut into ¼-inch-thick slices. Transfer the meat to a serving platter, spoon the remaining pan sauce over the lamb, and serve.

Broiled Lamb Chops—in the Oven or on the Grill

Serves 4

8 double-cut Colorado lamb chops, trimmed
    and frenched
4 tablespoons olive oil
4 teaspoons garlic powder
6 sprigs fresh rosemary, leaves only, plus extra
    for garnish
Kosher salt and freshly ground black pepper

Preheat the oven to 375°F. If using a grill, grease well and preheat on high for at least 15 minutes.

Place the chops on a large sheet of parchment paper. Lightly brush both sides of each chop with the olive oil, and generously season with the garlic powder, rosemary leaves, salt, and pepper.

TO COOK IN THE OVEN:
Preheat the oven to 350°F.

Transfer the chops to a baking sheet or shallow baking pan. Cook for 10 minutes on each side for medium.

Switch to broil, and broil for 1 minute more, or until the chops are deep brown with a hint of char.

Transfer the chops to individual plates. Garnish each with a sprig of fresh rosemary, and serve.

TO COOK ON THE GRILL:

Using long grilling tongs, place the chops on the grill. Quickly slide each chop front to back, about four times. Repeat when grilling the opposite sides. This helps ensure that the chops don't stick to the grill. Grill for 4 minutes on each side for medium-rare, or 5 minutes on each side for medium.

Transfer the chops to individual plates, garnish each with a sprig of fresh rosemary, and serve.

Chicken

Rao's Lemon Chicken—in the Oven or on the Grill

Serves 4

1 cup olive oil
2 cups fresh lemon juice
1 tablespoon red wine vinegar
1½ teaspoons minced garlic
½ teaspoon dried oregano
4 tablespoons chopped fresh Italian parsley
Kosher salt and freshly ground black pepper
Two 2½- to 3-pound chickens, halved
1 lemon, cut into wedges

In a large mixing bowl or large glass measuring cup, combine the olive oil, lemon juice, vinegar, garlic, oregano, 2 tablespoons of the parsley, and salt and pepper to taste. Whisk until evenly blended.

Using a sharp chef's knife, cut each broiled or grilled chicken half into 6 pieces (leg, thigh, wing, and three breast pieces). Transfer the pieces to a clean baking sheet.

Whisk the lemon marinade again, and pour over the chicken. Return the chicken on the baking sheet to the oven or onto the grill. When the marinade begins to bubble, turn the chicken pieces and evenly coat them all around in the marinade. Cook for 3 to 4 minutes, or until the chicken pieces are cooked through, turning often.

Transfer the chicken to a warmed serving platter and top with the sauce remaining on the baking sheet. Sprinkle with the remaining 2 tablespoons parsley and garnish with the lemon wedges. Serve hot.

IF USING THE OVEN:
Preheat the broiler for 15 minutes. Place the chicken halves, skin side down, on a greased baking sheet or in a greased shallow baking pan. Broil for 15 minutes on each side. Remove from the oven and let rest until cool to the touch. Leave the broiler on.

IF USING A GRILL:
Generously grease the grill and preheat to 450°F for 15 minutes. Using long grilling tongs, place the chicken halves, skin side down, on the grates. Slide the halves rapidly back to front. This will help release some of the fat in the chicken skin and prevent the chicken from sticking to the grill. Reduce the grill temperature to 350°F. Cook the chicken for 15 minutes on both sides. Remove from the grill and rest until cool to the touch.

Chicken Scarpariello

Serves 4

¼ cup corn oil
3 garlic cloves, smashed
½ pound hot Italian sausage, cut into bite-size
pieces
½ pound sweet Italian sausage, cut into bite-
size pieces
One 2-pound chicken, cut into 12 pieces (2 legs,
2 thighs, 2 wings, 2 backs, 4 half-breasts)
2 large bell peppers (any color), seeded and
cut lengthwise into ¼-inch strips
1 large yellow onion, halved and sliced ⅛ inch
thick
½ cup dry white wine
¼ cup chicken broth
½ cup pickled hot cherry peppers, seeded and
halved
½ cup pickled sweet cherry pepper brine
½ teaspoon chopped fresh oregano
Kosher salt and freshly ground black pepper
2 tablespoons chopped fresh Italian parsley

Heat the corn oil in a large sauté pan over medium-high heat and add 2 of the garlic cloves. When the garlic begins to shimmer, add the sausage and sauté for 8 minutes, or until lightly browned. Reduce the heat to medium. Transfer the sausage to a plate lined with paper towels and set aside.

Using tongs, carefully place the chicken pieces into the pan, skin side down. Cook for 8 minutes on each side, or until the chicken is golden brown and crispy. Add the bell peppers and onion and sauté for 5 minutes more.

Pour off the excess oil from the pan and return the pan to the heat. Return the sausage to the pan. Add the wine and chicken broth, and bring to a boil. Stir in the cherry peppers, cherry pepper brine, and oregano and season lightly with salt and black pepper and return to a boil. Reduce the heat to low and simmer for 10 minutes, or until the sauce has noticeably reduced and thickened.

 Transfer to a large serving platter, sprinkle with parsley, and serve.

Chicken Cacciatore

Serves 4

¼ cup corn oil

3 garlic cloves, smashed

One 2-pound chicken, cut into 12 pieces (2 legs, 2 thighs, 2 wings, 2 backs, 4 half-breasts)

2 large bell peppers (any color), cut lengthwise into ¼-inch slices

1 large yellow onion, halved and cut into ¼-inch slices

6 cups canned San Marzano tomatoes, hand crushed with juice

½ cup dry white wine

½ teaspoon finely chopped fresh oregano

¼ cup chicken broth

Kosher salt and freshly ground black pepper

2 tablespoons chopped fresh Italian parsley

Heat the corn oil in a large sauté pan over medium-high heat and add the garlic. When the garlic begins to shimmer, using tongs, carefully place the chicken pieces into the pan, skin side down. Cook for 8 minutes on each side, or until the chicken pieces are golden brown and crispy. Add the bell peppers and onion, and sauté for 5 minutes more.

Pour off the excess oil from the pan. Return the pan to the heat, add the crushed tomatoes, wine, oregano, and chicken broth, and bring to a boil. Reduce the heat to low and simmer for 10 minutes, or until the flavors have blended and the sauce has noticeably reduced and thickened. Taste and season with salt and pepper as needed.

Transfer to a serving platter, sprinkle with the parsley, and serve.

Aunt Anna's Southern Fried Chicken

Whenever I make this dish I use a trick that I learned from my Aunt Anna. Before flouring the chicken parts, score the thickest part of the meat on the drumsticks with a sharp knife. This ensures that drumsticks cook evenly throughout. Serves 4 to 6

Two 2½-pound chickens, cut into 24 pieces
3 cups all-purpose flour
3 tablespoons kosher salt
3 tablespoons freshly ground black pepper
2 cups vegetable oil
3 tablespoons chopped fresh Italian parsley
1 lemon, cut into wedges

Spread the chicken pieces out on a large baking sheet lined with a sheet of parchment paper. Pat the chicken dry with paper towels.

With a sharp chef's knife, deeply score (to the bone) each leg perpendicular to the bone.

In a large baking pan, combine the flour, salt, and pepper and mix well until the salt and pepper are evenly dispersed throughout the flour. Line a clean baking sheet with paper towels.

Dredge the chicken parts in the seasoned flour, patting off any excess flour, and return to the parchment paper. Set aside.

Heat the vegetable oil in a large sauté pan over medium heat for 3 minutes.

Using tongs, carefully place the chicken into the hot oil. Cook in batches as necessary to avoid crowding, turning occasionally while frying, for 13 to 15 minutes or until the chicken is golden brown and crispy. Transfer the chicken to the paper towel–lined baking sheet to absorb the excess oil.

Arrange the fried chicken on a large serving platter. Sprinkle with the parsley, garnish with the lemon wedges, and serve.

Chicken Parmigiano

When purchasing the chicken cutlets for this recipe, have your butcher trim and pound the cutlets for you. It will save you a lot of time and effort. As with all breading recipes, I also strongly recommend that you set up a breading assembly line, with the different coatings exactly in the order described. That will make preparing the dish hassle-free and easy as can be. Serves 4

1 cup all-purpose flour
2 cups plain bread crumbs
4 large eggs
½ cup grated Pecorino Romano cheese
¼ cup plus 2 teaspoons chopped fresh Italian parsley
Kosher salt and freshly ground black pepper
2 pounds chicken breast cutlets, trimmed and pounded
1 cup vegetable oil
½ cup grated Parmigiano Reggiano cheese
4 cups Homemade Marinara Sauce (page 113), warmed
8 slices mozzarella cheese, ¼-inch thick

Put the flour in a wide, shallow bowl or baking pan. Put the bread crumbs in a similar container. Whisk together the eggs, Pecorino Romano cheese, and 2 teaspoons of the parsley in a medium mixing bowl. Season the egg wash with the salt and pepper.

Set the flour, egg wash, and bread crumbs on your work surface in a row, in that order. Place a baking sheet lined with parchment paper next to the bread crumbs.

Holding a chicken cutlet by the tip, lightly dredge it in the flour. Gently shake off any excess, then dip it in the egg wash. Hold the cutlet over the bowl and let any excess drip off. Press the cutlet into the bread crumbs, coating it on all sides, and transfer to the baking sheet. Repeat to bread the remaining cutlets.

Heat the vegetable oil in a large sauté pan over medium-high heat for 2 minutes. Line a baking sheet with paper towels.

Carefully place the cutlets into the hot oil, and cook for 3 to 4 minutes per side, or until golden brown, frying in batches if necessary to avoid overcrowding.

Transfer the cutlets to the paper towel–lined baking sheet. Press the top of the cutlets with more paper towels to remove any excess oil.

Preheat the broiler.

Place the fried cutlets on an unlined baking sheet, leaving at least ¼ inch between each. Sprinkle each cutlet with the grated Parmigiano Reggiano cheese and top with about ½ cup of the marinara sauce, spreading it evenly across the top. Place 2 slices of mozzarella on top of the sauce, covering the cutlet. Place a dollop of marinara sauce on top of the mozzarella and gently spread over the cheese.

Broil the cutlets on the center rack of the oven for 4 to 6 minutes, or until the cheese has melted and begun to blister.

Transfer the cutlets to individual plates. Sprinkle with the remaining ¼ cup parsley and serve.

Roasted Chicken with Potatoes

Serves 6

One 5-pound roasting chicken
4 tablespoons (½ stick) salted butter, at room
    temperature
Kosher salt and freshly ground black pepper
6 fresh rosemary sprigs; 2 sprigs leaves only
1 lemon, cut into wedges
1 onion, quartered
8 fingerling potatoes, scrubbed and quartered
2 cups chicken broth
¼ cup olive oil
1 cup water

Preheat the oven to 350°F.

Remove the innards from the chicken. Rinse the chicken and cavities and pat dry.

Place the chicken on a large sheet of parchment paper. Grease the chicken all over with the butter and season liberally with salt and pepper.

Cut a piece of cheesecloth large enough to hold the rosemary sprigs, lemons, and onion. Pull the corners up and knot them to form a bouquet garni pouch; put it inside the chicken.

In a large roasting pan, combine the potatoes and rosemary leaves and season with salt and pepper. Add the chicken broth, olive oil, and water.

Place the chicken onto a V-shaped rack, and set in the roasting pan over the potatoes. Loosely cover the chicken with aluminum foil and roast for 1½ hours.

As the chicken roasts, occasionally turn the potatoes, remove the foil, and baste the chicken with the liquid in the pan. Replace the foil and continue to roast.

For the last 15 minutes of the roasting time, remove the foil so that the chicken skin browns and crisps. When a meat thermometer placed into the thickest part of the thigh registers 165°F, remove the chicken from the oven, transfer to a cutting board, and let rest for 15 minutes.

Carve the chicken and transfer the pieces to a large serving platter. Discard the bouquet garni. Surround the chicken with the potatoes and serve.

Wings on the Grill

Serves 4 to 6

½ cup olive oil
3 garlic cloves, smashed
1 cup pickled sweet cherry peppers, seeded
    and halved
1 cup pickled hot cherry peppers, seeded and
    halved
1 cup pickled cherry pepper brine
1 cup dry white wine
1 tablespoon salted butter
4 pounds chicken wings
Kosher salt and freshly ground black pepper
2 tablespoons chopped fresh Italian parsley

Grease the grates and preheat the grill on high with the lid closed. Line a large baking sheet or baking pan with parchment paper.

Heat ¼ cup of the olive oil in a large skillet on the grill grates and add the garlic. Cook for 2 minutes. Add the cherry peppers, cherry pepper brine, wine, and butter and bring to a boil. Cook until the sauce has reduced by half, 8 to 10 minutes.

Remove and set aside. (The sauce can be made up to 2 hours ahead.)

Place the wings onto the lined baking sheet or baking pan. Lightly grease the wings all over with the remaining ¼ cup olive oil and generously season with salt and black pepper.

Reduce the grill heat to medium-low. Place the wings on the grill, spacing them at least 2 inches apart. This will allow for even cooking, and provide sufficient space for turning the wings without a hassle. Cook for 20 minutes, until golden brown and crisp, turning the wings every 4 to 6 minutes. As the wings cook, baste them with the cherry pepper sauce.

Transfer the wings to a baking pan and pour the remaining cherry pepper sauce on top. Place the pan on the grill, increase the heat to high, and bring the sauce to a boil. Turn the wings frequently until evenly coated with the sauce, and cook 30 seconds on each side.

Transfer the wings to a large serving platter. Pour the sauce from the pan over the wings. Sprinkle with the parsley and serve.

VEGETABLES

Broccoli Rabe

Serves 4

¼ cup extra virgin olive oil
4 garlic cloves, smashed
2 bunches broccoli rabe, trimmed and steamed
¼ cup chicken broth
Kosher salt and freshly ground black pepper

Heat the olive oil in a large sauté pan over medium heat and add the garlic. When the garlic begins to shimmer, add the broccoli rabe and chicken broth and season with salt and pepper. Toss frequently while the broccoli rabe cooks, 4 to 6 minutes.

Transfer to a serving plate and serve hot.

"You feel it the moment you step into the place. Even at six in the evening, when it is just coming to life, or at one in the morning, when things are just winding down. There is an undeniable magic in the room and it draws you in every time. Countless nights we stopped in for a quick drink and were still there four hours later. Of course, the mystique is legendary, but this is no ordinary restaurant. There are the 'regulars' ensconced in their coveted wooden booths who have been coming every week for decades. Then you see the 'first-timers' giddy with anticipation, eager for a glimpse of glamour and hoping to spy a famous face at this East Harlem oasis."

—TOM AND LINDA

Artie's Stuffed Italian Frying Peppers

Serves 6

12 Italian frying peppers
½ cup plain bread crumbs
¼ cup grated Pecorino Romano cheese
¼ cup anchovy fillets
½ cup extra-virgin olive oil, plus more for
    drizzling
4 garlic cloves
1 tablespoon red wine vinegar
Pinch of dried oregano
¼ teaspoon crushed red pepper flakes
Kosher salt and freshly ground black pepper

Cut the tops off the peppers and discard. Slit the peppers lengthwise down one side and remove the seeds.

Toast the bread crumbs in a large sauté pan over medium heat, 3 to 5 minutes. Transfer the bread crumbs to a mixing bowl and combine with the grated cheese, anchovies, and ¼ cup olive oil. Mix well until the bread crumbs have completely absorbed the oil, and the seasoning is evenly integrated throughout.

Heat the remaining ¼ cup of olive oil in the sauté pan over medium heat and add the garlic. When the garlic begins to shimmer, add the frying peppers and cover the pan. Reduce the heat to low and steam the peppers for 15 minutes, turning occasionally.

Using tongs, transfer the peppers to a large bowl and set aside. Leave the pan on the burner.

Add the vinegar, oregano, and red pepper flakes, and salt and black pepper to taste, to the pan on the burner. Cook for 2 minutes, remove the pan from the heat, and set aside to cool.

When the peppers are cool to the touch, gently open them and spoon 3 tablespoons of the stuffing into each pepper.

Arrange the peppers on a serving platter, top with the sauce, drizzle with olive oil, and serve at room temperature.

Grilled Vegetables

Serves 4 to 6

- 1 large zucchini, trimmed and cut into ½-inch slices
- 1 large yellow squash, trimmed and cut into ½-inch slices
- 1 large fennel bulb, trimmed and cut into ½-inch slices
- 1 medium eggplant, trimmed and cut into ½-inch slices
- 1 head radicchio, trimmed and quartered
- ¼ cup extra-virgin olive oil, plus more for drizzling
- 1 tablespoon kosher salt
- 1 teaspoon freshly ground black pepper

Grease the grill grates. Preheat the grill to 400°F. (Or use a grill pan on your stovetop, over medium-high heat.)

In a large mixing bowl, combine the vegetables, ¼ cup of olive oil, and the salt and pepper. Toss until the vegetables are evenly coated.

Using long grilling tongs, place the vegetables on the grill (or on the grill pan).

Grill about 4 minutes on each side, or until the vegetables are browned and crisp.

Note that the veggies will char a little bit on the grill. This adds another dimension of flavor. Keep the grill lid closed for the first 4 minutes of cooking. This will help keep the vegetables tender, and allow them to cook evenly.

Transfer the vegetables to a serving platter. Sprinkle with salt and pepper, drizzle with olive oil, and serve.

Senior's Artichokes

Serves 6

6 large artichokes
Juice of 1 lemon
1½ cups plain bread crumbs
1½ cups grated Pecorino Romano cheese
1 tablespoon chopped fresh Italian parsley
1 garlic clove, smashed
Kosher salt and freshly ground black pepper
1 cup extra-virgin olive oil

Rinse the artichokes under cold water. Cut about ½ inch off of the tops of the artichokes and remove the stems. Using scissors, cut off the tips of the remaining leaves. Place each artichoke upside down on a hard surface and press down firmly to open the leaves. Hold each artichoke right side up and scrape out the choke with a small spoon.

Add the lemon juice to a large bowl of cold water. Place the prepped artichokes in the water, and set aside.

In a mixing bowl, combine the bread crumbs, cheese, parsley, garlic, and salt and pepper to taste. Mix thoroughly until completely combined. Set aside.

Remove the artichokes from the water. Place the artichokes upside down on a few layers of paper towels to drain. When drained, pat the artichokes dry.

Turn the artichokes right side up and generously stuff with the bread crumb mixture, pushing it down into the spaces between the leaves.

In a deep pot with 1 inch of water, add 1 tablespoon salt and ½ cup of the olive oil. Place the artichokes in the pot, breaded side up. Drizzle the remaining ½ cup of olive oil over the artichokes. Cover the pot and bring to a simmer over high heat.

Reduce the heat to medium-low and let the artichokes steam for 45 minutes, or until the bottoms are tender when pierced with a sharp knife. (If the pan goes dry before the artichokes fully cook, add more water.)

Use tongs to remove the artichokes. Divide the liquid from the pot among 6 individual soup bowls. Place 1 artichoke in each bowl and serve hot.

Potatoes, Peppers, and Onions

This preparation is fantastic as a topping for frankfurters, steaks, burgers, or toasted Italian bread. If you're fond of spicy foods, add crushed red pepper flakes to the bell peppers and onions in the pan. Trust me, these are lip-smacking good! Serves 6

¼ cup olive oil
2 garlic cloves, smashed
4 fingerling potatoes, rinsed and cut into ¼-inch slices
1 large onion, halved and cut into ¼-inch slices
1 red bell pepper, seeded and cut into ¼-inch slices
One 8-ounce can whole San Marzano tomatoes, hand crushed with juice (optional)
Crushed red pepper flakes (optional)
Kosher salt and freshly ground black pepper

Heat the olive oil in a medium sauté pan over medium heat and add the garlic. When the garlic begins to shimmer, add the potatoes. Fry until they are lightly browned and fork-tender.

Add the onion and bell pepper and sauté for 10 minutes, or until tender and lightly browned. Add the tomatoes and red pepper flakes, if using, at this point. Cook for 5 minutes more. Taste and season with salt and black pepper as needed.

Transfer the vegetables to a serving bowl and serve hot as a side dish, or use as a topping.

Stuffed Mushroom Caps

Serves 4

12 large white mushrooms, stems removed and finely chopped, caps left whole
1 cup plain bread crumbs
2 garlic cloves, minced
½ teaspoon kosher salt
¼ teaspoon freshly ground black pepper
¼ cup finely chopped fresh Italian parsley, plus extra for garnish
¼ cup grated Parmigiano Reggiano cheese
¼ cup olive oil, plus more for drizzling
¼ cup chicken broth

Preheat the oven to 425°F. Grease a baking sheet.

In a medium mixing bowl, combine the chopped mushroom stems, bread crumbs, garlic, salt, pepper, parsley, grated cheese, ¼ cup of olive oil, and the broth. Mix until completely combined.

Place the mushroom caps upside down on the prepared baking sheet. Generously fill each mushroom cap with the stuffing and drizzle each with olive oil. Bake for 15 minutes, or until the mushrooms are cooked through and the breading is golden brown and crisp.

Transfer the mushrooms to a serving platter, sprinkle with chopped parsley, and serve.

Potato Croquettes

Makes 12 croquettes

1 pound russet potatoes, peeled, cooked, and
mashed
3 cups plus 3 tablespoons vegetable oil
½ cup finely chopped prosciutto
½ cup finely diced yellow onion
3 large egg yolks
½ pound mozzarella cheese, finely diced
1 pound plus ¼ cup grated Pecorino Romano
cheese
3 tablespoons plus 2 teaspoons finely chopped
fresh Italian parsley
4 large eggs
Kosher salt and freshly ground black pepper
1½ cups all-purpose flour
¾ cup plain bread crumbs

Prepare the mashed potatoes. Set aside.

Heat 3 tablespoons of the vegetable oil in
a medium sauté pan over medium-high heat.
Add the prosciutto and onions and sauté for 5
minutes.

In a large mixing bowl, combine the
mashed potatoes, onions, and prosciutto and
mix with a wooden spoon until completely
combined.

Add the egg yolks, the diced mozzarella
cheese, 1 pound of the grated Pecorino
Romano cheese, and the 3 tablespoons of
parsley and mix until evenly blended.

Wearing a pair of kitchen latex gloves,
shape the potato mixture into 12 balls of equal
size. Set aside.

In a large mixing bowl, combine the
eggs, the ¼ cup of grated cheese, and the 2
teaspoons parsley. Season liberally with salt
and pepper. Whisk until completely blended.

Put the flour in a shallow bowl or baking
pan. Pour the bread crumbs into a separate
shallow bowl or baking pan.

Arrange the flour, egg wash, and bread
crumbs in that order, left to right, to set up a
breading system. Grease a baking sheet and
set next to the stove.

Carefully dredge each croquette in
the flour, patting off any excess. Dip each
croquette in the egg wash, allowing any excess
to drip off. Roll the croquette in the bread
crumbs until evenly coated all around. Repeat
until all the croquettes are breaded. Set them
on the greased baking sheet.

Heat the remaining 3 cups vegetable oil
in a large, deep pot or a deep fryer, until a
thermometer registers 365°F. Line a baking
sheet with paper towels.

Using tongs, carefully lower the croquettes
into the hot oil a few at a time. Fry for 2
minutes, turning frequently, until golden
brown and crisp. Transfer the croquettes to
the paper towel–lined baking sheet. Allow to
cool for at least 5 minutes before serving.

Roasted Potatoes

Serves 6

2 pounds fingerling potatoes, rinsed and
    halved
4 garlic cloves, smashed
⅓ cup extra-virgin olive oil
4 sprigs fresh rosemary; 3 sprigs leaves only, 1
    whole sprig for garnish
Kosher salt and freshly ground black pepper

Preheat the oven to 375°F.

In a large saucepan over high heat, cover the potatoes with 2 inches of cold water. Salt lightly and bring to a boil. Boil for 3 minutes. Drain and pat the potatoes dry. Transfer the potatoes with the garlic to a baking dish. Drizzle with the olive oil. Sprinkle the rosemary leaves over the potatoes and season liberally with salt and pepper. Toss to coat.

Roast the potatoes for 25 minutes, or until golden brown and crisp. Transfer to a serving bowl and serve hot, garnishing with the sprig of rosemary held in reserve.

Asparagus with Parmigiano Reggiano Cheese

Serves 6

2 pounds asparagus, tough ends removed and
    stems peeled
Kosher salt
6 tablespoons (¾ stick) unsalted butter, melted
1 cup grated Parmigiano Reggiano cheese

Preheat the oven to 400°F.

In large, deep pan over medium-high heat,
cover the asparagus with cold water by 1 inch.
Salt lightly, bring to a boil, and cover. Reduce
the heat to simmer and cook the asparagus for
4 minutes, or just until tender. Drain and pat
dry.

Arrange the asparagus, tips pointing in the
same direction, into 6 separate servings on a
baking sheet. Drizzle the melted butter over
each serving and generously sprinkle with the
cheese.

Bake the asparagus for 5 minutes, or
until the cheese has melted. Using a spatula,
carefully transfer each serving to individual
plates and serve.

Sautéed Mushrooms

Serves 6

¼ cup extra-virgin olive oil
2 garlic cloves, smashed
1¼ pounds of shitake, oyster, and other wild
    mushrooms, sliced
¼ cup dry white wine
Kosher salt and freshly ground black pepper
2 tablespoons chopped fresh Italian parsley

Heat the olive oil in a large sauté pan over medium heat. Add the garlic and sauté for 3 minutes, or until golden brown. Remove and discard the garlic.

Add the mushrooms and sauté for 5 minutes, or until tender but still firm.

Add the wine and salt and pepper to taste. Bring to a boil and cook for 1 minute. Stir in the parsley and serve hot.

Sautéed Cabbage

Serves 4

¼ cup extra-virgin olive oil
4 garlic cloves, smashed
1 head cabbage, cored, quartered, and
    blanched
¼ cup chicken broth
Kosher salt and freshly ground black pepper.

Heat the olive oil in a large sauté pan over medium heat and add the garlic. When the garlic begins to shimmer, add the cabbage and chicken broth. Season to taste with the salt and pepper. Toss and cook until heated through, 4 to 6 minutes.

Serve hot.

Sautéed Escarole

Serves 4

¼ cup extra-virgin olive oil
4 garlic cloves, smashed
1 head escarole, trimmed and blanched
¼ cup chicken broth
Kosher salt and freshly ground black pepper

Heat the olive oil in a large sauté pan over medium heat and add the garlic. When the garlic begins to shimmer, add the escarole and chicken broth. Season to taste with salt and pepper. Toss and cook until heated through, 4 to 6 minutes.

Serve hot.

Aunt Stella's Batter-Fried Vegetables

Serves 4

3 large eggs
3 tablespoons all-purpose flour
3 tablespoons baking powder
¼ teaspoon kosher salt
¼ teaspoon freshly ground black pepper
Pinch of garlic powder
¼ cup chopped fresh Italian parsley
¼ cup grated Pecorino Romano cheese
¾ cup vegetable oil
½ head broccoli, florets only
½ head cauliflower, florets only
3 zucchini, trimmed and quartered lengthwise

In a large mixing bowl, combine the eggs, flour, baking powder, salt, pepper, garlic powder, parsley, and grated cheese. Heat the vegetable oil in a large sauté pan over medium-high heat for 2 minutes. (The oil is ready for frying when it registers 375°F.) Line a plate with paper towels.

Working in batches, dip the broccoli, cauliflower, and zucchini in the egg batter, coating the pieces completely and letting any extra drip off. Carefully place them in the hot oil. Fry each batch for 2 to 3 minutes, or until golden brown.

Using tongs, transfer the fried vegetables to the paper towel-lined plate. Allow to cool for 3 to 5 minutes, then serve.

Peas with Prosciutto and Onions

Serves 4

¼ cup extra-virgin olive oil
4 garlic cloves, smashed
¾ cup coarsely chopped prosciutto
¾ cup diced onion
4 cups fresh peas (or substitute frozen)
Kosher salt and freshly ground black pepper

Heat the olive oil in a large sauté pan over medium heat. Add the garlic, prosciutto, and onions and cook for 3 minutes.

When the garlic begins to shimmer, add the peas. Toss and cook until the peas are heated through, 4 to 6 minutes. Taste and season with salt and pepper as needed.

Serve hot.

Baked Beefsteak Tomatoes

Serves 4 to 6

6 ripe beefsteak tomatoes
½ cup chopped fresh Italian parsley
2 teaspoons chopped fresh oregano
2 garlic cloves, minced
1 cup plain bread crumbs
1 cup shredded mozzarella cheese
½ cup grated Parmigiano Reggiano cheese
¼ cup shredded fresh basil leaves
½ cup extra-virgin olive oil, plus more for drizzling
2 teaspoons kosher salt
1 teaspoon black pepper

Preheat the oven to 350°F.

Cut the top off of each tomato. Hollow the tomato out, reserving the pulp. Chop the pulp.

In a medium mixing bowl, combine the chopped tomato pulp, parsley, oregano, garlic, bread crumbs, shredded mozzarella, grated Parmigiano Reggiano, basil, ½ cup of the olive oil, and the salt and pepper. Mix thoroughly with a fork.

Stuff the tomatoes with the mixture. Arrange the tomatoes on a baking sheet just large enough to hold the tomatoes upright. Drizzle each tomato with olive oil.

Bake the stuffed tomatoes for 30 minutes. During the last 2 minutes, switch to broil to brown and crisp the tops.

Transfer the tomatoes to a serving platter and serve hot.

DESSERTS

Oreo Cheesecake

Serves 10 to 12

FOR THE CRUST:
15 Oreo cookies (or substitute other chocolate sandwich cookies)
2 tablespoons unsalted butter, melted

FOR THE FILLING:
1 pound cream cheese, at room temperature
1¼ cups granulated sugar
½ cup vanilla yogurt
1 tablespoon pure vanilla extract
⅛ cup heavy cream
4 large eggs
One 16.4-ounce package Oreo cookies (or substitute other chocolate sandwich cookies)

TO MAKE THE CRUST: Preheat the oven to 325°F.

In the bowl of a food processor, coarsely chop the cookies. Transfer to a medium mixing bowl, combine with the melted butter, and stir until evenly moistened.

Press the mixture into a 10-inch springform pan and bake the crust for 5 minutes.

TO MAKE THE FILLING: In the bowl of a stand mixer fitted with the paddle, beat the cream cheese on low speed until smooth. Add the sugar and cream until smooth and fluffy, scraping down the inside of the bowl as needed.

In a small bowl, combine the yogurt, vanilla, and heavy cream and whisk until blended. Slowly pour the yogurt mixture into the cream cheese. Mix on medium speed until smooth, scraping down the bowl as needed.

Add the eggs, two at a time, scraping down the sides of the bowl in between each addition.

In the bowl of a food processor, finely chop the cookies. Mix three-quarters of the cookies into the filling. Reserve one-quarter of the cookies for the top.

Pour the filling into the springform pan, and scatter the reserved finely chopped cookies on top.

If the pan does not have a tight seal all the way around the bottom, nest the pan in a large sheet of aluminum foil, pressing it up the outside of the pan. This will prevent water getting into the cheesecake during baking. Set the pan in a baking pan or in a large roasting pan and add 1 inch of hot water to create a water bath.

Bake the cheesecake for 20 minutes. Reduce the heat to 275°F, and bake for 30 minutes more.

Remove the springform pan from the water bath; then remove the water bath from the oven. Continue to bake the cheesecake for 10 minutes more. Turn the oven off and leave the cheesecake inside for 30 minutes longer. The cheesecake will still be jiggly in the middle, but should look dry on top.

Remove the cheesecake from the oven and run a thin knife around the inside edge of the springform pan. Set the cheesecake aside to cool in the pan.

When cool, transfer the pan to the refrigerator and chill the cheesecake overnight.

When you're ready to serve, remove the cheesecake from the pan, slice, and serve.

Peanut Butter Pie

Serves 12 to 16

FOR THE CRUST:
  1½ cups graham cracker crumbs
  4 tablespoons (½ stick) unsalted butter, melted
  5 tablespoons peanut butter

FOR THE FILLING:
  Two 8-ounce packages cream cheese, softened
  1½ cups powdered sugar
  1 cup peanut butter (crunchy or smooth, your choice)
  ¼ cup whole milk
  1 cup heavy cream

FOR THE GANACHE:
  1 cup heavy cream
  9 ounces semisweet chocolate

TO MAKE THE CRUST: Preheat the oven to 350°F.

In a large bowl, combine the graham cracker crumbs, butter, and peanut butter. Stir with a fork until the mixture has an even texture throughout. Press the mixture into a 13 x 9-inch pan. Bake the crust for 3 to 5 minutes.

When you smell peanut butter, the crust it is done. Remove it from the oven and set aside to cool.

TO MAKE THE FILLING: In the bowl of a stand mixer fitted with the paddle, combine the cream cheese and powdered sugar and beat on low speed until smooth and fluffy, scraping down the sides of the bowl as necessary. Add the peanut butter and beat until smooth. With the mixer running, slowly add the milk and mix until the filling has a uniform texture.

In a separate medium bowl fitted with the wire whisk, whip the heavy cream to medium-hard peaks. Fold it into the filling.

Pour the filling into the cooled crust, and spread to even it out. Refrigerate the pie for 3 hours to let the filling set.

TO MAKE THE GANACHE: In a small pot over medium-high heat, warm the cream. (You can also do this in a microwave.) Add the chocolate and stir until it melts and the mixture is completely combined and smooth.

Pour the ganache over the set filling. Chill in the refrigerator for at least 2 to 3 hours. Slice, and serve.

Ricotta Cheesecake

Serves 10 to 12

FOR THE CRUST:
- 1½ cups graham cracker crumbs
- 2 tablespoons granulated sugar
- 6 tablespoons (½ stick plus 2 tablespoons) unsalted butter, melted

FOR THE FILLING:
- 20 ounces ricotta cheese
- 18 ounces cream cheese, at room temperature
- 1⅓ cups granulated sugar
- ½ cup honey
- Finely grated zest of ¾ of a lemon
- Finely grated zest of 1 orange
- 7 large eggs

TO MAKE THE CRUST: Preheat the oven to 325°F.

In a large bowl, combine the graham cracker crumbs, sugar, and butter. Mix with a fork until the crumbs are completely coated. Transfer to a 10-inch springform pan, and press down firmly on the bottom and sides. Bake the crust for 5 minutes, then set aside to cool.

Once cool to the touch, wrap the pan with aluminum foil, running it up the sides 2 to 3 inches (above the rim of the pan).

TO MAKE THE FILLING: Increase the oven temperature to 350°F.

In the bowl of a stand mixer fitted with the paddle (or in a mixing bowl if using a hand mixer), cream the ricotta on medium speed until smooth. Add the cream cheese and mix to combine, scraping down the sides of the bowl down as necessary.

Add the sugar and mix until incorporated. Add the honey, and lemon and orange zests, and mix thoroughly, scraping down the sides of the bowl as necessary.

Add the eggs, one at a time, scraping down the bowl after each addition.

Pour the filling into the cooled crust. Set the pan in a baking or roasting pan and add 1 inch of water to create a water bath.

Bake the cheesecake for 25 minutes. Lower the temperature to 300°F, and bake for 40 minutes more.

Turn the oven off, and leave the cheesecake in the oven for 30 minutes longer. The cheesecake is done when the center is jiggly but the top looks dry.

Let cool on a counter, then chill until ready to serve (it's best if the cheesecake chills overnight).

When ready to serve, remove the cheesecake from the springform pan, slice, and serve.

Cannoli

Serves 6 to 8

32 ounces ricotta cheese
1 ⅓ cup powdered sugar
2 teaspoons pure vanilla extract
1 tablespoon orange juice (or orange-flavored liqueur)
Finely grated zest from ½ orange
⅔ cup mini chocolate chips
⅛ cup diced candied fruit (optional)
1 package cannoli shells

In a large mixing bowl, combine the ricotta, sugar, vanilla, orange juice, and orange zest. Mix until thoroughly combined.

Add the chocolate chips and the candied fruit, if desired, and mix again.

Fill a pastry bag or a plastic bag with the filling, and snip off a corner. Pipe the mixture into the prepared cannoli shells.

"You and the whole staff at Rao's made us feel at home and the food was beyond compare."
—PETER FOGARTY

Red Velvet Shortcake

Serves 10 to 12

FOR THE BISCUITS
2½ cups all-purpose flour
2½ teaspoons baking powder
1 teaspoon kosher salt
2 tablespoons granulated sugar
1 tablespoon plus 1 teaspoon unsweetened cocoa powder
4 tablespoons (½ stick) cold unsalted butter, cubed
¾ cup buttermilk
1 large egg
1 tablespoon red food coloring

FOR THE TOPPING:
½ cup granulated sugar
½ cup water
6 ounces fresh raspberries
6 ounces fresh blueberries
6 ounces fresh blackberries
1 pint strawberries, hulled and quartered

FOR THE FILLING:
1½ cups heavy cream
1 teaspoon pure vanilla extract
One 8-ounce package cream cheese, at room temperature
2 tablespoons powdered sugar
Fresh mint

TO MAKE THE BISCUITS: Preheat the oven to 325°F.

In the bowl of a stand mixer fitted with the paddle (or in a large mixing bowl if using a hand mixer), combine the flour, baking powder, salt, granulated sugar, and cocoa powder. With the mixer running on medium speed, add the butter. Mix until the pieces of butter are about the size of a dime.

In a small bowl, combine the buttermilk, egg, and food coloring. Whisk until completely blended. Slowly add the wet mixture to the dry ingredients. Mix on low speed until a rough dough forms.

Turn the dough out onto a lightly floured work surface. Gently knead the dough just until it comes together; do not overwork. Roll the dough out to a thickness of ½ inch. Cut out biscuits with a round cutter or by cutting the dough into squares 2 ½ inches in diameter. Place the biscuits on a nonstick baking sheet, spacing them evenly.

Bake for 20 minutes. Rotate the sheet, and bake for another 5 to 10 minutes, or until the biscuits are deep golden brown.

TO MAKE THE TOPPING: In a small saucepan over high heat, combine the granulated sugar and water and bring to a boil. Boil until the sugar dissolves completely. Remove from the heat and let cool.

In a large bowl, combine the berries and rinse gently with cold water and drain. Return the berries to the rinsed bowl and pour the cooled syrup over them. Cover, and let macerate for 30 minutes to draw out the juices from the berries.

TO MAKE THE FILLING: In a large mixing bowl, combine the cream and vanilla. Whip to medium-soft peaks. Set aside.

In the bowl of a stand mixer, combine the cream cheese and powdered sugar. Mix on medium speed until smooth.

Fold in the whipped cream using the mixer on the same speed, and mix until smooth. Cover the bowl and chill in the refrigerator for 3 hours to stiffen up.

TO SERVE THE SHORTCAKES: Cut a biscuit horizontally in half, spoon a dollop of the filling in the middle, and top with a spoonful of the fruit topping. Garnish with a sprig of fresh mint and serve.

Blood Orange and Limoncello Panna Cotta

Serves 8

2 tablespoons limoncello
2 tablespoons Solerno (blood orange liqueur)
2 teaspoons powdered unflavored gelatin
2¼ cups heavy cream
½ cup granulated sugar
½ teaspoon finely grated lemon zest
½ teaspoon finely grated orange or blood orange zest

1 cup sour cream
Segments of orange or blood orange, for garnish
8 sprigs fresh mint

In a small bowl, combine the limoncello and Solerno. Sprinkle the gelatin on top of the liquid; do not stir. Let sit, undisturbed, for 4 minutes, or until the gelatin has softened and is ready to use.

In a medium saucepan over medium-high heat, combine the heavy cream, granulated sugar, and lemon and orange zests. Bring to simmer—be careful not to boil. Cook, stirring, until the sugar has dissolved. Remove the pan from the heat.

Microwave the gelatin mixture for 5 to 10 seconds on high to melt it down to a liquid. Pour the liquid gelatin into the saucepan with the cream mixture and stir until thoroughly combined. Whisk in the sour cream.

Divide the mixture among eight glasses (or whatever decorative serving container you prefer). Cover with plastic wrap, and chill for at least 5 hours, or up to overnight.

Serve each panna cotta garnished with an orange segment and a sprig of mint.

Note: Should you want to speed up the setting time, chill the mixture in the pan, set in an ice water bath, stirring the mixture constantly until it begins to thicken up. Then transfer to glasses and chill.

Coast-to-Coast Management

Joe Ciccone
general manager, NYC

Marie-Joe Tabet
general manager, LV

Patrick Hickey
general manager,
Hollywood

Andrea Slazar
assistant general
manager, LV

Tommy Nicolas Mora
assistant general
manager, NYC

Lou Farber
sommelier/assistant
general manager, LA

In loving memory of Bubbles

Dino Gatto
executive chef, NYC

Fatimah Madyun
executive chef, LV

Laura Cortez
pastry chef, LV

Michael Lanza
sous chef, NYC

Roast Beef
LA ambassador

Faces of Rao's

Alan
Los Vegas

Alex
Las Vegas

Ali
Las Vegas

Angela
Las Vegas

Arturo
Las Vegas

Baruch
Las Vegas

Baruch
Las Vegas

Big Rob
Las Vegas

Brian
Las Vegas

Caesar
Las Vegas

Charles Rao

Charlie
Las Vegas

Chucoo
Las Vags

Darling
New York City

Davis
Las Vegas

Davor
Las Vegas

Diamond
Los Angles

Dominick the Butcher
New York City

Duane
Las Vegas

Dwight
Las Vegas

Dylan
Las Vags

Flor
Las Vags

George
Las Vegas

Gerald
Las Vegas

Gerry
Las Vegas

Glenda
Las Vegas

Hilton
New York City

Howie
Las Vegas

Isidro
Las Vegas

Jaymie
Las Vegas

Jesús
Las Vegas

Jesús
Las Vegas

Jimmy
Las Vegas

Jovanny
Las Vegas

John
Las Vegas

Jose
Las Vegas

Jose
Las Vegas

Josh
Las Vegas

Juan
Las Vegas

Junior
Las Vegas

Karma
Las Vegas

Kevin
Los Angeles

Lauren
Las Vegas

Leslie
Las Vegas

Luz
Las Vegas

Lydia
New York City

Marc
Los Angeles

Maria
Las Vegas

Marisa
Las Vegas

Matt
Las Vegas

Michael
Las Vegas

Miguel
Las Vegas

Mike Waz
Las Vegas

Nick
Las Vegas

Nicky the Vest
New York City

Niki
Las Vegas

Oscar
Las Vegas

Paul
Las Vegas

Paulie
New York City

Peter
Las Vegas

Rebecca
Las Vegas

Rene
Las Vegas

Roger
Las Vegas

Rose
Las Vegas

Russ
Las Vegas

Sean
Las Vegas

Super Nick
New York City

Sylvia
Las Vegas

Therasa
New York City

Terry
Las Vegas

AFTERWORD

I work at Rao's in the daytime. I've been part of the daily running of this wonderful restaurant for the last twenty-three years. I watch the deliveries come in; the floors get washed; the kitchen scrubbed down—all the movements that get the restaurant ready for another night of dining. The kitchen staff arrives. I inhale the aroma of the peppers roasting, the sauce simmering; the calamari boiling to edible softness, the meatballs frying. Heavenly scents that always make me feel comforted. I see the dining room with the chairs upside down on the tables after the floors are done. It looks like any other restaurant.

In the early afternoon, the chairs come down, the tables are set, the festive Christmas lights go on and the dining room sparkles. The clean white linens await the spills and drops of food shared family style. No fancy china or matched flatware is in sight, plain glass goblets only as we serve the diners. As I finish my work and prepare to leave, I sit in the back of the empty dining room and take it all in. The walls are covered with photos: beloved customers, family, staff, celebrities—all witness to the magic that takes place here each night. Smiling down like patron saints ensuring a wonderful delicious dining event, they are ready, waiting for tonight's group of diners. They are part of the fun, the camaradarie!

Many call the experience at Rao's magical; representing all that is good about dining out. I look out at the dining room to welcome familiar faces and new faces. All enter to eat or just sit at the bar and take in what has come to be known as Rao's! How does the magic begin? For me it's when the first diners arrive, happily anticipating what is to come. Faces rosy red from the cold, or flush with summer's heat. No matter the weather, when they are inside the red doors, it's all good. They arrive and the room comes alive with talk and laughter and hugs and kisses. The ambiance is warm and comforting. The staff smiles at everyone, happy to see regulars and happy to welcome newcomers. Frank Pellegrino stops at each table to greet guests—after all, this is his home—and he makes sure that all feel welcome and appreciated. That is Frank's style, and it is the heart of Rao's. Each night produces a different magic; each group of diners creates a different aura. I guess the magic has a lot to do with the consistency of what Rao's offers. There is so much change in our lives; it is lovely to be part of something that stays the same year after year. Each member of the family at Rao's plays a part in the magic, in the smiling faces as diners enter and the contented look on those same faces as they walk out the red doors.

—*Cousin Susan Paolercio*
March 16, 2016

INDEX